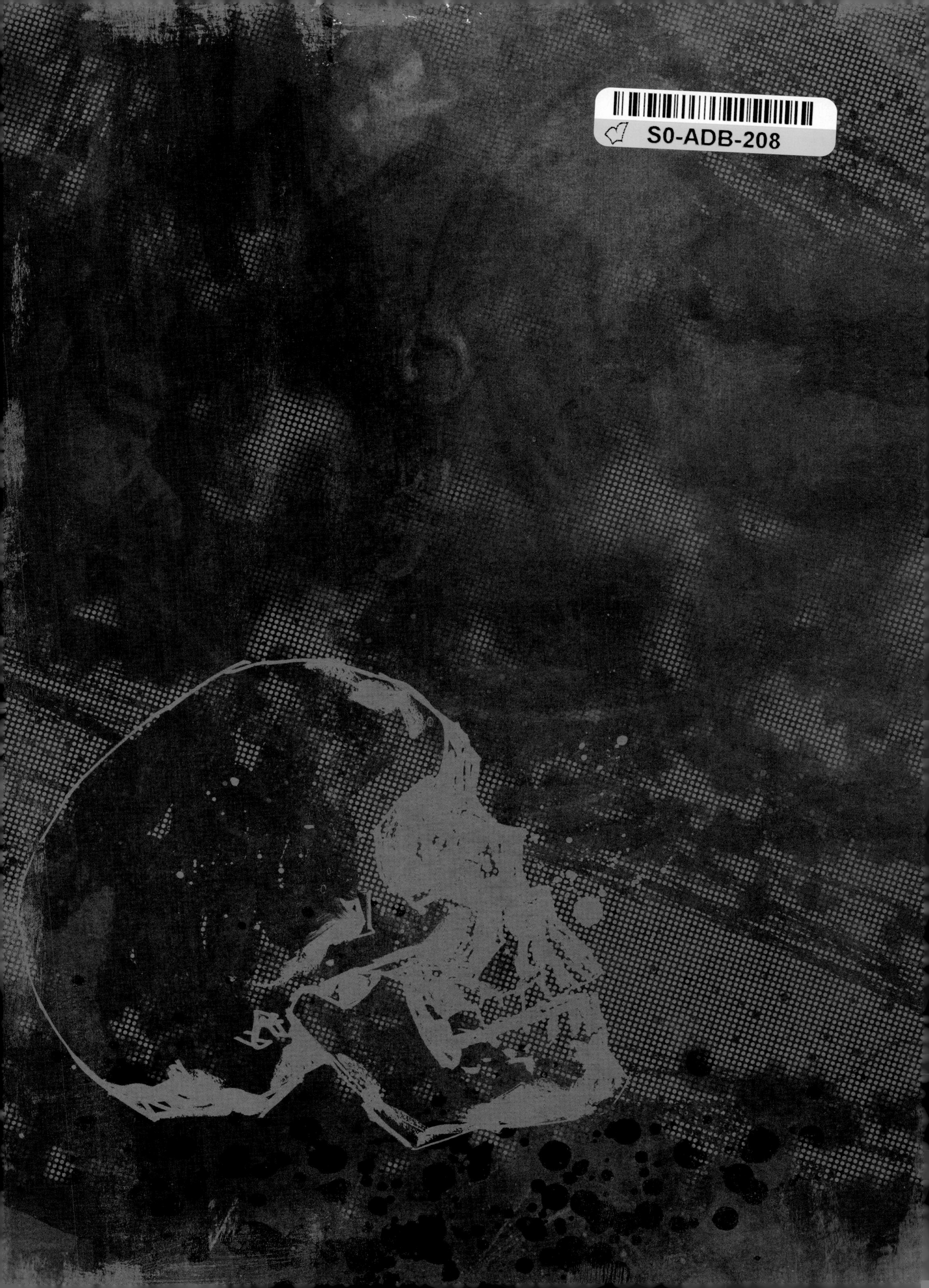

IVAN BRANDON   NIC KLEIN
VIKING™
THE LONG
COLD FIRE.

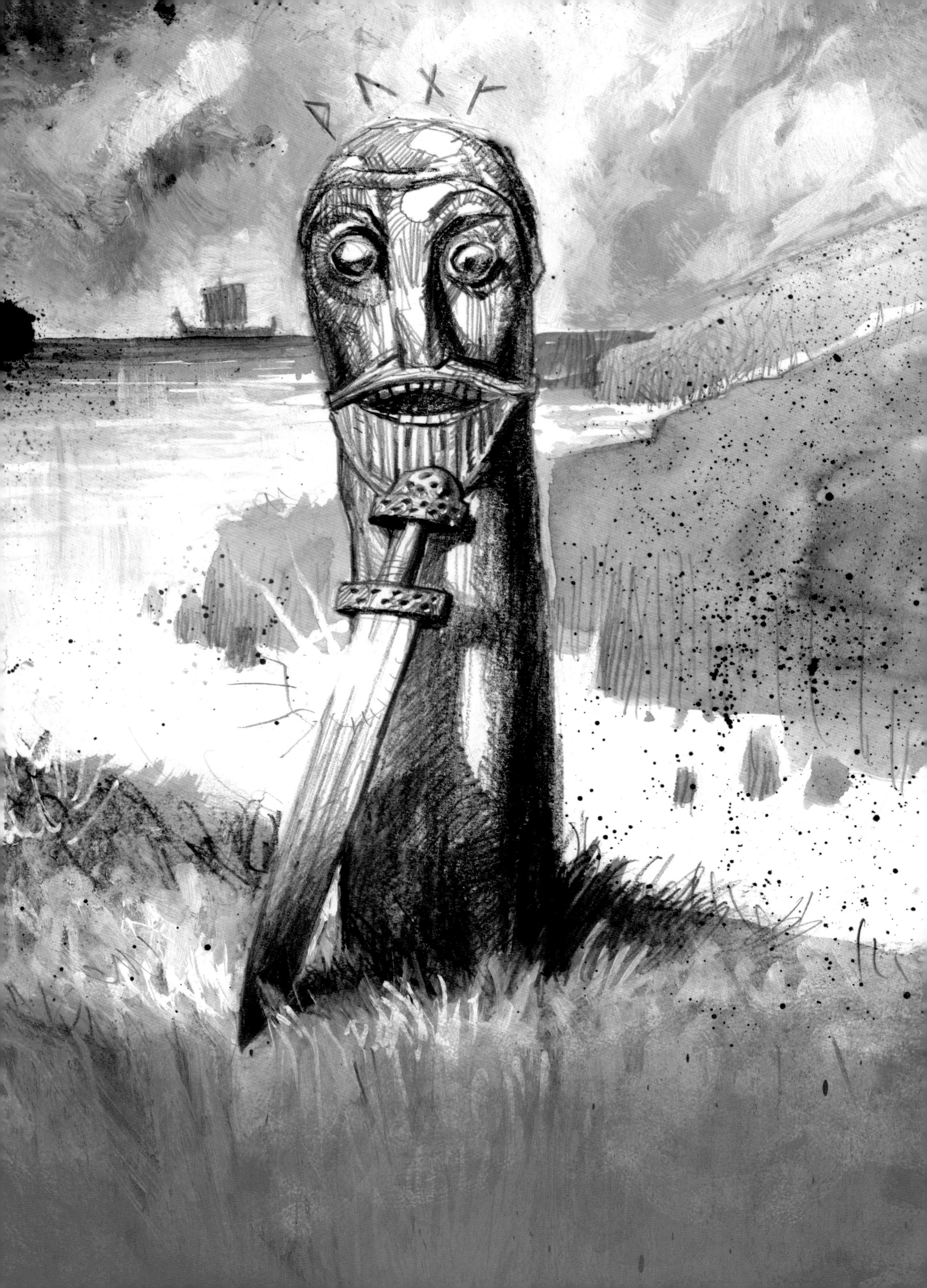

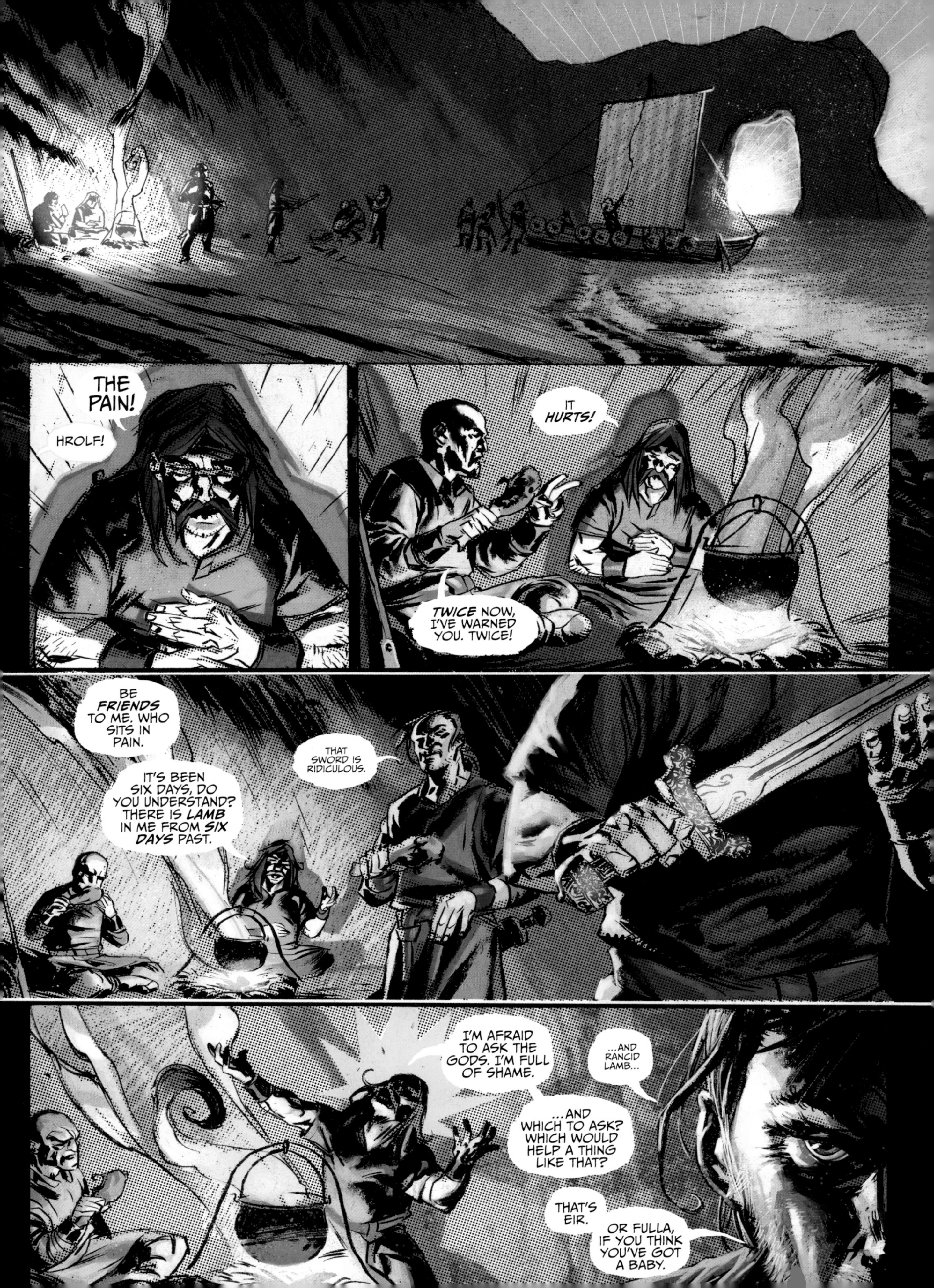
THE PAIN!
HROLF!
IT HURTS!
TWICE NOW, I'VE WARNED YOU. TWICE!
BE FRIENDS TO ME. WHO SITS IN PAIN.
IT'S BEEN SIX DAYS, DO YOU UNDERSTAND? THERE IS LAMB IN ME FROM SIX DAYS PAST.
THAT SWORD IS RIDICULOUS.
I'M AFRAID TO ASK THE GODS. I'M FULL OF SHAME.
...AND RANCID LAMB...
...AND WHICH TO ASK? WHICH WOULD HELP A THING LIKE THAT?
THAT'S EIR.
OR FULLA, IF YOU THINK YOU'VE GOT A BABY.

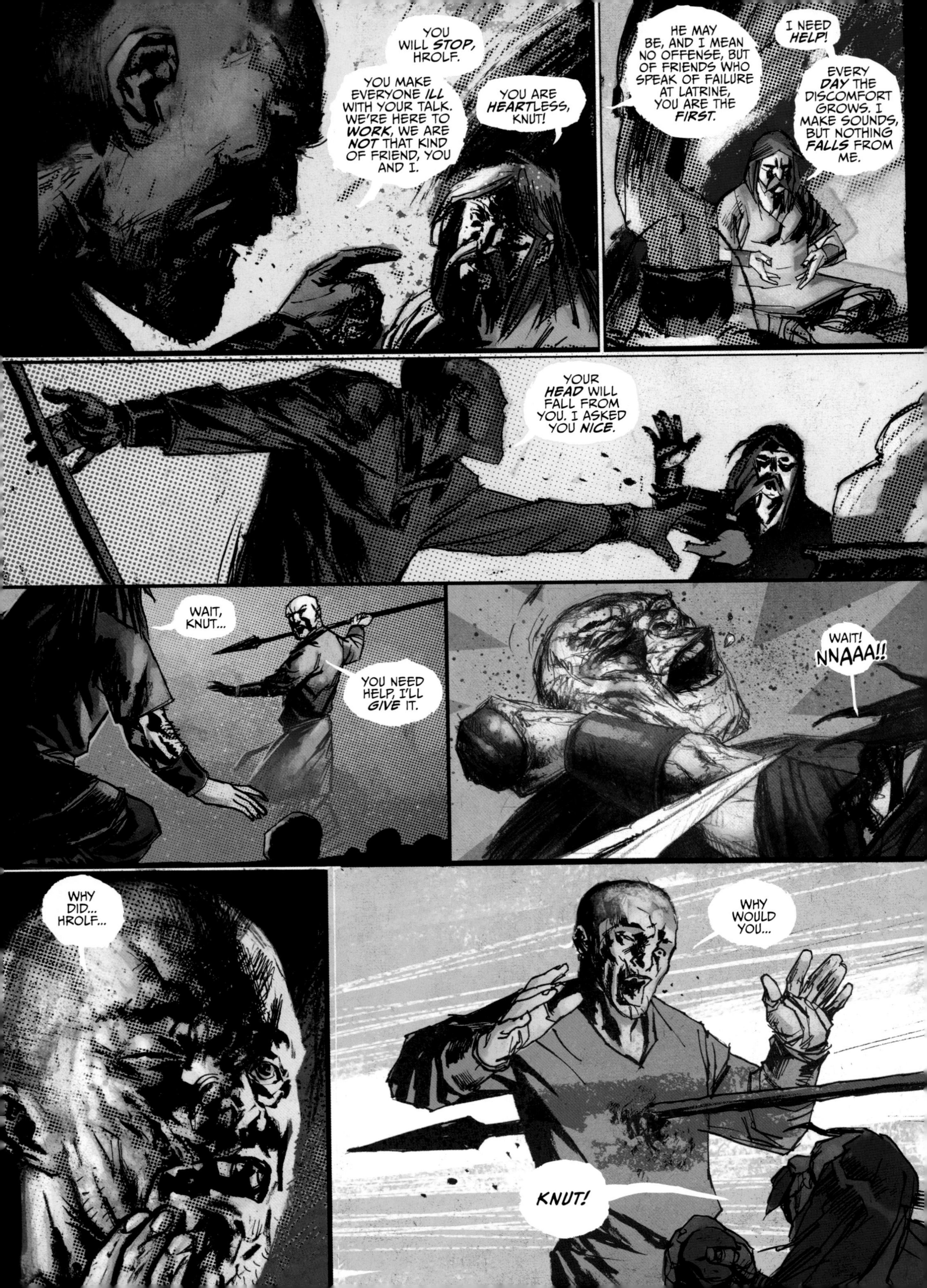

YOU WILL STOP, HROLF.
YOU MAKE EVERYONE ILL WITH YOUR TALK. WE'RE HERE TO WORK, WE ARE NOT THAT KIND OF FRIEND, YOU AND I.
YOU ARE HEARTLESS, KNUT!
HE MAY BE, AND I MEAN NO OFFENSE, BUT OF FRIENDS WHO SPEAK OF FAILURE AT LATRINE, YOU ARE THE FIRST.
I NEED HELP!
EVERY DAY THE DISCOMFORT GROWS. I MAKE SOUNDS, BUT NOTHING FALLS FROM ME.
YOUR HEAD WILL FALL FROM YOU. I ASKED YOU NICE.
WAIT, KNUT...
YOU NEED HELP, I'LL GIVE IT.
WAIT! NNAAA!!
WHY DID... HROLF...
WHY WOULD YOU...
KNUT!

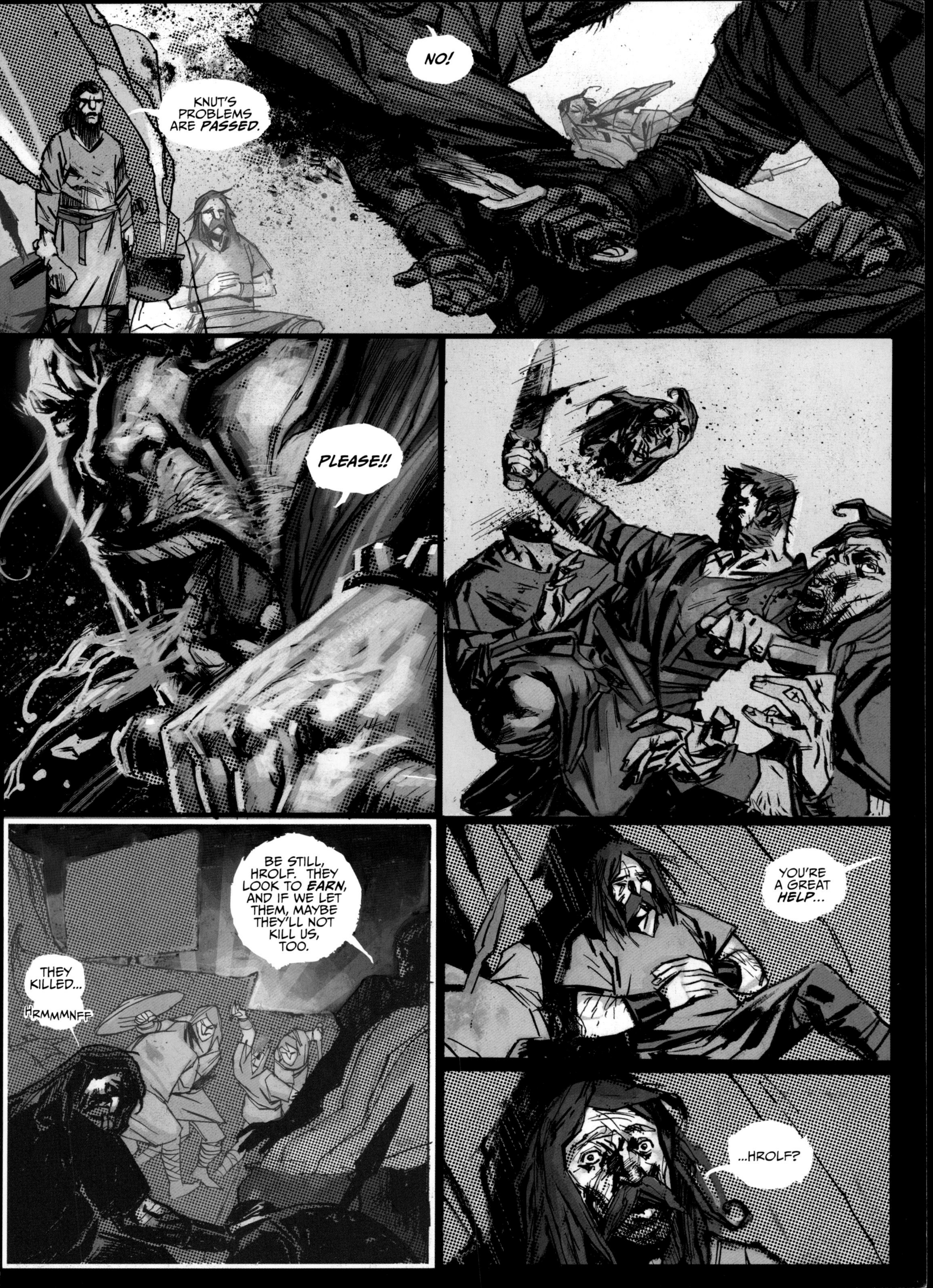

KNUT'S PROBLEMS ARE PASSED.
NO!
PLEASE!!
BE STILL, HROLF. THEY LOOK TO EARN, AND IF WE LET THEM, MAYBE THEY'LL NOT KILL US, TOO.
THEY KILLED...
HRMMMNFF
YOU'RE A GREAT HELP...
...HROLF?

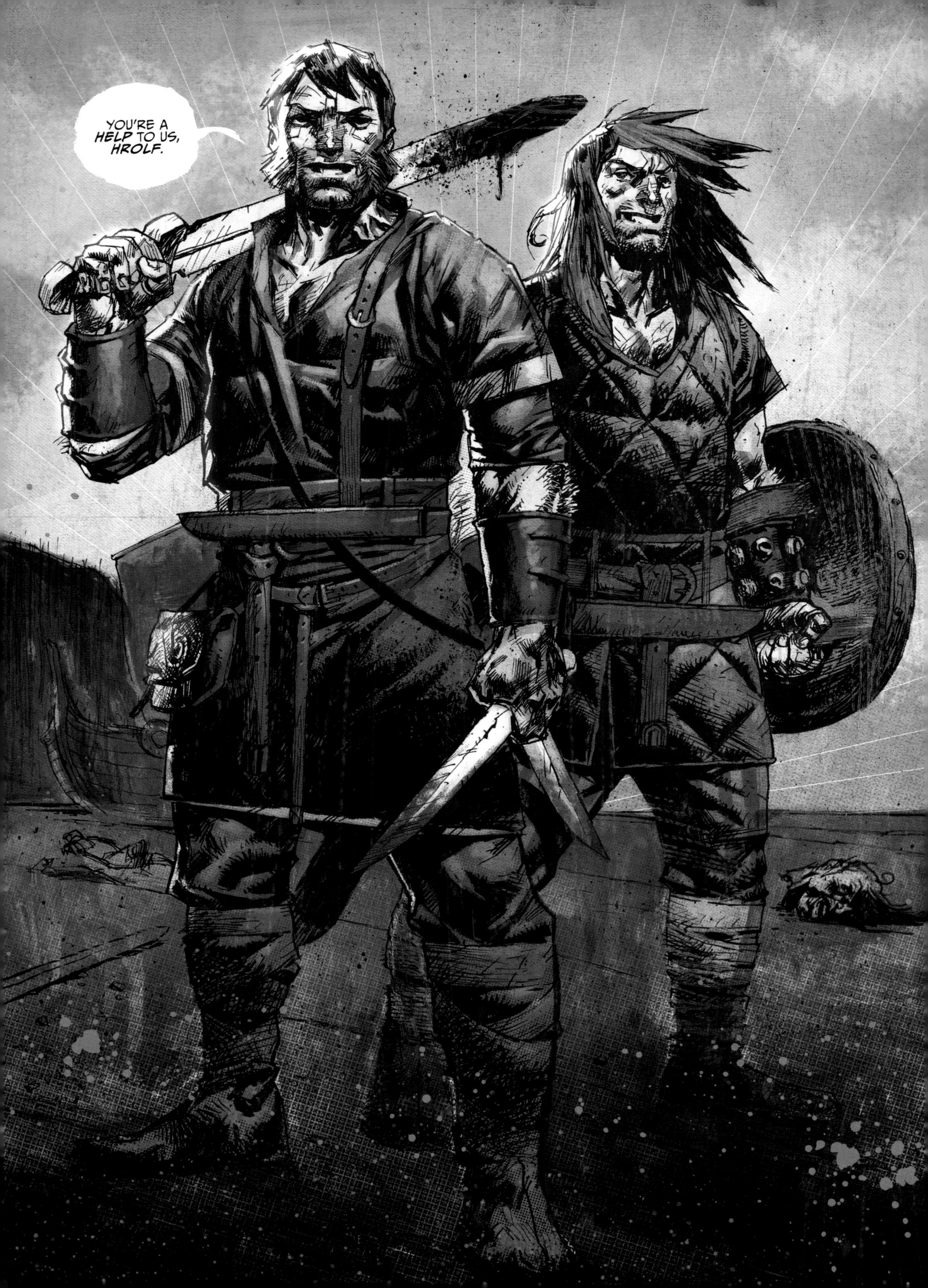
YOU'RE A HELP TO US, HROLF.

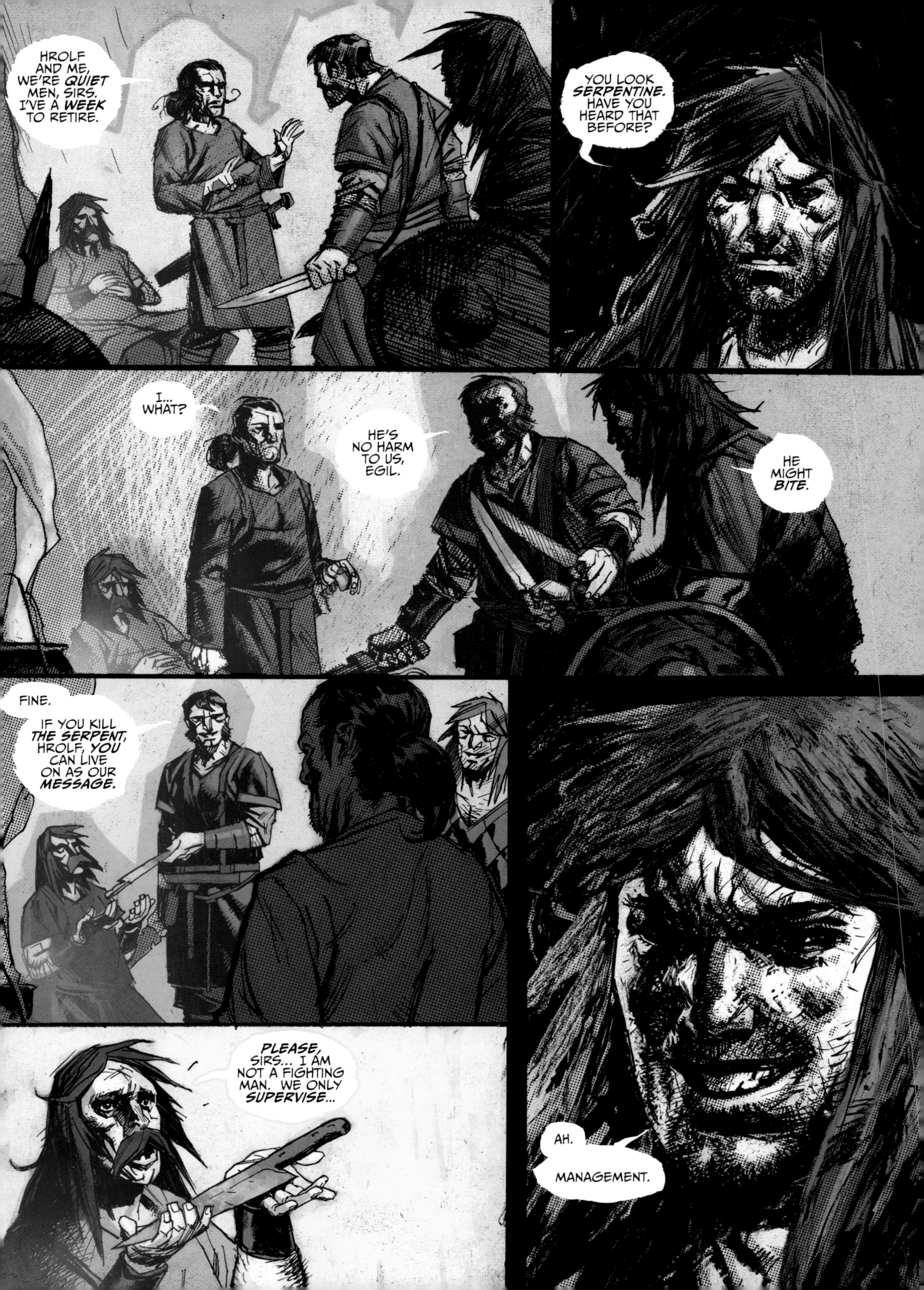
HROLF AND ME, WE'RE *QUIET* MEN, SIRS. I'VE A *WEEK* TO RETIRE.
YOU LOOK *SERPENTINE.* HAVE YOU HEARD THAT BEFORE?
I... WHAT?
HE'S NO HARM TO US, EGIL.
HE MIGHT *BITE.*
FINE.
IF YOU KILL *THE SERPENT,* HROLF, *YOU* CAN LIVE ON AS OUR *MESSAGE.*
PLEASE, SIRS... I AM NOT A FIGHTING MAN. WE ONLY *SUPERVISE*...
AH.
MANAGEMENT.

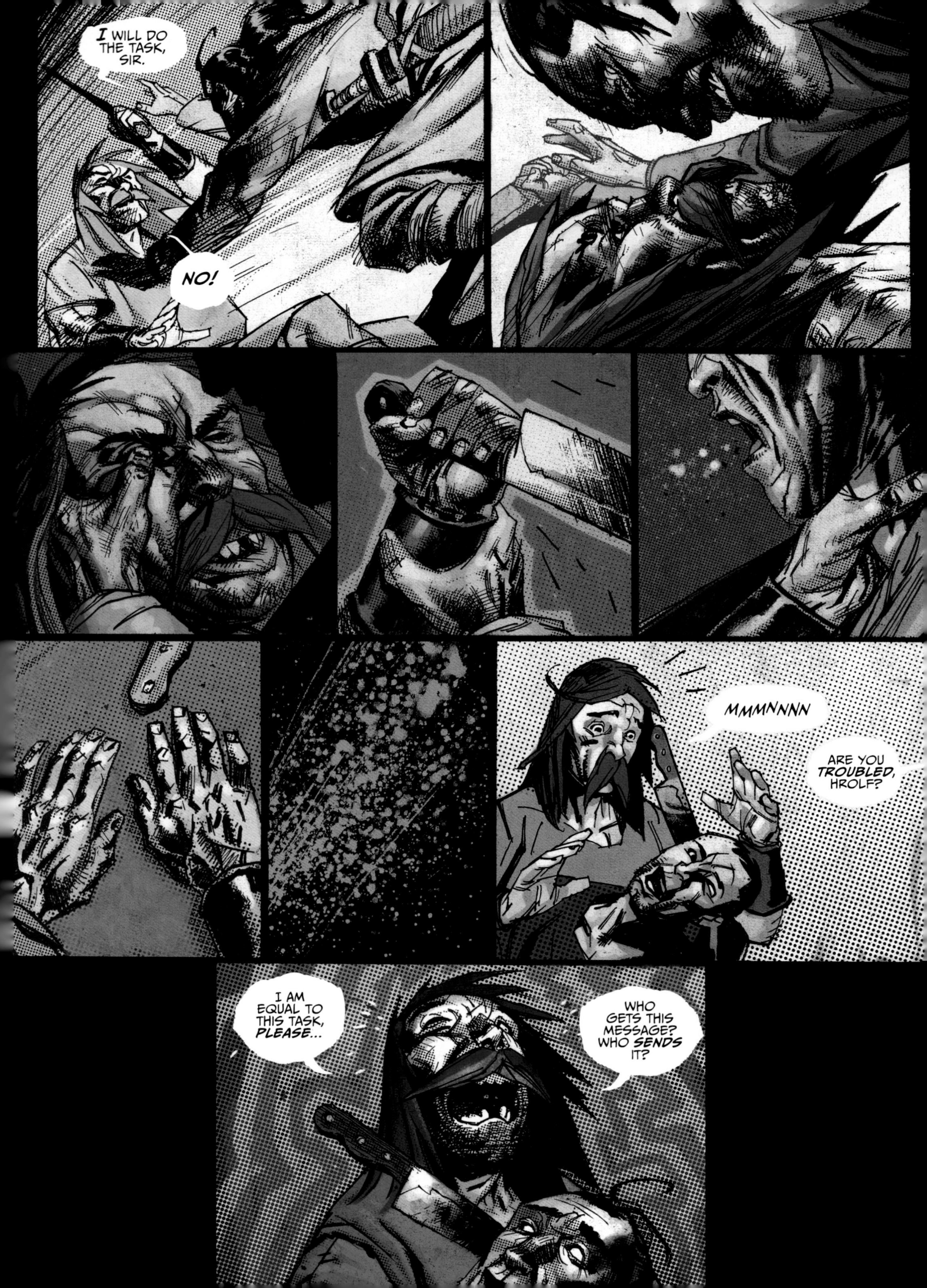
I WILL DO THE TASK, SIR.
NO!
MMMNNNN
ARE YOU TROUBLED, HROLF?
I AM EQUAL TO THIS TASK, PLEASE...
WHO GETS THIS MESSAGE? WHO SENDS IT?

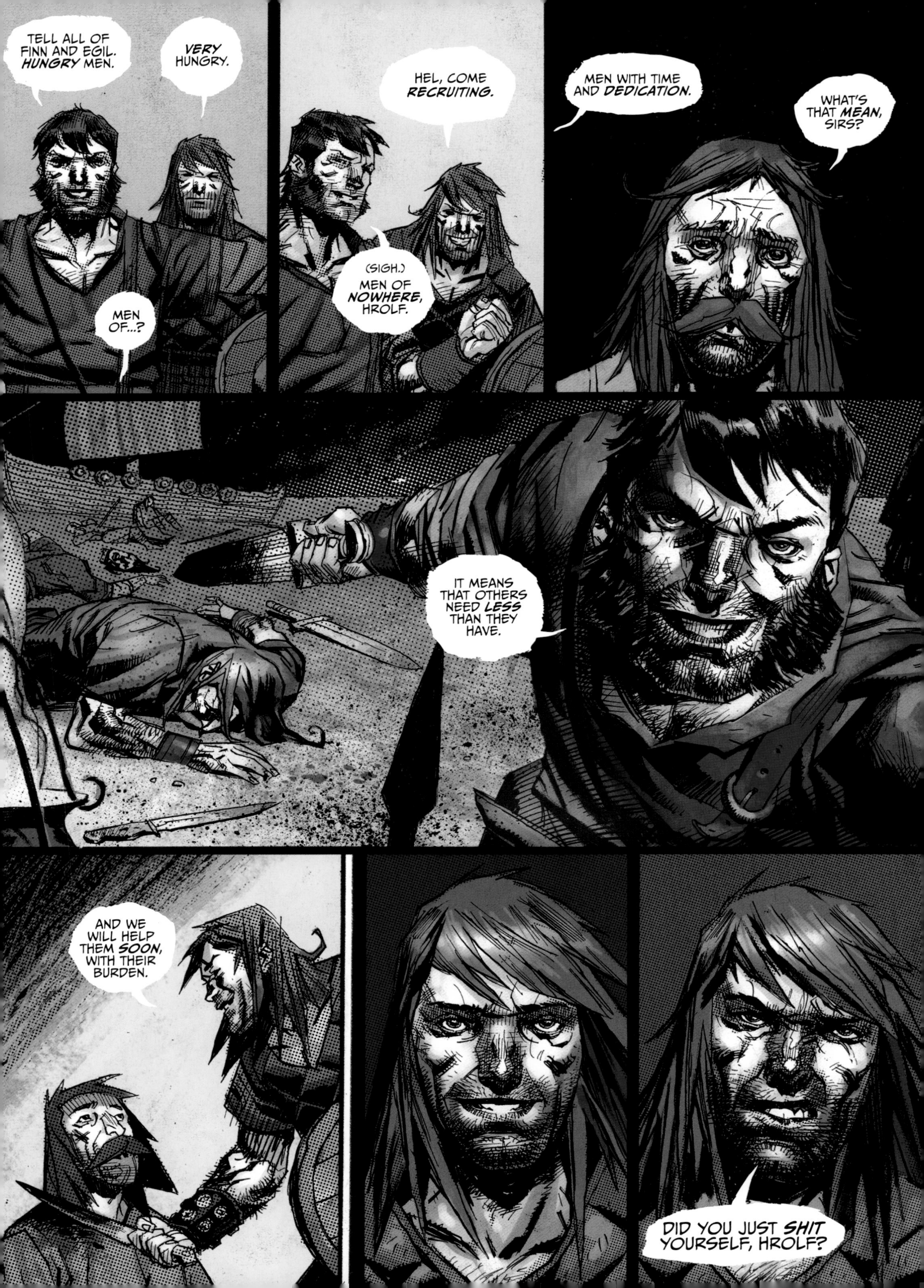
TELL ALL OF FINN AND EGIL. *HUNGRY* MEN.
VERY HUNGRY.
MEN OF...?
HEL, COME *RECRUITING.*
(SIGH.) MEN OF *NOWHERE,* HROLF.
MEN WITH TIME AND *DEDICATION.*
WHAT'S THAT *MEAN,* SIRS?
IT MEANS THAT OTHERS NEED *LESS* THAN THEY HAVE.
AND WE WILL HELP THEM *SOON,* WITH THEIR BURDEN.
DID YOU JUST *SHIT* YOURSELF, HROLF?

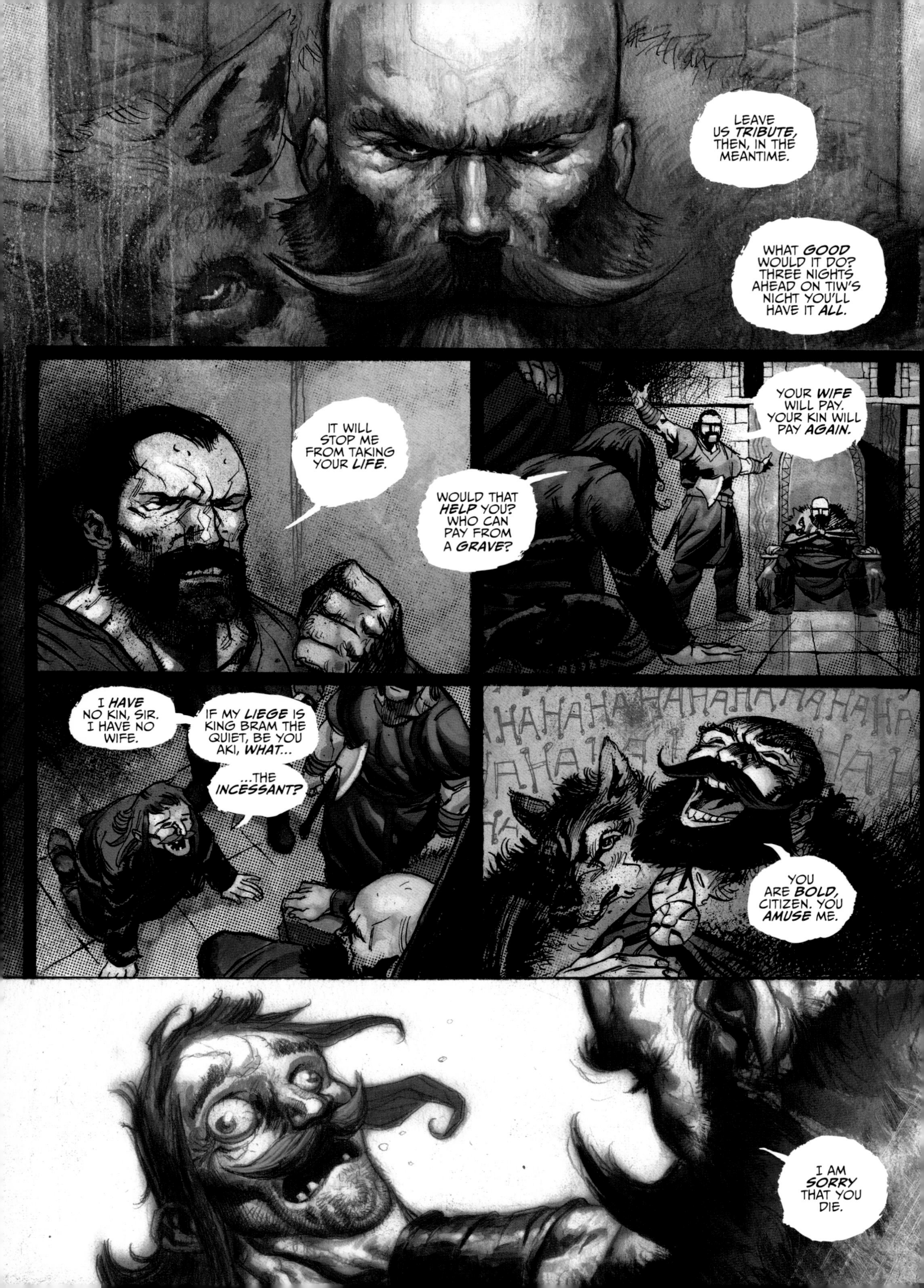

LEAVE US TRIBUTE, THEN, IN THE MEANTIME.
WHAT GOOD WOULD IT DO? THREE NIGHTS AHEAD ON TIW'S NIGHT YOU'LL HAVE IT ALL.
IT WILL STOP ME FROM TAKING YOUR LIFE.
WOULD THAT HELP YOU? WHO CAN PAY FROM A GRAVE?
YOUR WIFE WILL PAY. YOUR KIN WILL PAY AGAIN.
I HAVE NO KIN, SIR. I HAVE NO WIFE.
IF MY LIEGE IS KING BRAM THE QUIET, BE YOU AKI, WHAT...
...THE INCESSANT?
HAHAHAHAHAHAHAHA
YOU ARE BOLD, CITIZEN. YOU AMUSE ME.
I AM SORRY THAT YOU DIE.

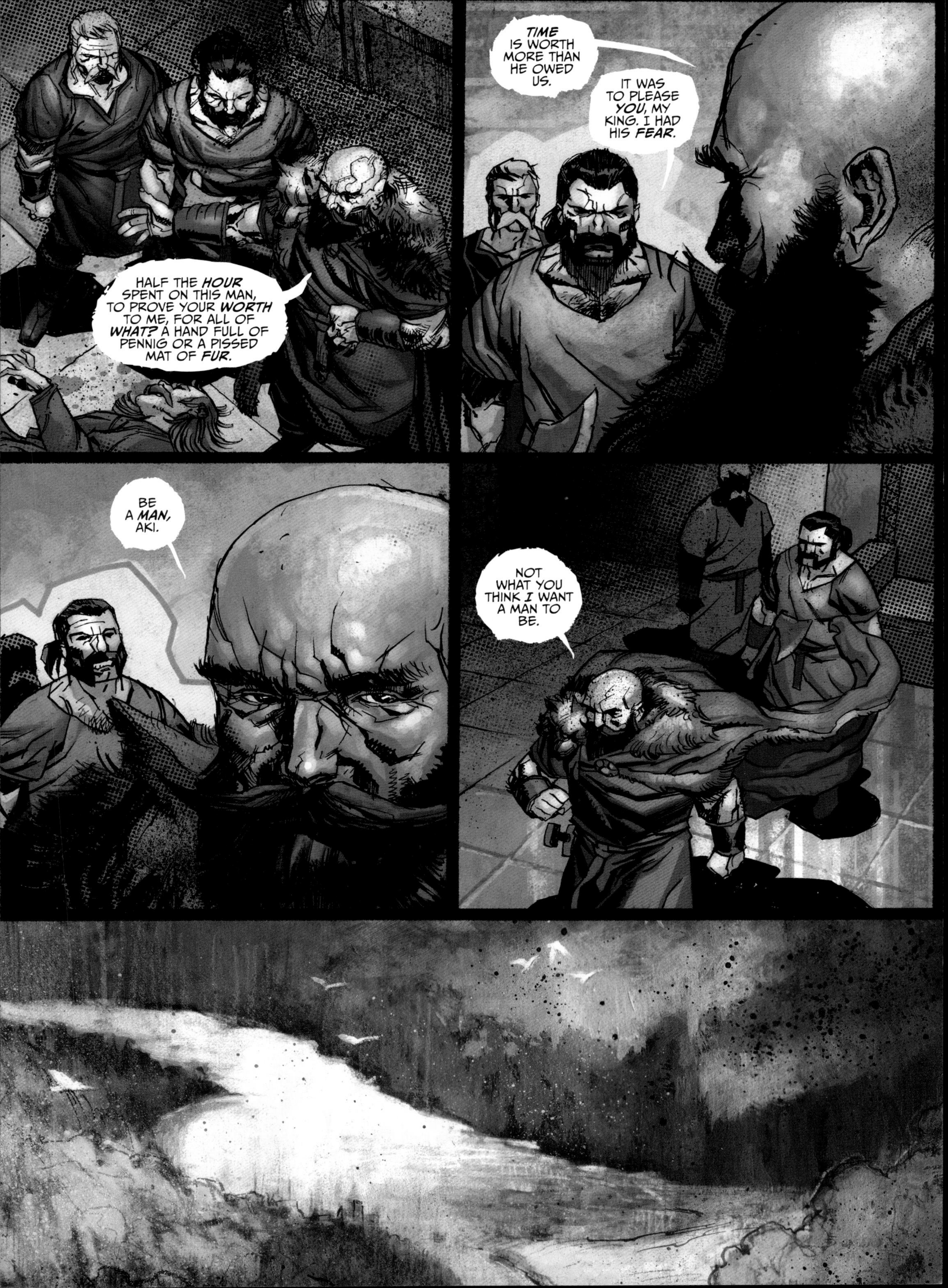

HALF THE HOUR SPENT ON THIS MAN, TO PROVE YOUR WORTH TO ME, FOR ALL OF WHAT? A HAND FULL OF PENNIG OR A PISSED MAT OF FUR.
TIME IS WORTH MORE THAN HE OWED US.
IT WAS TO PLEASE YOU, MY KING. I HAD HIS FEAR.
BE A MAN, AKI.
NOT WHAT YOU THINK I WANT A MAN TO BE.

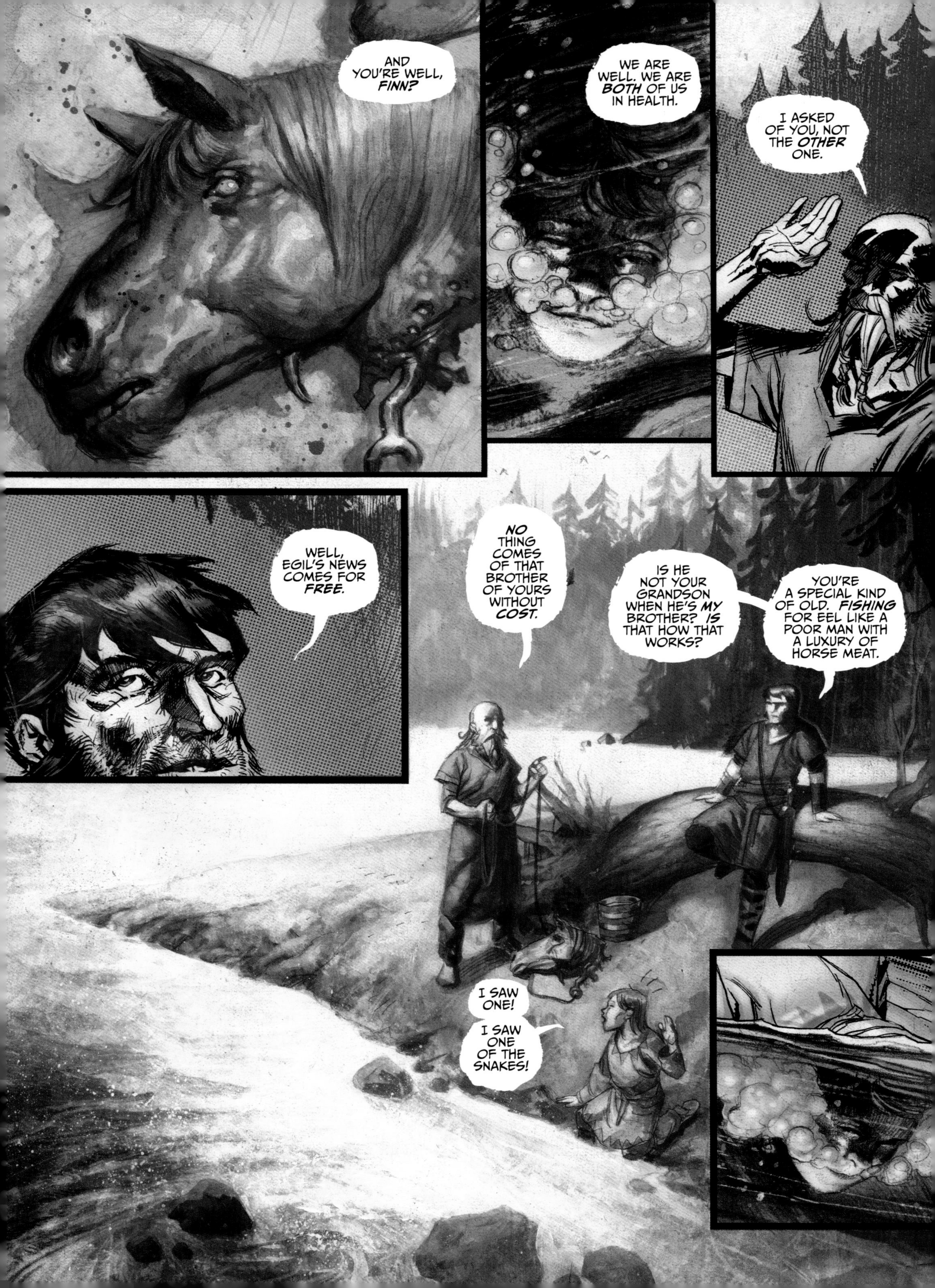

AND YOU'RE WELL, FINN?
WE ARE WELL. WE ARE BOTH OF US IN HEALTH.
I ASKED OF YOU, NOT THE OTHER ONE.
WELL, EGIL'S NEWS COMES FOR FREE.
NO THING COMES OF THAT BROTHER OF YOURS WITHOUT COST.
IS HE NOT YOUR GRANDSON WHEN HE'S MY BROTHER? IS THAT HOW THAT WORKS?
YOU'RE A SPECIAL KIND OF OLD. FISHING FOR EEL LIKE A POOR MAN WITH A LUXURY OF HORSE MEAT.
I SAW ONE!
I SAW ONE OF THE SNAKES!

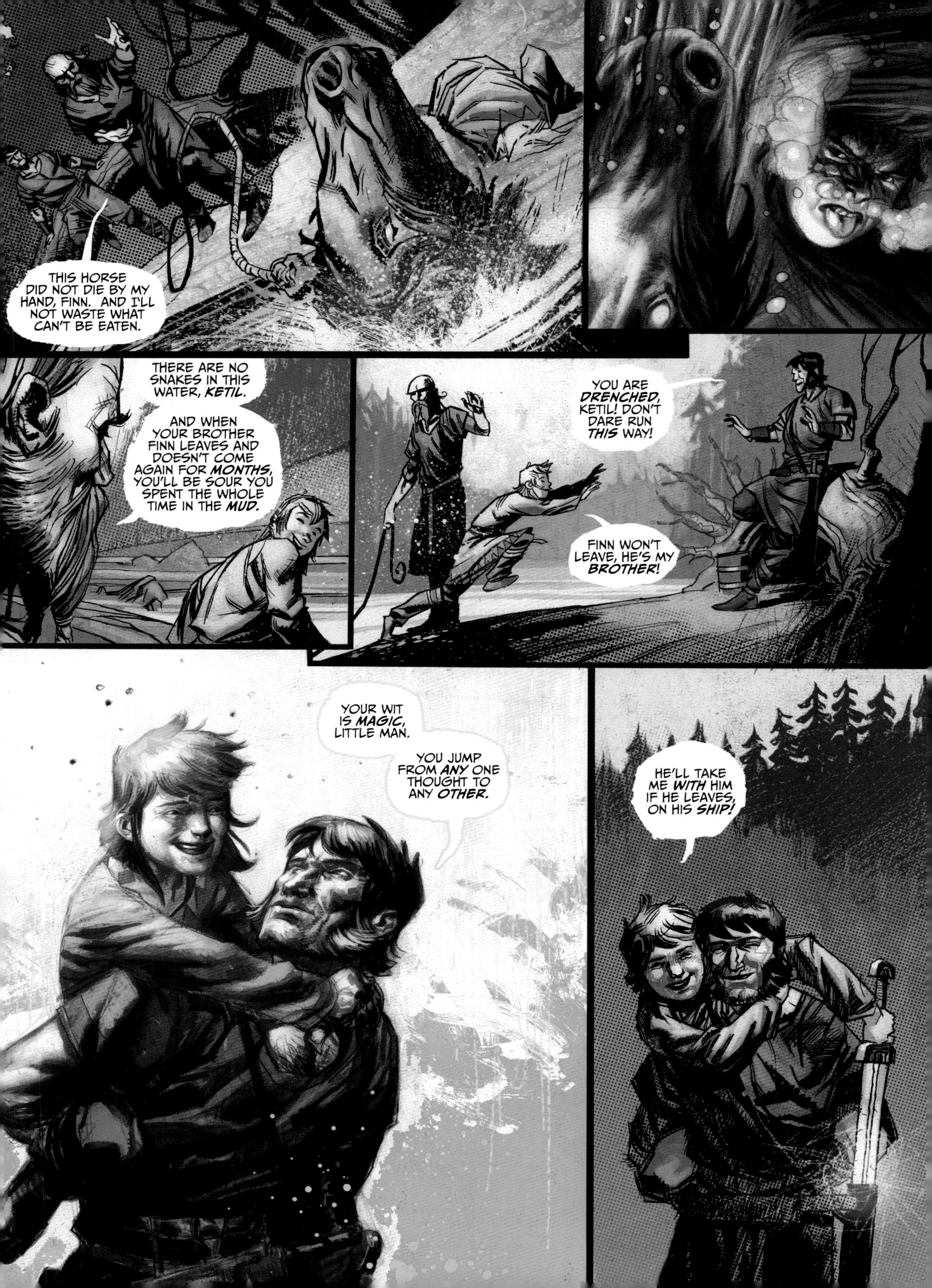

THIS HORSE DID NOT DIE BY MY HAND, FINN. AND I'LL NOT WASTE WHAT CAN'T BE EATEN.
THERE ARE NO SNAKES IN THIS WATER, *KETIL.*
AND WHEN YOUR BROTHER FINN LEAVES AND DOESN'T COME AGAIN FOR *MONTHS,* YOU'LL BE SOUR YOU SPENT THE WHOLE TIME IN THE *MUD.*
YOU ARE *DRENCHED,* KETIL! DON'T DARE RUN *THIS* WAY!
FINN WON'T LEAVE, HE'S MY *BROTHER!*
YOUR WIT IS *MAGIC,* LITTLE MAN.
YOU JUMP FROM *ANY* ONE THOUGHT TO ANY *OTHER.*
HE'LL TAKE ME *WITH* HIM IF HE LEAVES, ON HIS *SHIP!*

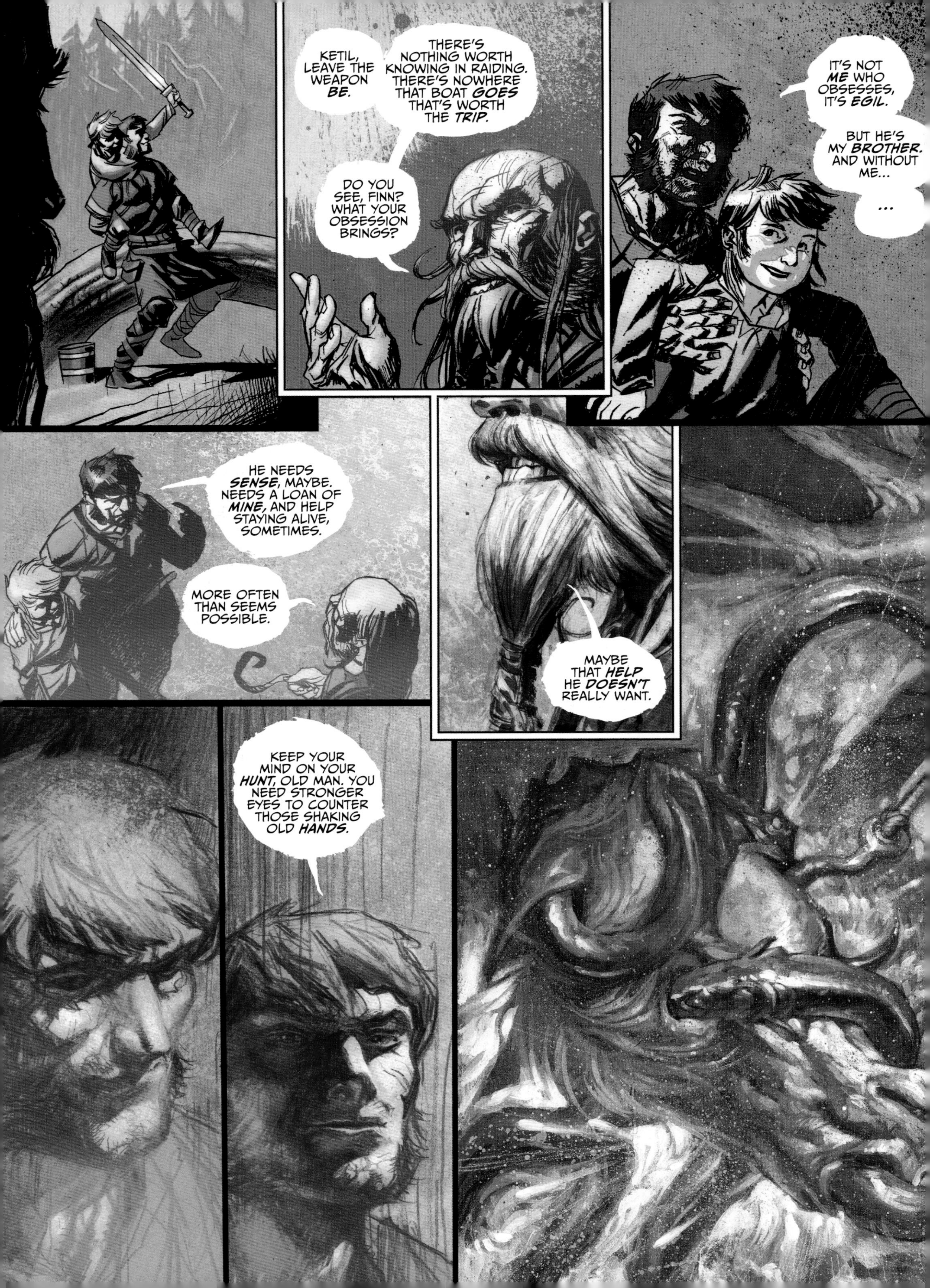
KETIL, LEAVE THE WEAPON BE.
THERE'S NOTHING WORTH KNOWING IN RAIDING. THERE'S NOWHERE THAT BOAT GOES THAT'S WORTH THE TRIP.
DO YOU SEE, FINN? WHAT YOUR OBSESSION BRINGS?
IT'S NOT ME WHO OBSESSES, IT'S EGIL.
BUT HE'S MY BROTHER. AND WITHOUT ME...
...
HE NEEDS SENSE, MAYBE. NEEDS A LOAN OF MINE, AND HELP STAYING ALIVE, SOMETIMES.
MORE OFTEN THAN SEEMS POSSIBLE.
MAYBE THAT HELP HE DOESN'T REALLY WANT.
KEEP YOUR MIND ON YOUR HUNT, OLD MAN. YOU NEED STRONGER EYES TO COUNTER THOSE SHAKING OLD HANDS.

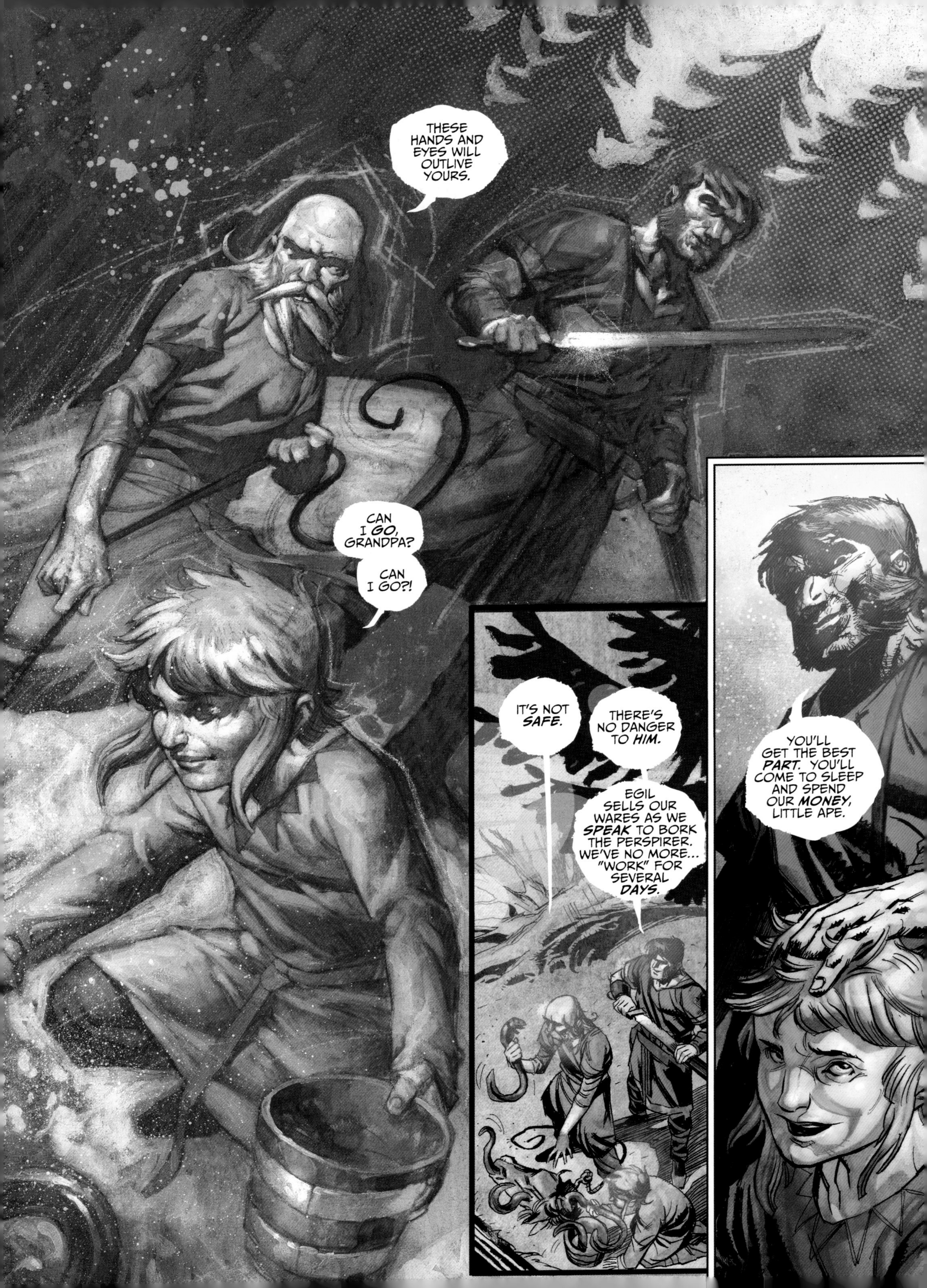
THESE HANDS AND EYES WILL OUTLIVE YOURS.
CAN I GO, GRANDPA?
CAN I GO?!
IT'S NOT SAFE.
THERE'S NO DANGER TO HIM.
EGIL SELLS OUR WARES AS WE SPEAK TO BORK THE PERSPIRER. WE'VE NO MORE... "WORK" FOR SEVERAL DAYS.
YOU'LL GET THE BEST PART. YOU'LL COME TO SLEEP AND SPEND OUR MONEY, LITTLE APE.

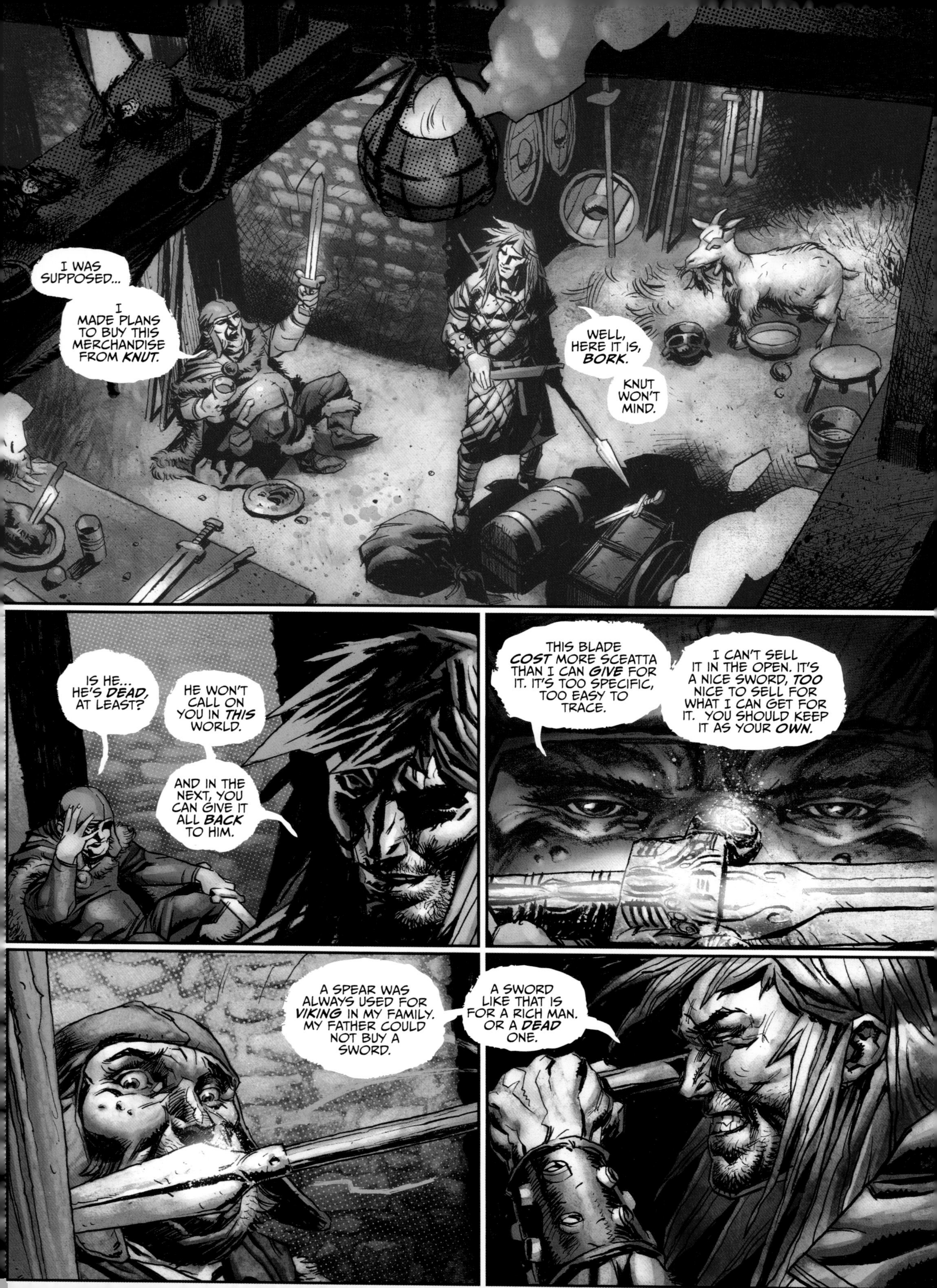
I WAS SUPPOSED...
I MADE PLANS TO BUY THIS MERCHANDISE FROM KNUT.
WELL, HERE IT IS, BORK.
KNUT WON'T MIND.
IS HE... HE'S DEAD, AT LEAST?
HE WON'T CALL ON YOU IN THIS WORLD.
AND IN THE NEXT, YOU CAN GIVE IT ALL BACK TO HIM.
THIS BLADE COST MORE SCEATTA THAN I CAN GIVE FOR IT. IT'S TOO SPECIFIC, TOO EASY TO TRACE.
I CAN'T SELL IT IN THE OPEN. IT'S A NICE SWORD, TOO NICE TO SELL FOR WHAT I CAN GET FOR IT. YOU SHOULD KEEP IT AS YOUR OWN.
A SPEAR WAS ALWAYS USED FOR VIKING IN MY FAMILY. MY FATHER COULD NOT BUY A SWORD.
A SWORD LIKE THAT IS FOR A RICH MAN. OR A DEAD ONE.

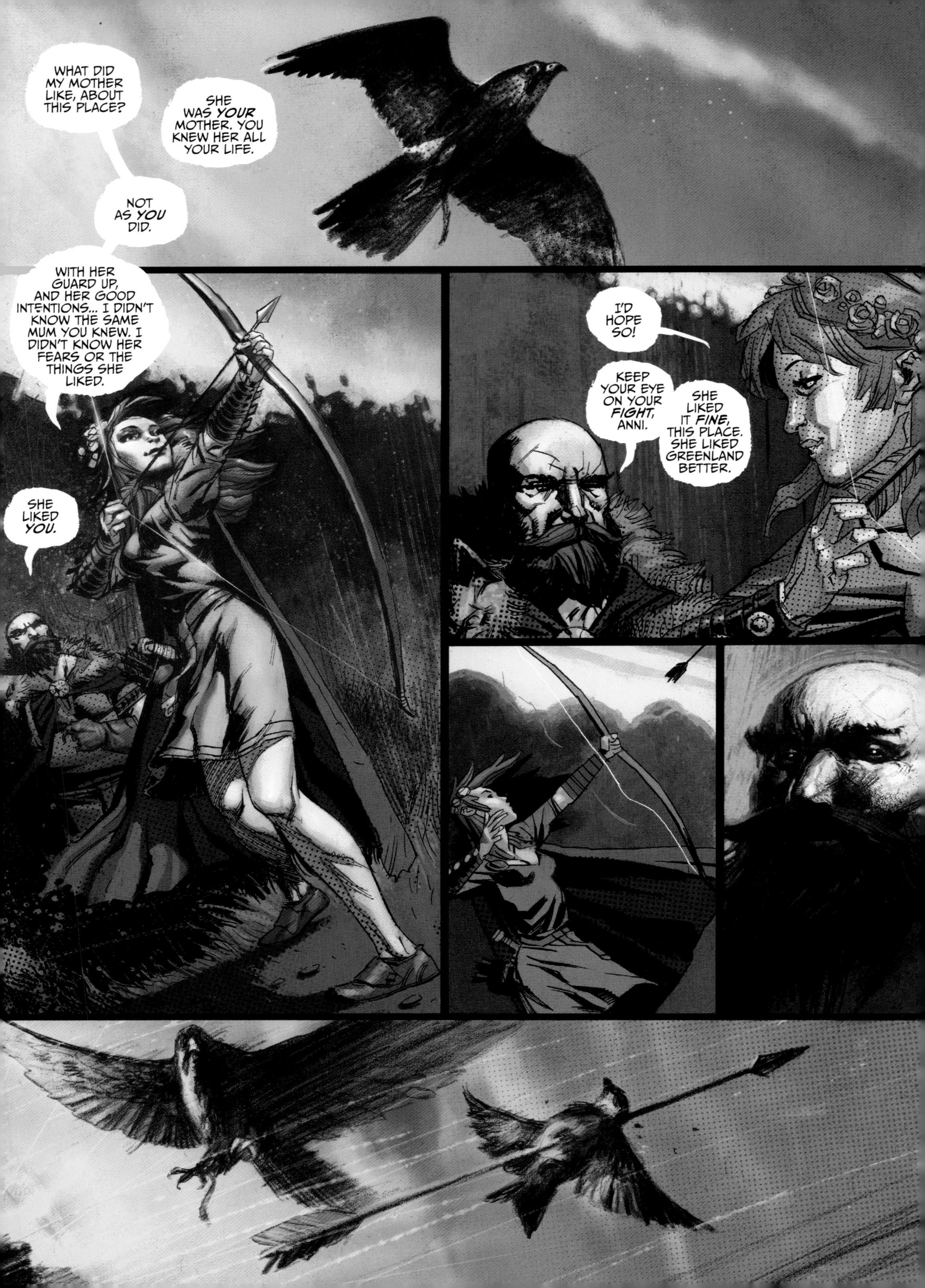
WHAT DID MY MOTHER LIKE, ABOUT THIS PLACE?
SHE WAS YOUR MOTHER. YOU KNEW HER ALL YOUR LIFE.
NOT AS YOU DID.
WITH HER GUARD UP, AND HER GOOD INTENTIONS... I DIDN'T KNOW THE SAME MUM YOU KNEW. I DIDN'T KNOW HER FEARS OR THE THINGS SHE LIKED.
SHE LIKED YOU.
I'D HOPE SO!
KEEP YOUR EYE ON YOUR FIGHT, ANNI.
SHE LIKED IT FINE, THIS PLACE. SHE LIKED GREENLAND BETTER.

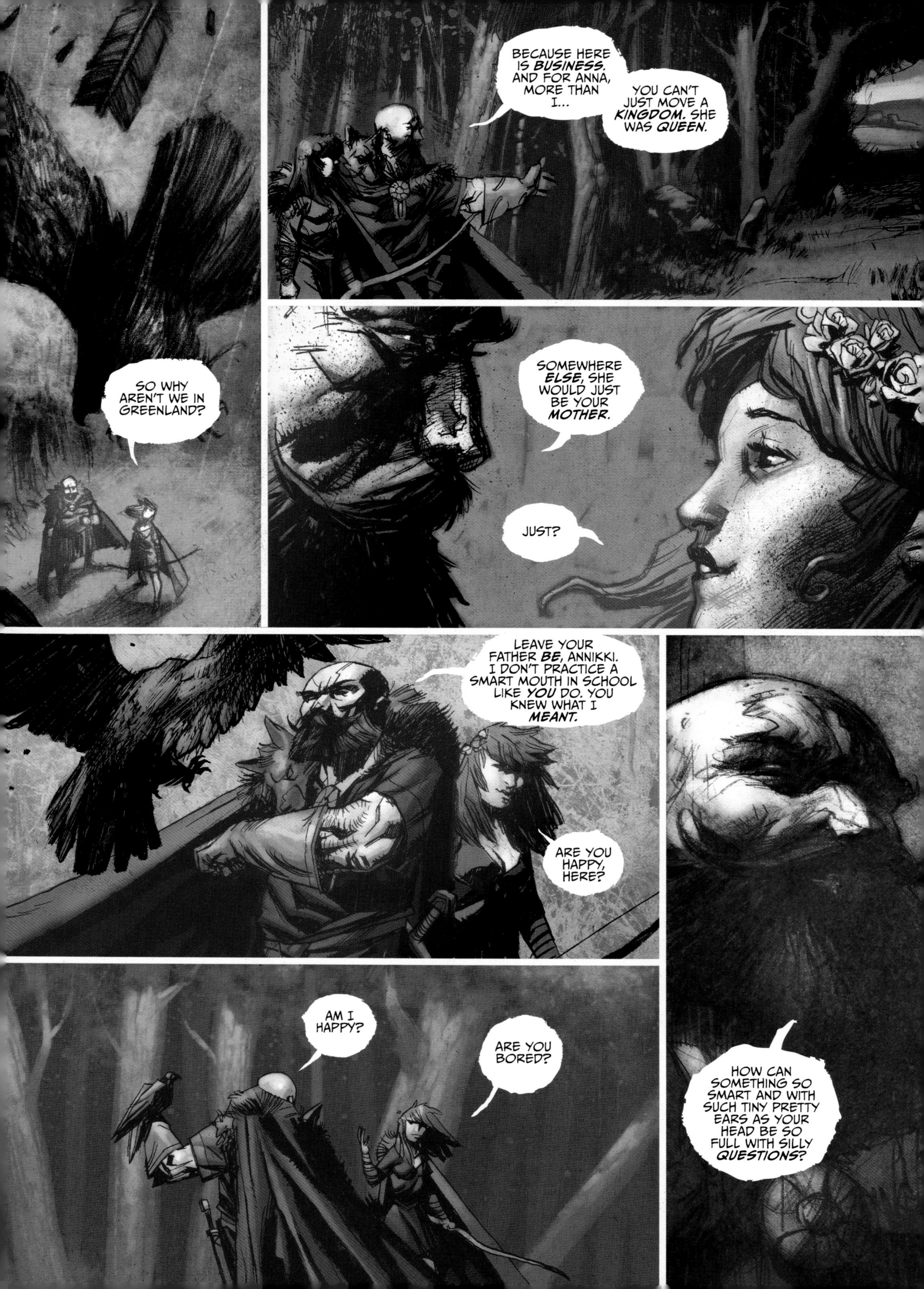
SO WHY AREN'T WE IN GREENLAND?
BECAUSE HERE IS BUSINESS. AND FOR ANNA, MORE THAN I...
YOU CAN'T JUST MOVE A KINGDOM. SHE WAS QUEEN.
SOMEWHERE ELSE, SHE WOULD JUST BE YOUR MOTHER.
JUST?
LEAVE YOUR FATHER BE, ANNIKKI. I DON'T PRACTICE A SMART MOUTH IN SCHOOL LIKE YOU DO. YOU KNEW WHAT I MEANT.
ARE YOU HAPPY, HERE?
AM I HAPPY?
ARE YOU BORED?
HOW CAN SOMETHING SO SMART AND WITH SUCH TINY PRETTY EARS AS YOUR HEAD BE SO FULL WITH SILLY QUESTIONS?

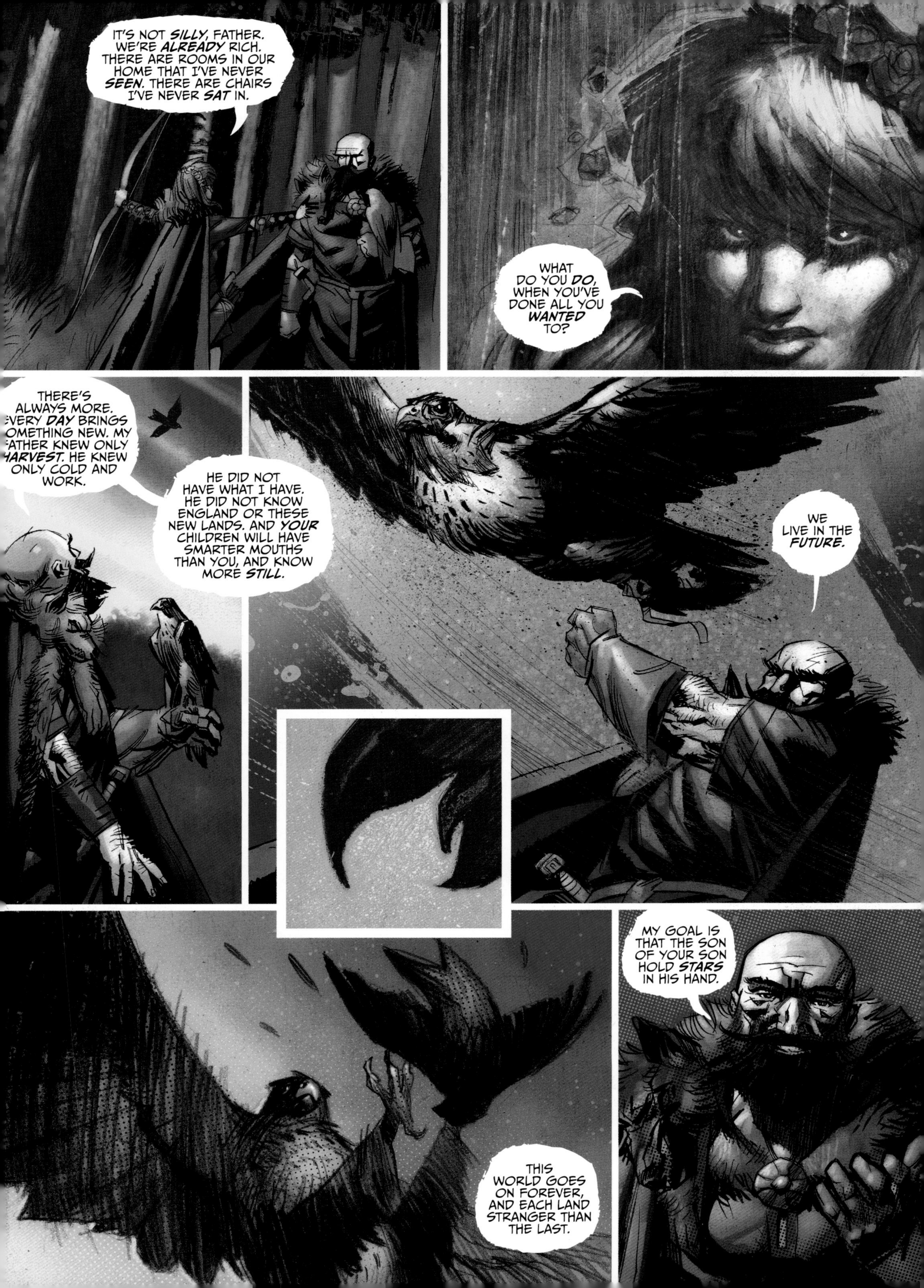
IT'S NOT *SILLY*, FATHER. WE'RE *ALREADY* RICH. THERE ARE ROOMS IN OUR HOME THAT I'VE NEVER *SEEN*. THERE ARE CHAIRS I'VE NEVER *SAT* IN.
WHAT DO YOU *DO*, WHEN YOU'VE DONE ALL YOU *WANTED* TO?
THERE'S ALWAYS MORE. VERY *DAY* BRINGS OMETHING NEW. MY ATHER KNEW ONLY *ARVEST.* HE KNEW ONLY COLD AND WORK.
HE DID NOT HAVE WHAT I HAVE. HE DID NOT KNOW ENGLAND OR THESE NEW LANDS. AND *YOUR* CHILDREN WILL HAVE SMARTER MOUTHS THAN YOU, AND KNOW MORE *STILL*.
WE LIVE IN THE *FUTURE.*
MY GOAL IS THAT THE SON OF YOUR SON HOLD *STARS* IN HIS HAND.
THIS WORLD GOES ON FOREVER, AND EACH LAND STRANGER THAN THE LAST.

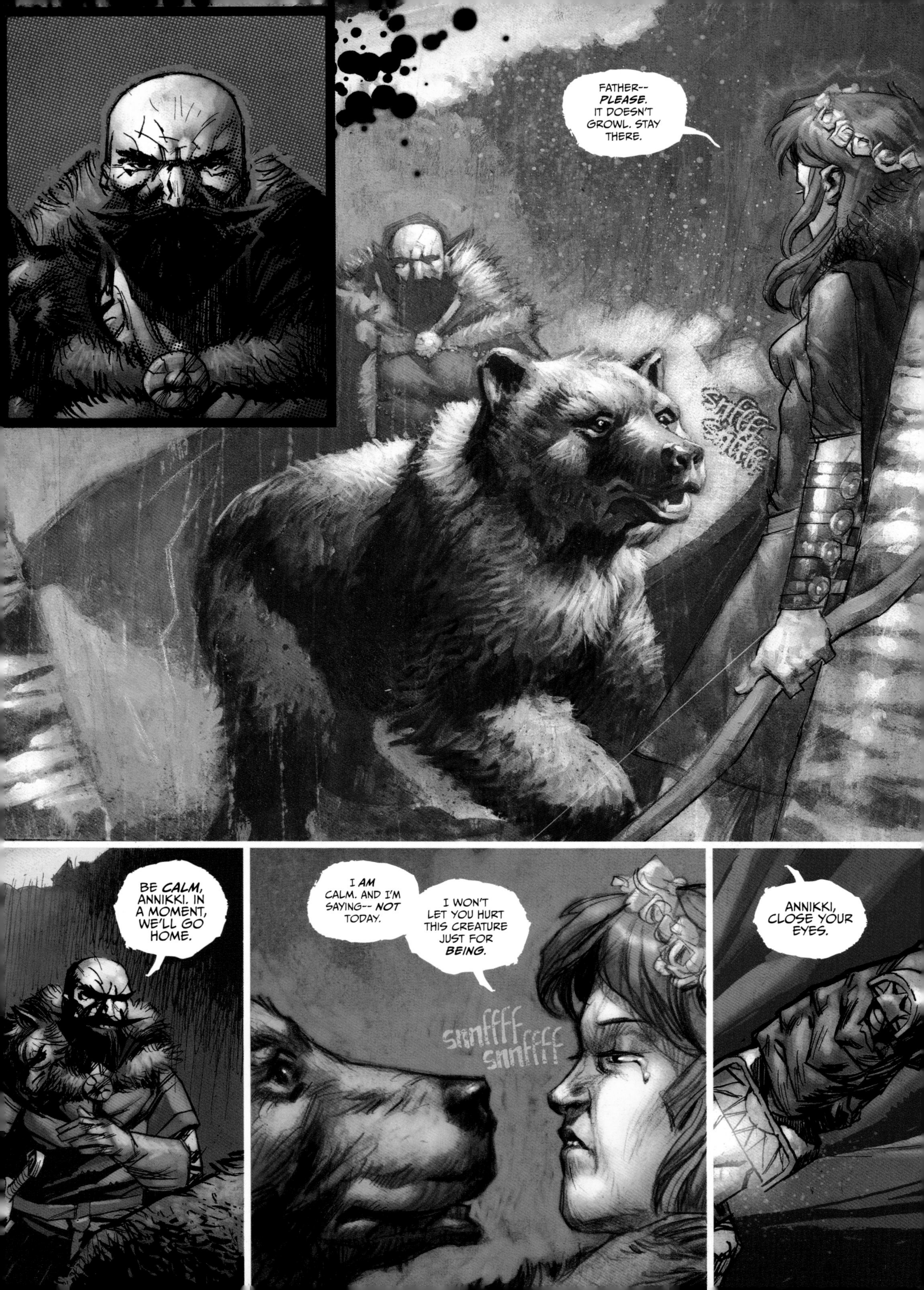
FATHER-- *PLEASE.* IT DOESN'T GROWL. STAY THERE.
BE *CALM,* ANNIKKI. IN A MOMENT, WE'LL GO HOME.
I *AM* CALM. AND I'M SAYING-- *NOT* TODAY.
I WON'T LET YOU HURT THIS CREATURE JUST FOR *BEING.*
snnffff
snnffff
ANNIKKI, CLOSE YOUR EYES.

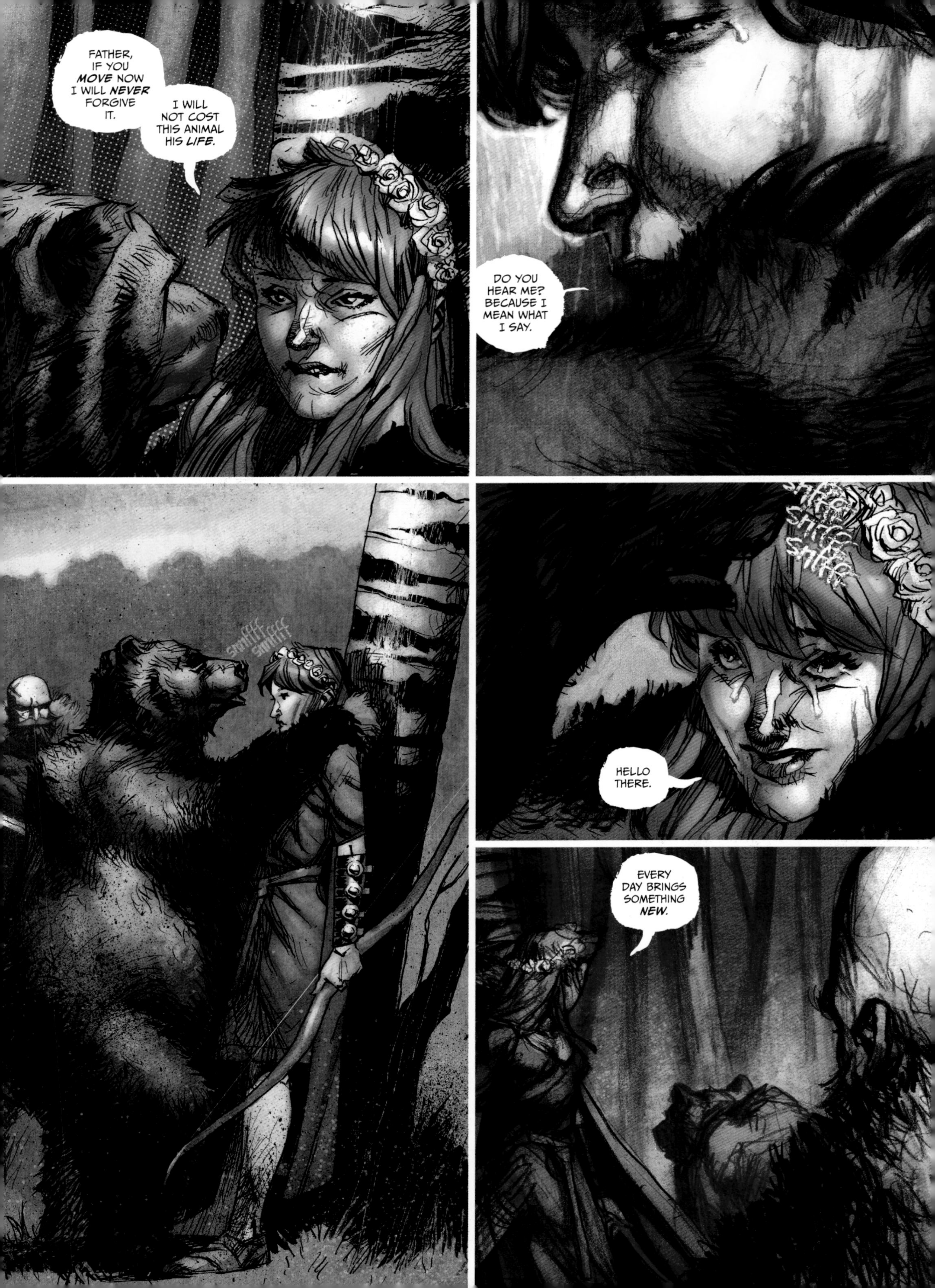
FATHER, IF YOU *MOVE* NOW I WILL *NEVER* FORGIVE IT.
I WILL NOT COST THIS ANIMAL HIS *LIFE*.
DO YOU HEAR ME? BECAUSE I MEAN WHAT I SAY.
HELLO THERE.
EVERY DAY BRINGS SOMETHING *NEW*.

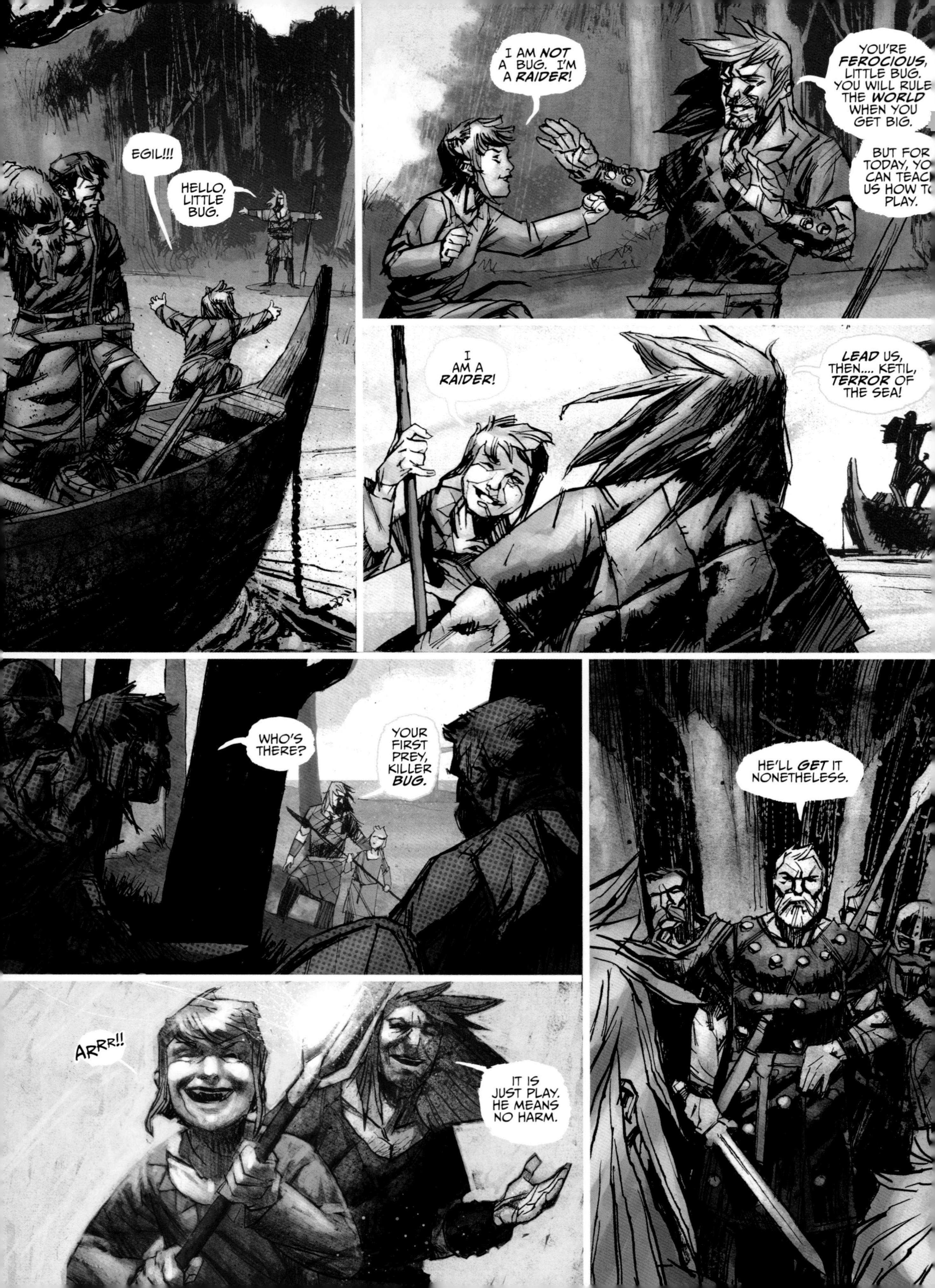

EGIL!!!
HELLO, LITTLE BUG.
I AM NOT A BUG. I'M A RAIDER!
YOU'RE FEROCIOUS, LITTLE BUG. YOU WILL RULE THE WORLD WHEN YOU GET BIG.
BUT FOR TODAY, YOU CAN TEACH US HOW TO PLAY.
I AM A RAIDER!
LEAD US, THEN.... KETIL, TERROR OF THE SEA!
WHO'S THERE?
YOUR FIRST PREY, KILLER BUG.
ARRR!!
IT IS JUST PLAY. HE MEANS NO HARM.
HE'LL GET IT NONETHELESS.

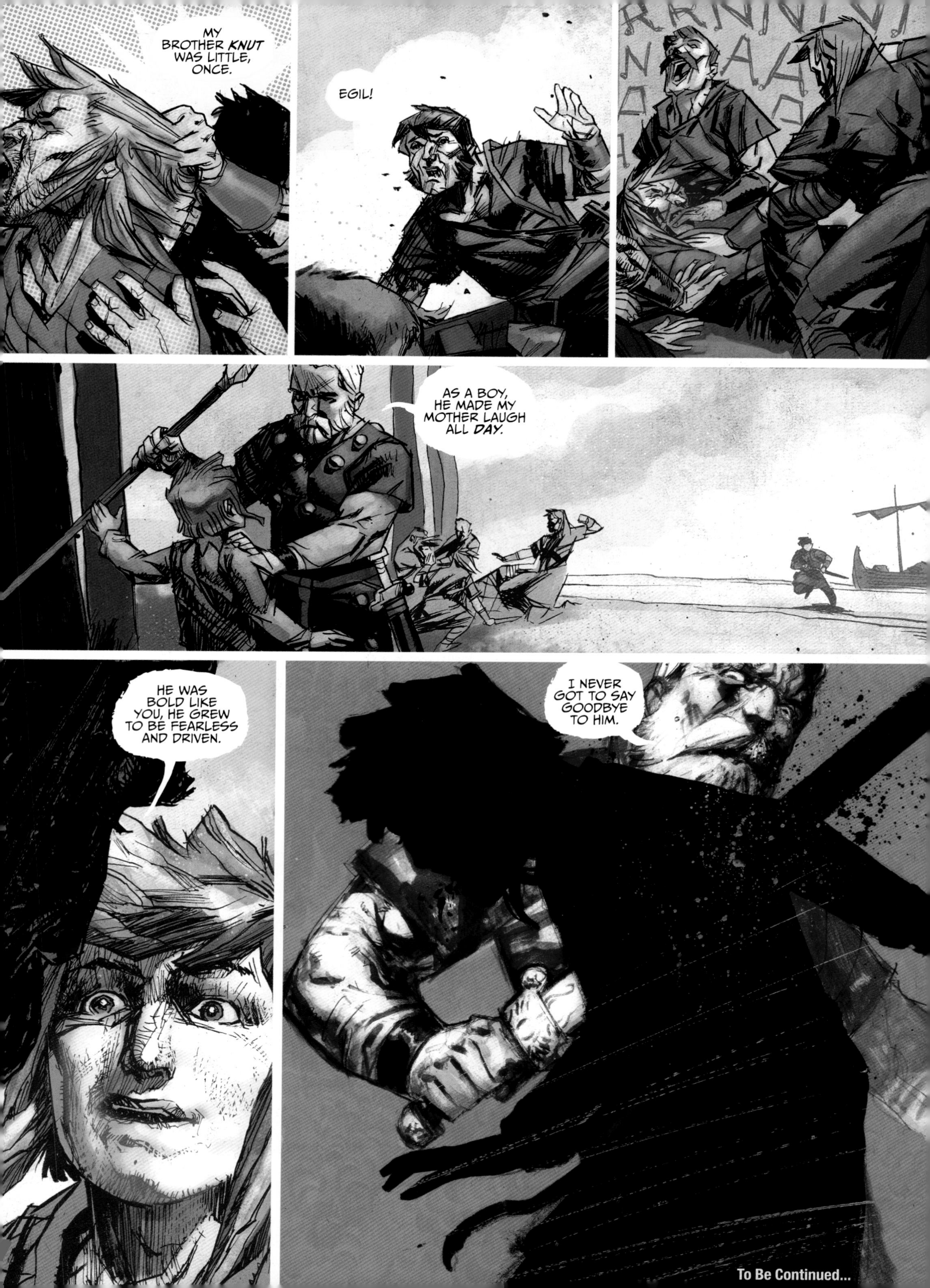
MY BROTHER KNUT WAS LITTLE, ONCE.
EGIL!
AS A BOY, HE MADE MY MOTHER LAUGH ALL DAY.
HE WAS BOLD LIKE YOU, HE GREW TO BE FEARLESS AND DRIVEN.
I NEVER GOT TO SAY GOODBYE TO HIM.
To Be Continued...

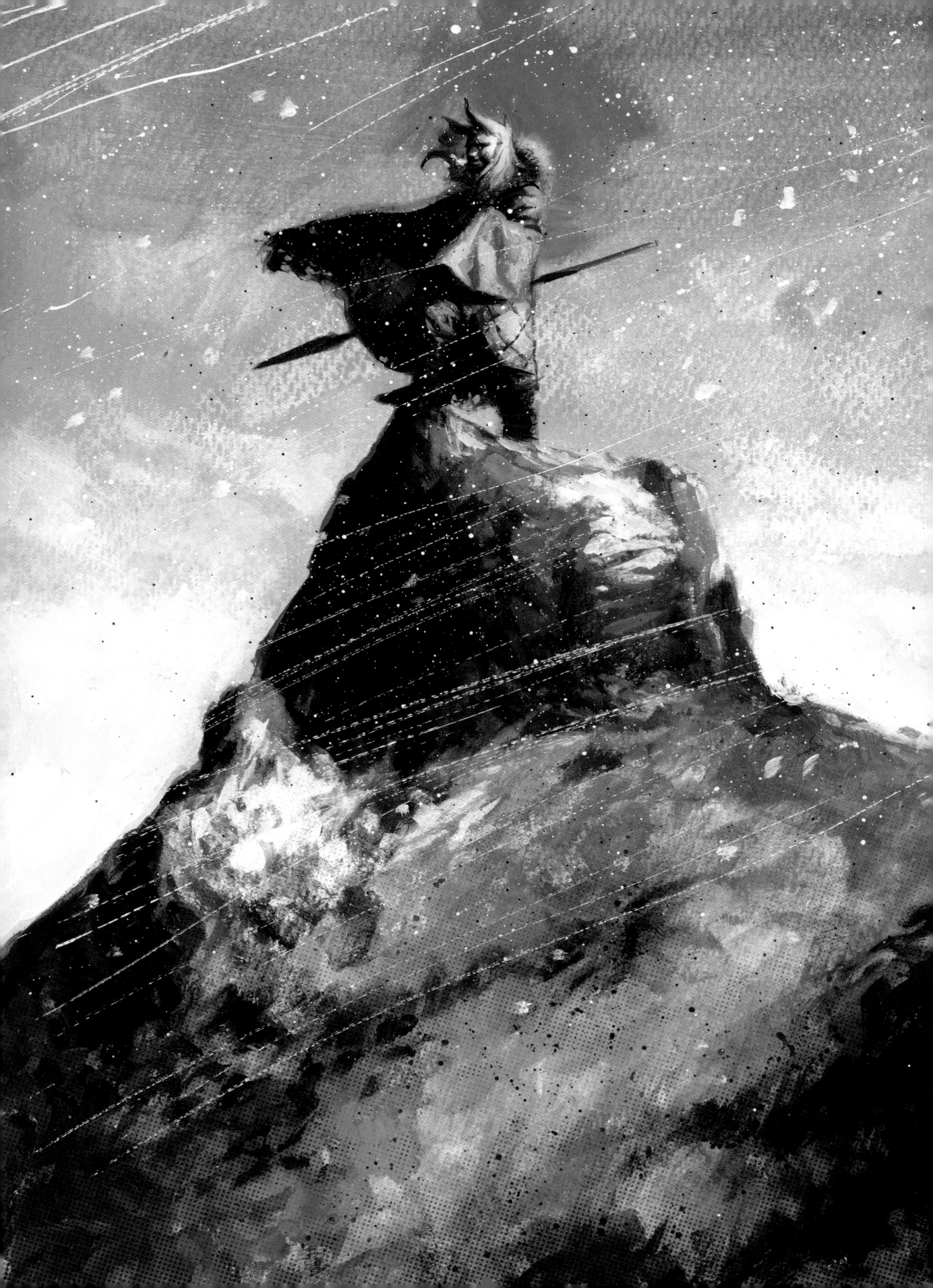

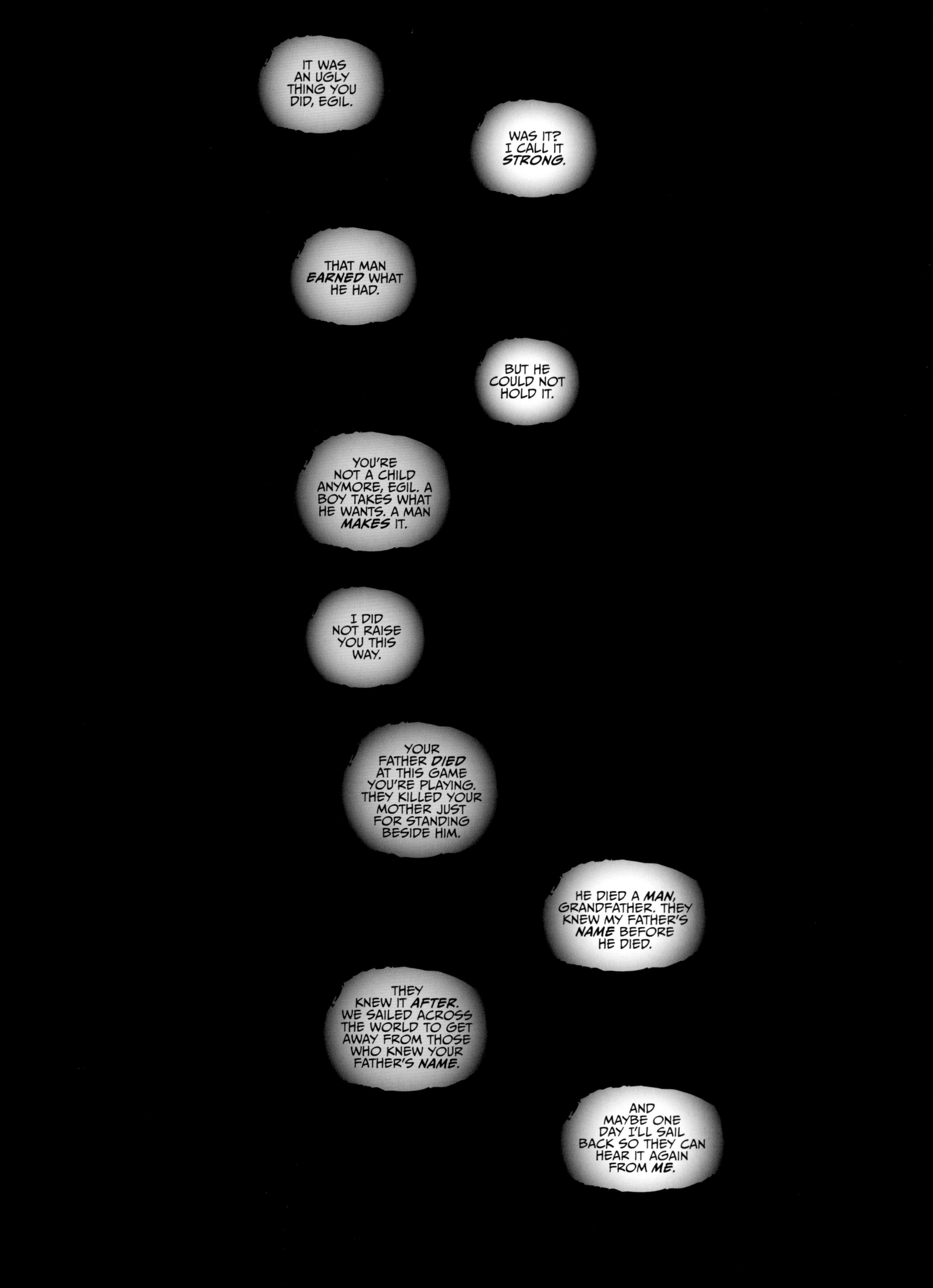
IT WAS AN UGLY THING YOU DID, EGIL.
WAS IT? I CALL IT *STRONG*.
THAT MAN *EARNED* WHAT HE HAD.
BUT HE COULD NOT HOLD IT.
YOU'RE NOT A CHILD ANYMORE, EGIL. A BOY TAKES WHAT HE WANTS. A MAN *MAKES* IT.
I DID NOT RAISE YOU THIS WAY.
YOUR FATHER *DIED* AT THIS GAME YOU'RE PLAYING. THEY KILLED YOUR MOTHER JUST FOR STANDING BESIDE HIM.
HE DIED A *MAN*, GRANDFATHER. THEY KNEW MY FATHER'S *NAME* BEFORE HE DIED.
THEY KNEW IT *AFTER*. WE SAILED ACROSS THE WORLD TO GET AWAY FROM THOSE WHO KNEW YOUR FATHER'S *NAME*.
AND MAYBE ONE DAY I'LL SAIL BACK SO THEY CAN HEAR IT AGAIN FROM *ME*.

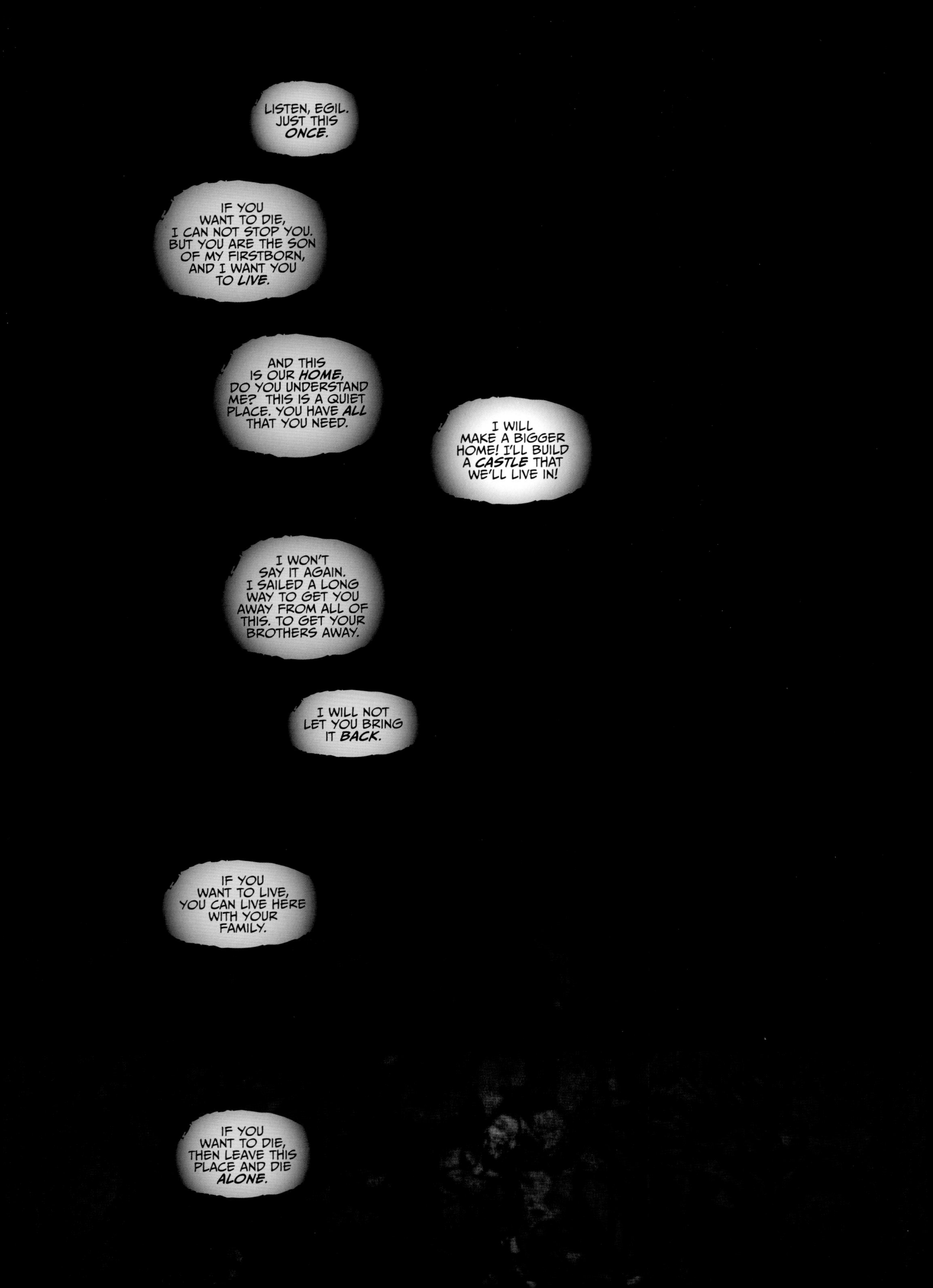
LISTEN, EGIL. JUST THIS ONCE.
IF YOU WANT TO DIE, I CAN NOT STOP YOU. BUT YOU ARE THE SON OF MY FIRSTBORN, AND I WANT YOU TO LIVE.
AND THIS IS OUR HOME, DO YOU UNDERSTAND ME? THIS IS A QUIET PLACE. YOU HAVE ALL THAT YOU NEED.
I WILL MAKE A BIGGER HOME! I'LL BUILD A CASTLE THAT WE'LL LIVE IN!
I WON'T SAY IT AGAIN. I SAILED A LONG WAY TO GET YOU AWAY FROM ALL OF THIS. TO GET YOUR BROTHERS AWAY.
I WILL NOT LET YOU BRING IT BACK.
IF YOU WANT TO LIVE, YOU CAN LIVE HERE WITH YOUR FAMILY.
IF YOU WANT TO DIE, THEN LEAVE THIS PLACE AND DIE ALONE.

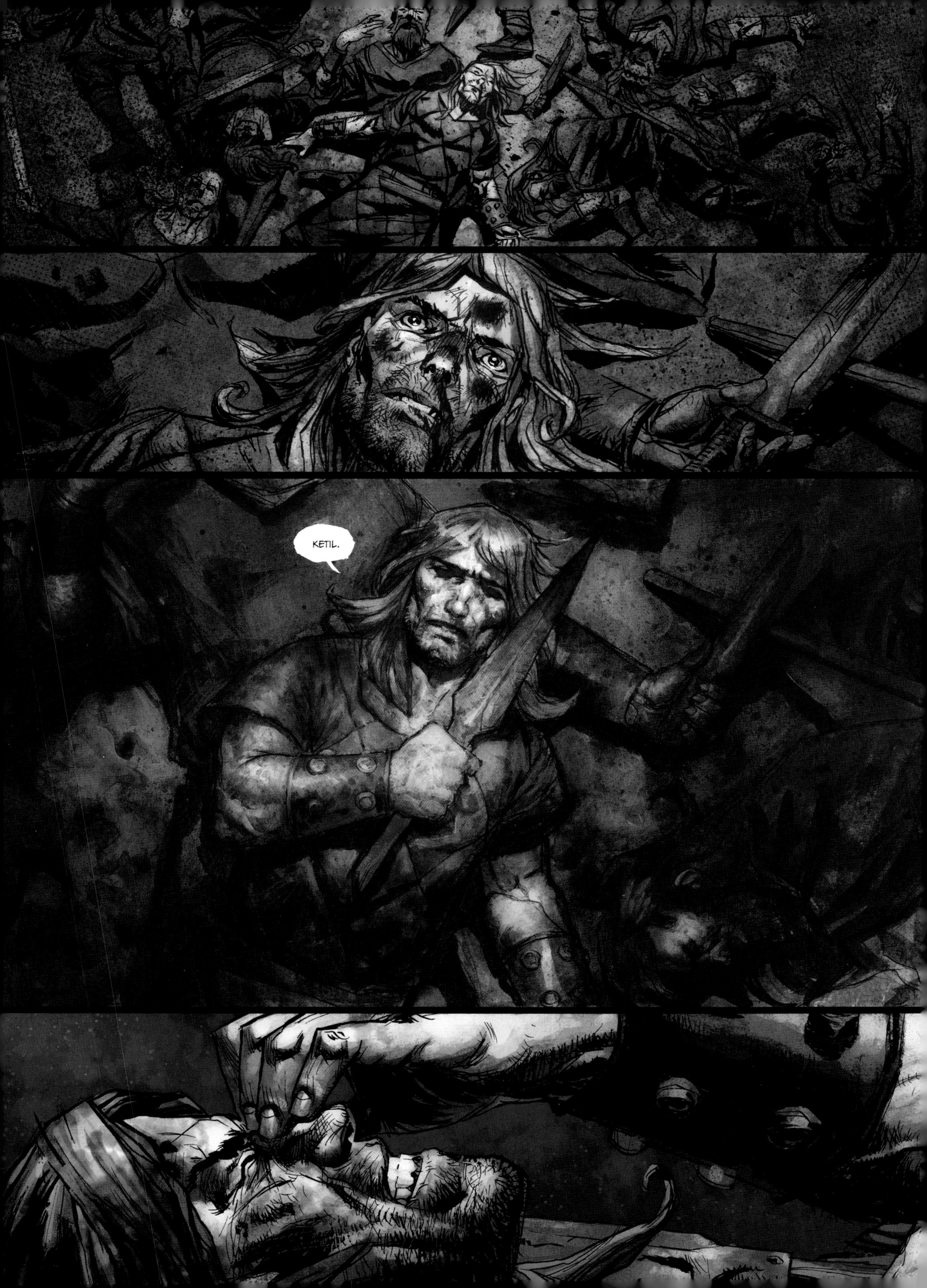
KETIL.

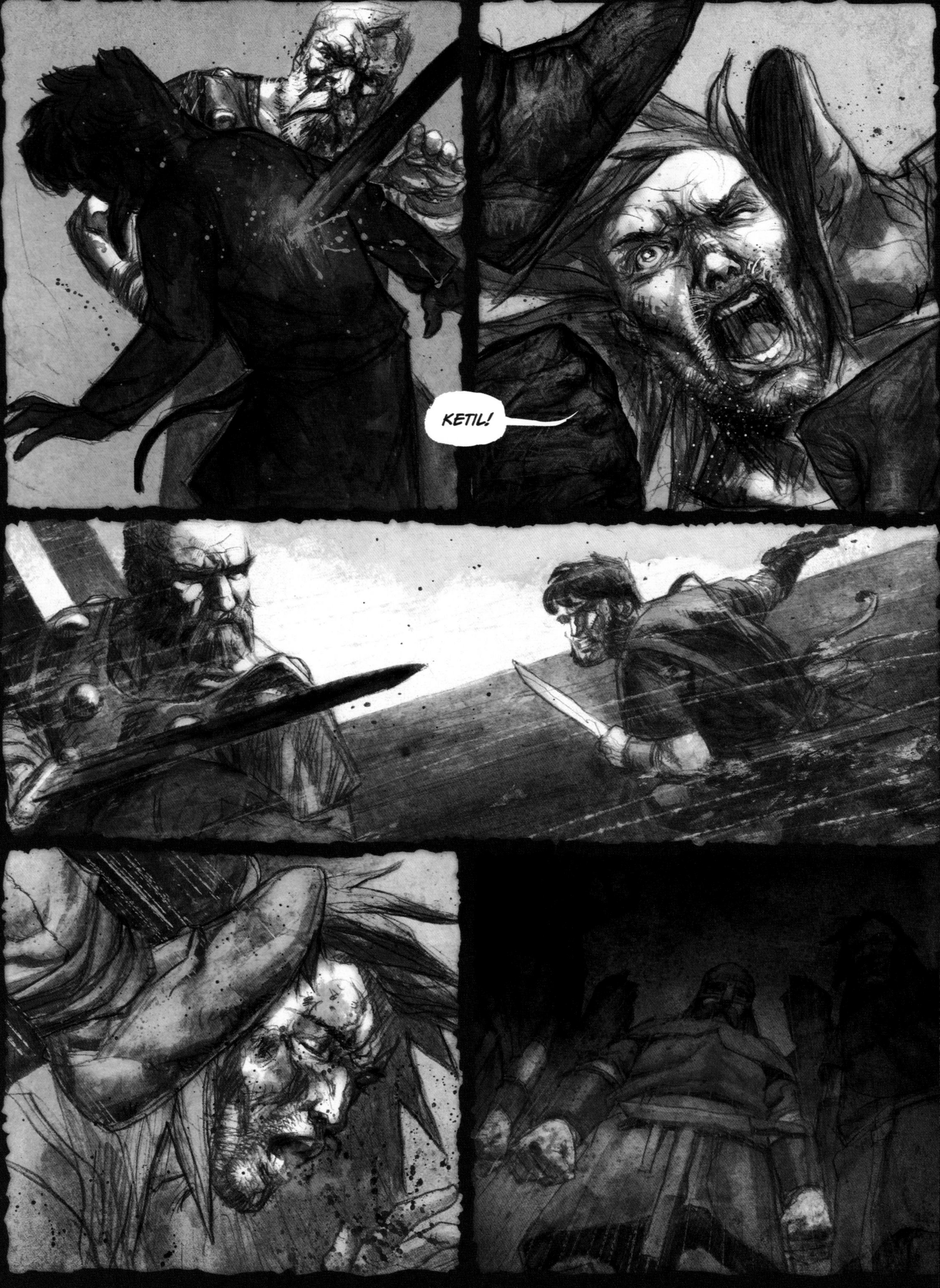
KETIL!

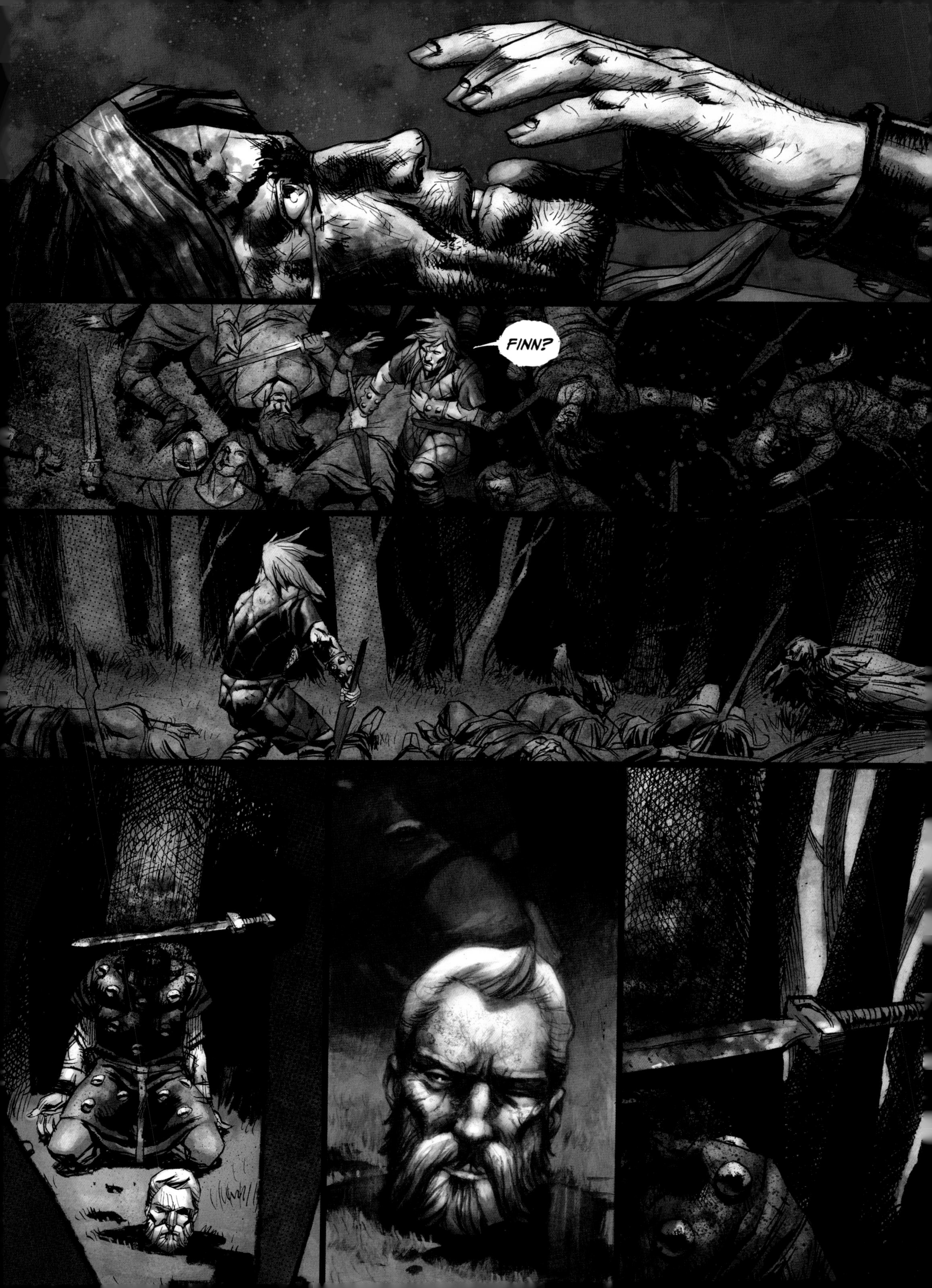
FINN?

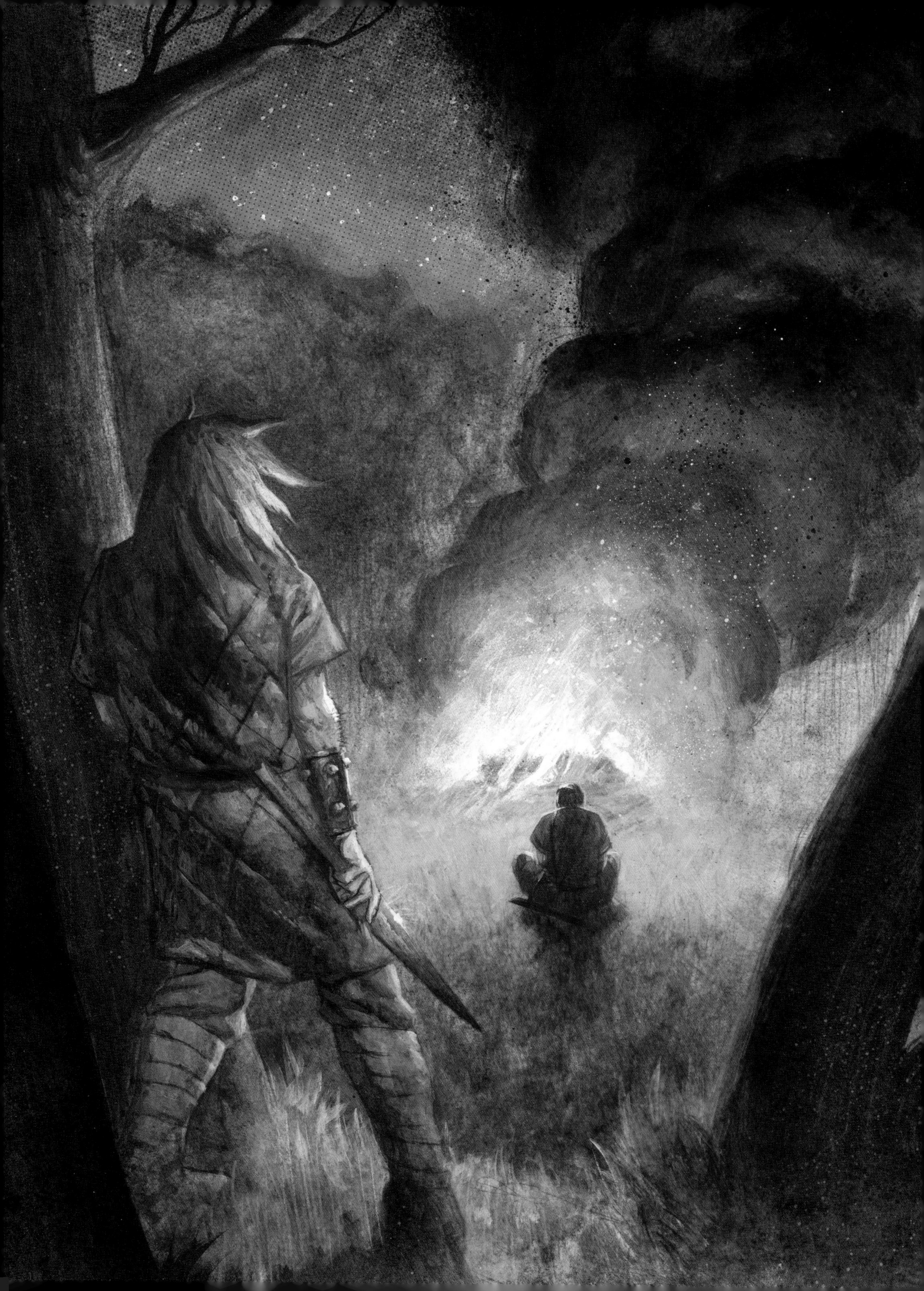

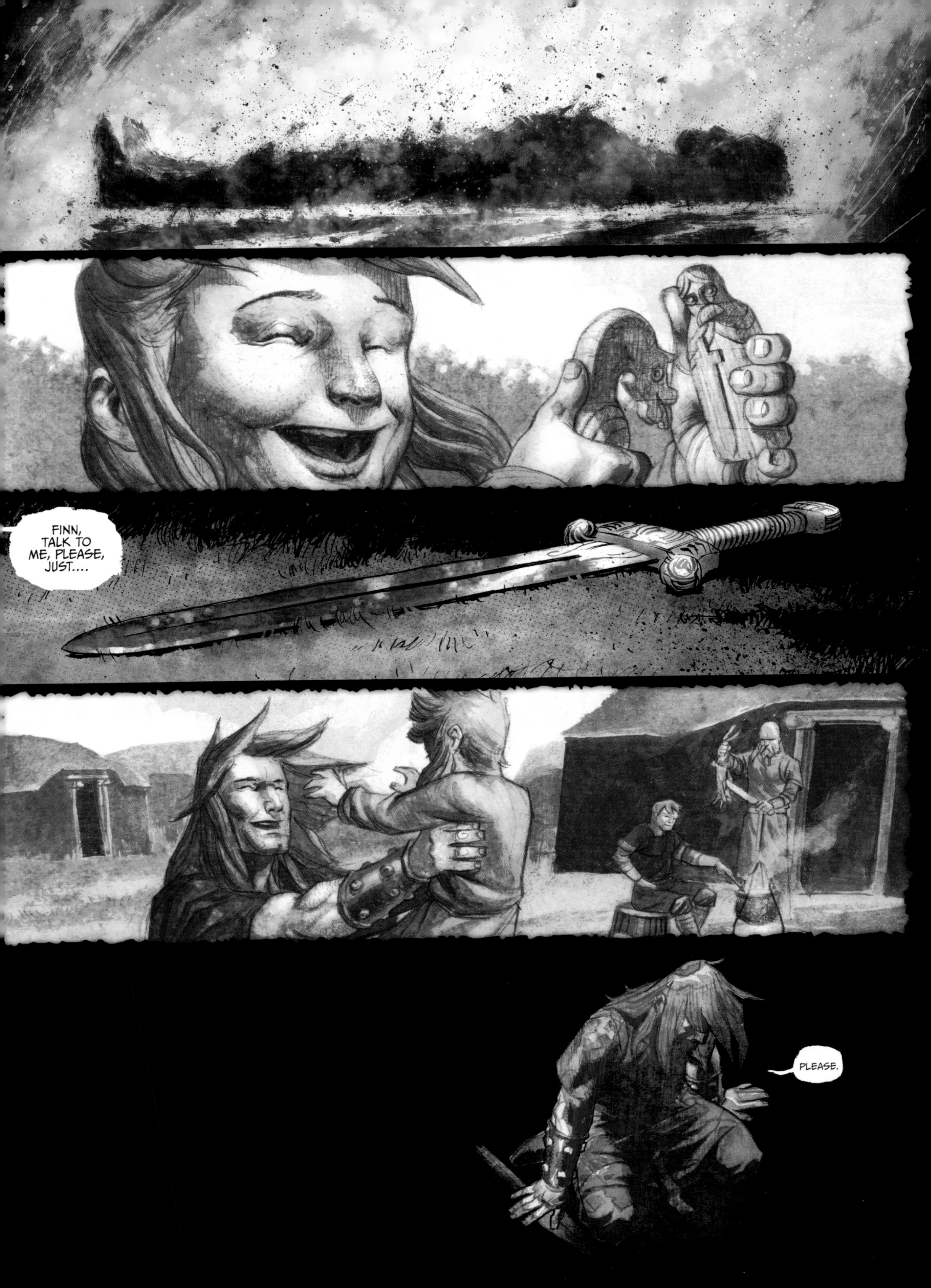
FINN, TALK TO ME, PLEASE, JUST....
PLEASE.

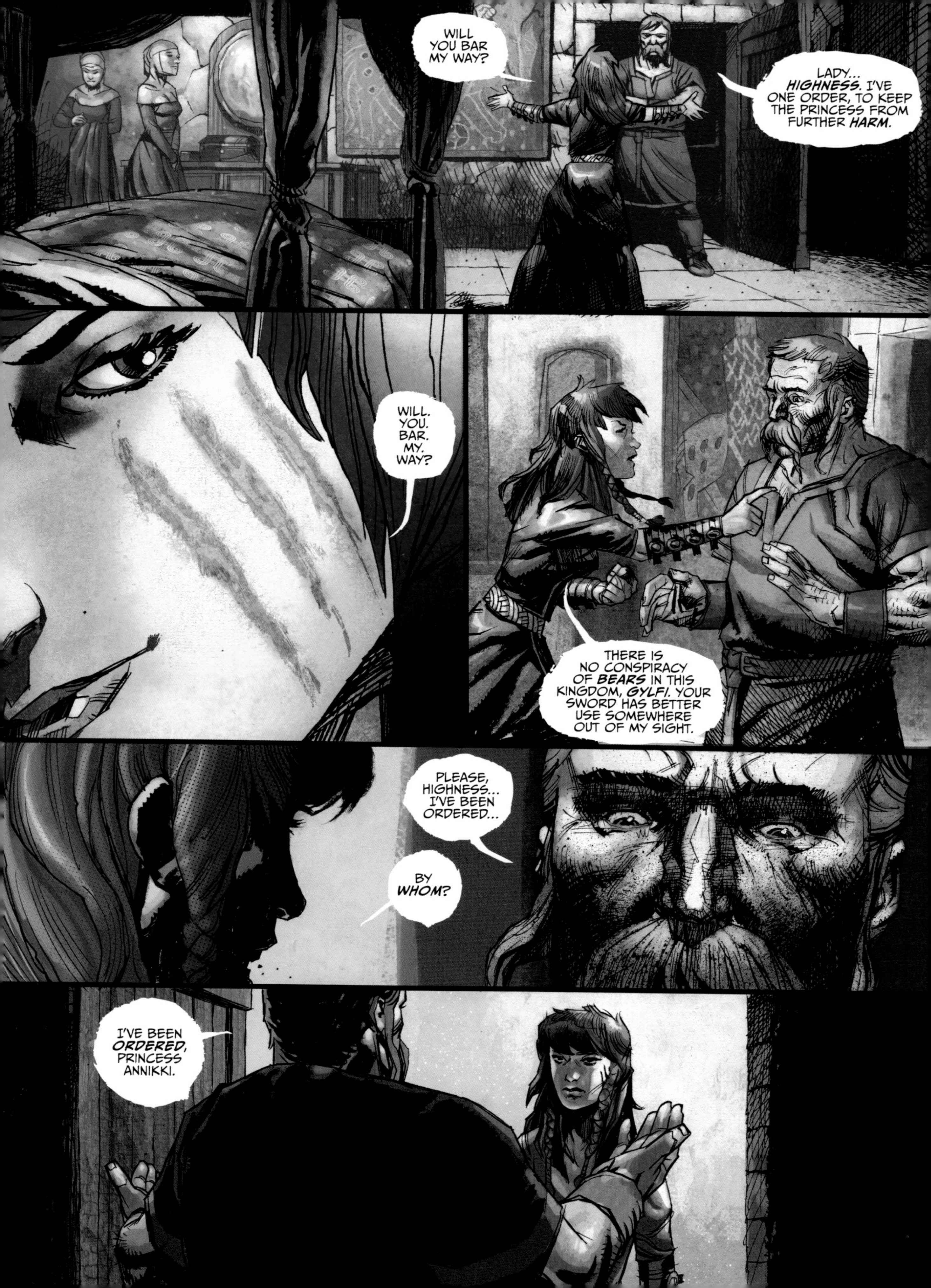
WILL YOU BAR MY WAY?
LADY... HIGHNESS. I'VE ONE ORDER, TO KEEP THE PRINCESS FROM FURTHER HARM.
WILL. YOU. BAR. MY. WAY?
THERE IS NO CONSPIRACY OF BEARS IN THIS KINGDOM, GYLFI. YOUR SWORD HAS BETTER USE SOMEWHERE OUT OF MY SIGHT.
PLEASE, HIGHNESS... I'VE BEEN ORDERED...
BY WHOM?
I'VE BEEN ORDERED, PRINCESS ANNIKKI.

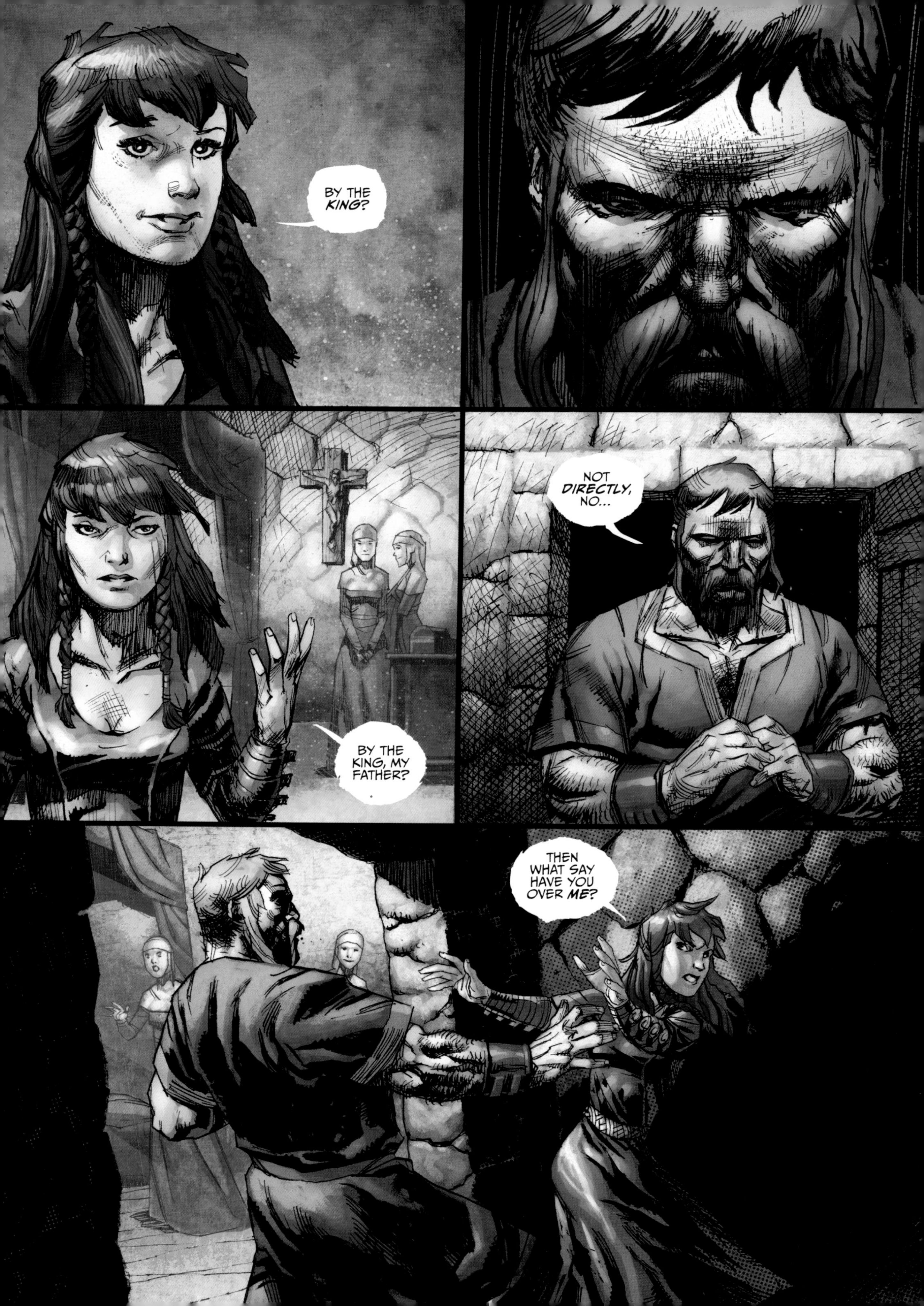
BY THE *KING*?
NOT *DIRECTLY*, NO...
BY THE KING, MY FATHER?
THEN WHAT SAY HAVE YOU OVER *ME*?

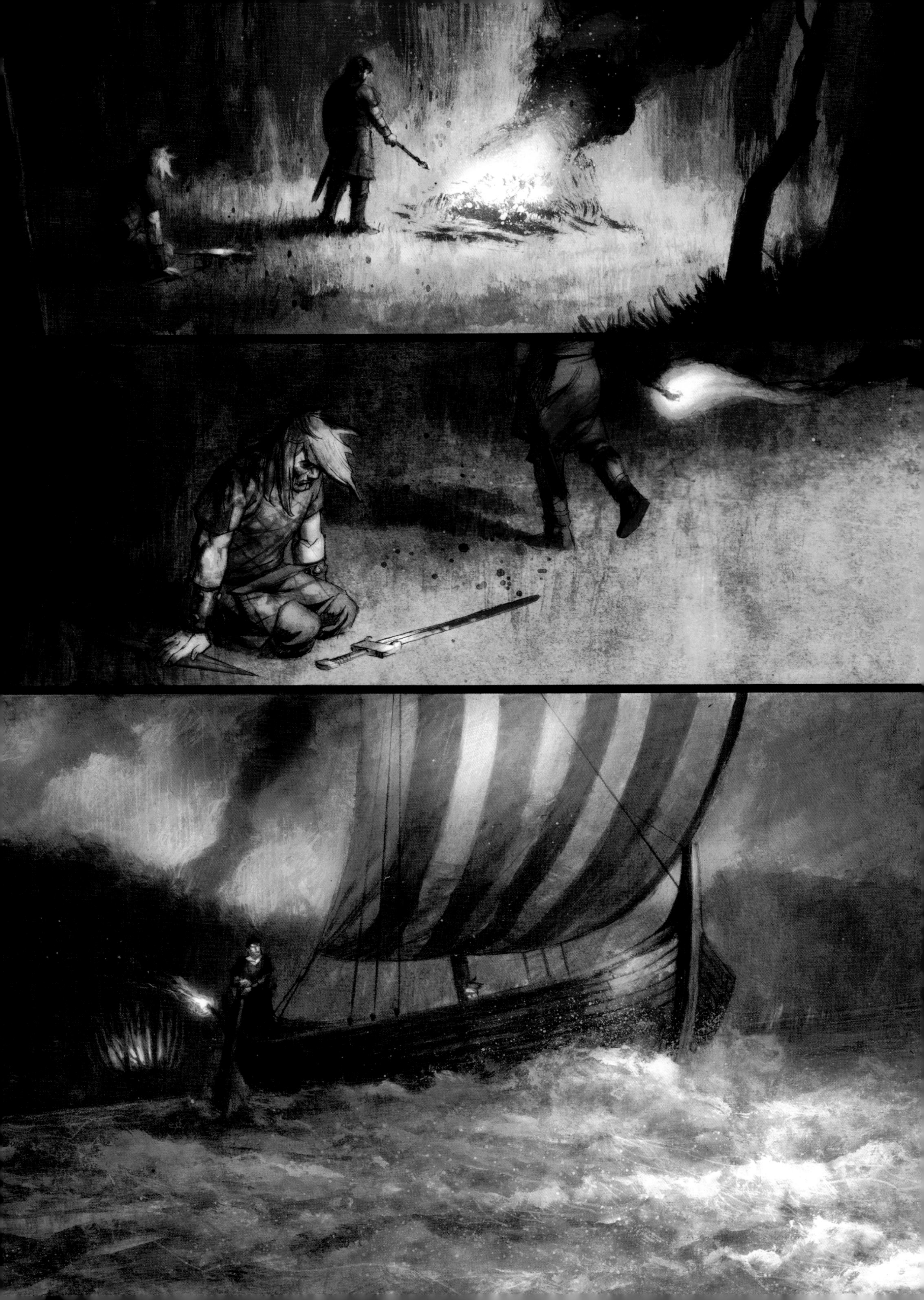

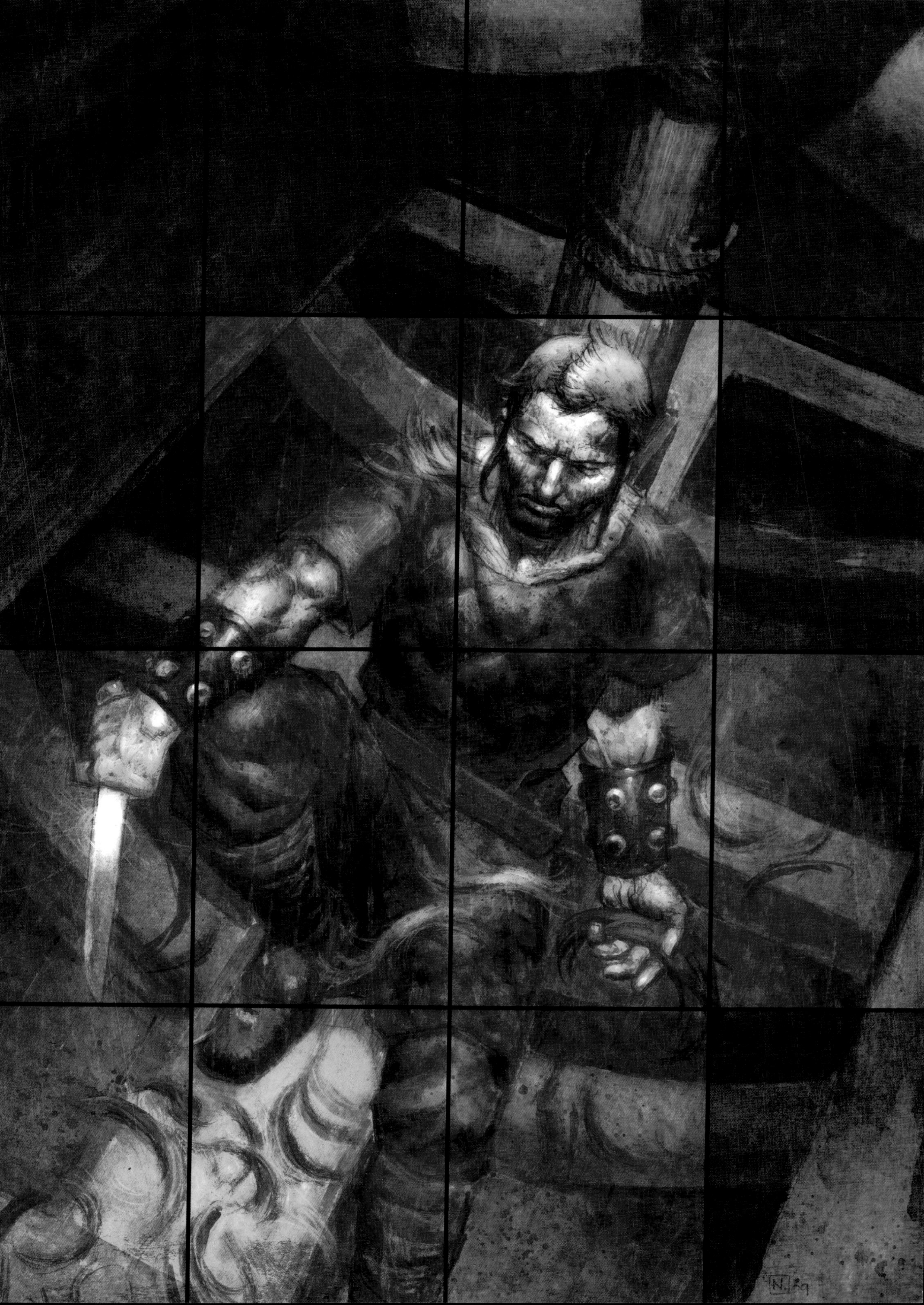

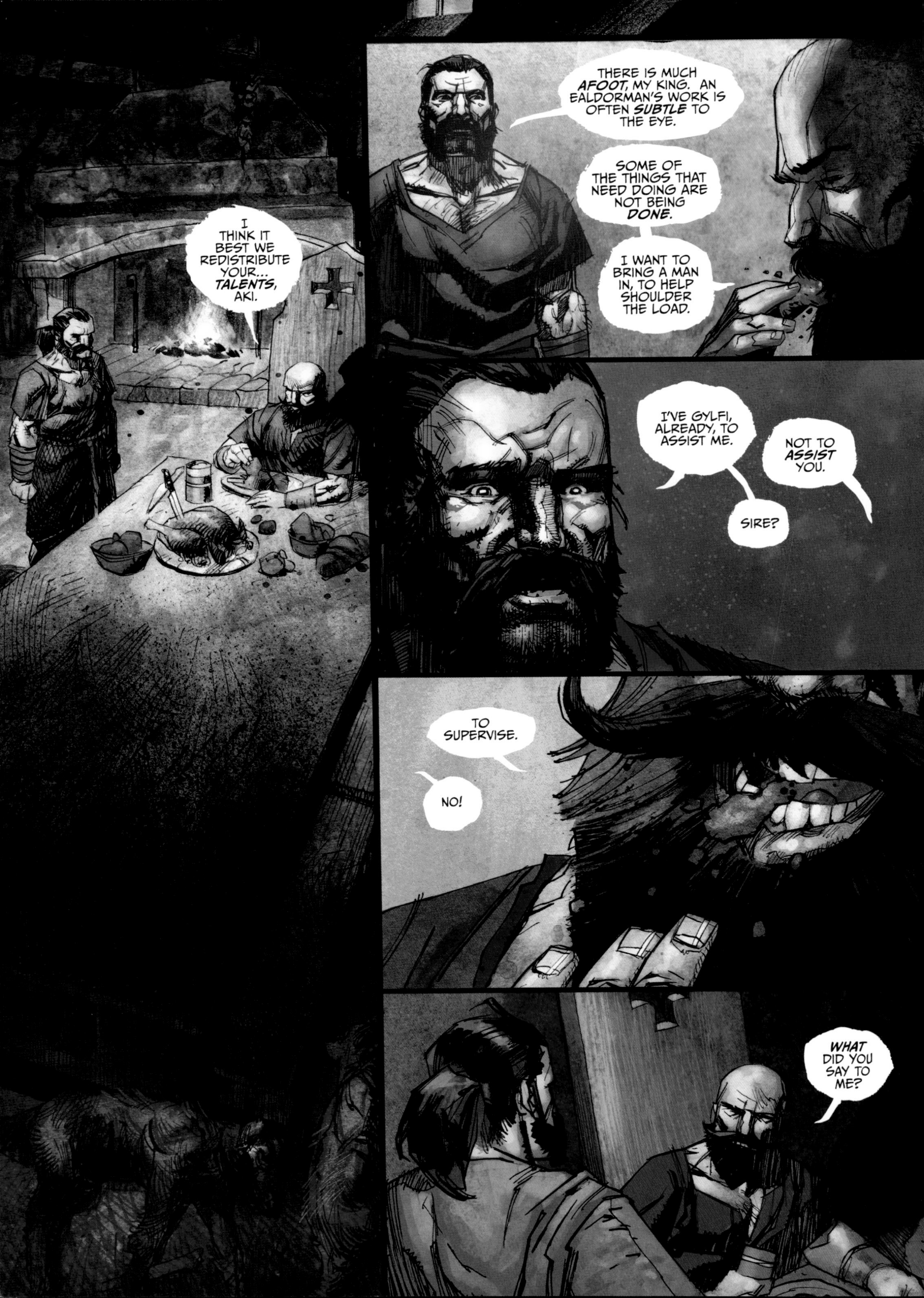
I THINK IT BEST WE REDISTRIBUTE YOUR... *TALENTS,* AKI.
THERE IS MUCH *AFOOT,* MY KING. AN EALDORMAN'S WORK IS OFTEN *SUBTLE* TO THE EYE.
SOME OF THE THINGS THAT NEED DOING ARE NOT BEING *DONE.*
I WANT TO BRING A MAN IN, TO HELP SHOULDER THE LOAD.
I'VE GYLFI, ALREADY, TO ASSIST ME.
SIRE?
NOT TO *ASSIST* YOU.
TO SUPERVISE.
NO!
WHAT DID YOU SAY TO ME?

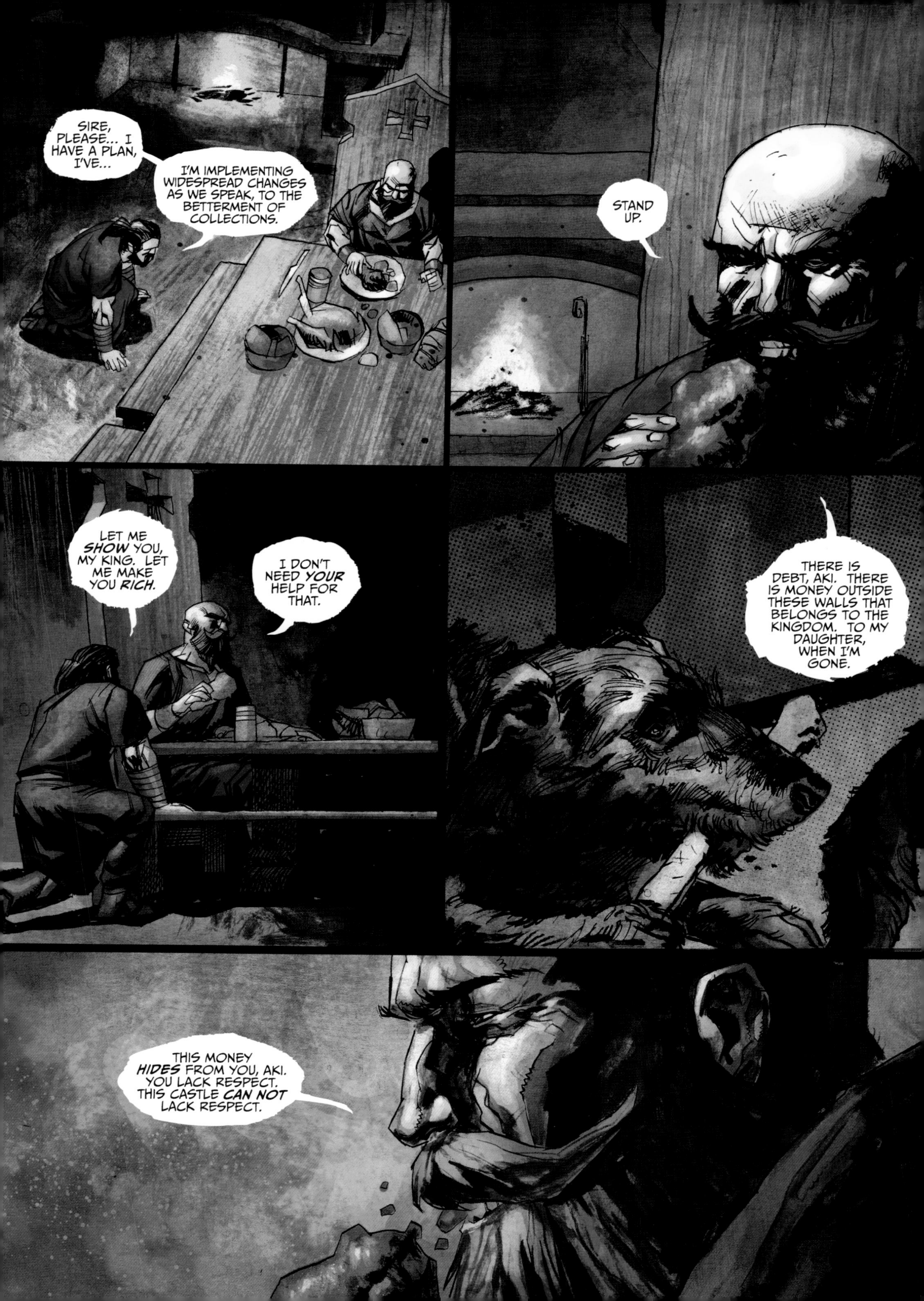
SIRE, PLEASE... I HAVE A PLAN, I'VE...
I'M IMPLEMENTING WIDESPREAD CHANGES AS WE SPEAK, TO THE BETTERMENT OF COLLECTIONS.
STAND UP.
LET ME SHOW YOU, MY KING. LET ME MAKE YOU RICH.
I DON'T NEED YOUR HELP FOR THAT.
THERE IS DEBT, AKI. THERE IS MONEY OUTSIDE THESE WALLS THAT BELONGS TO THE KINGDOM. TO MY DAUGHTER, WHEN I'M GONE.
THIS MONEY HIDES FROM YOU, AKI. YOU LACK RESPECT. THIS CASTLE CAN NOT LACK RESPECT.

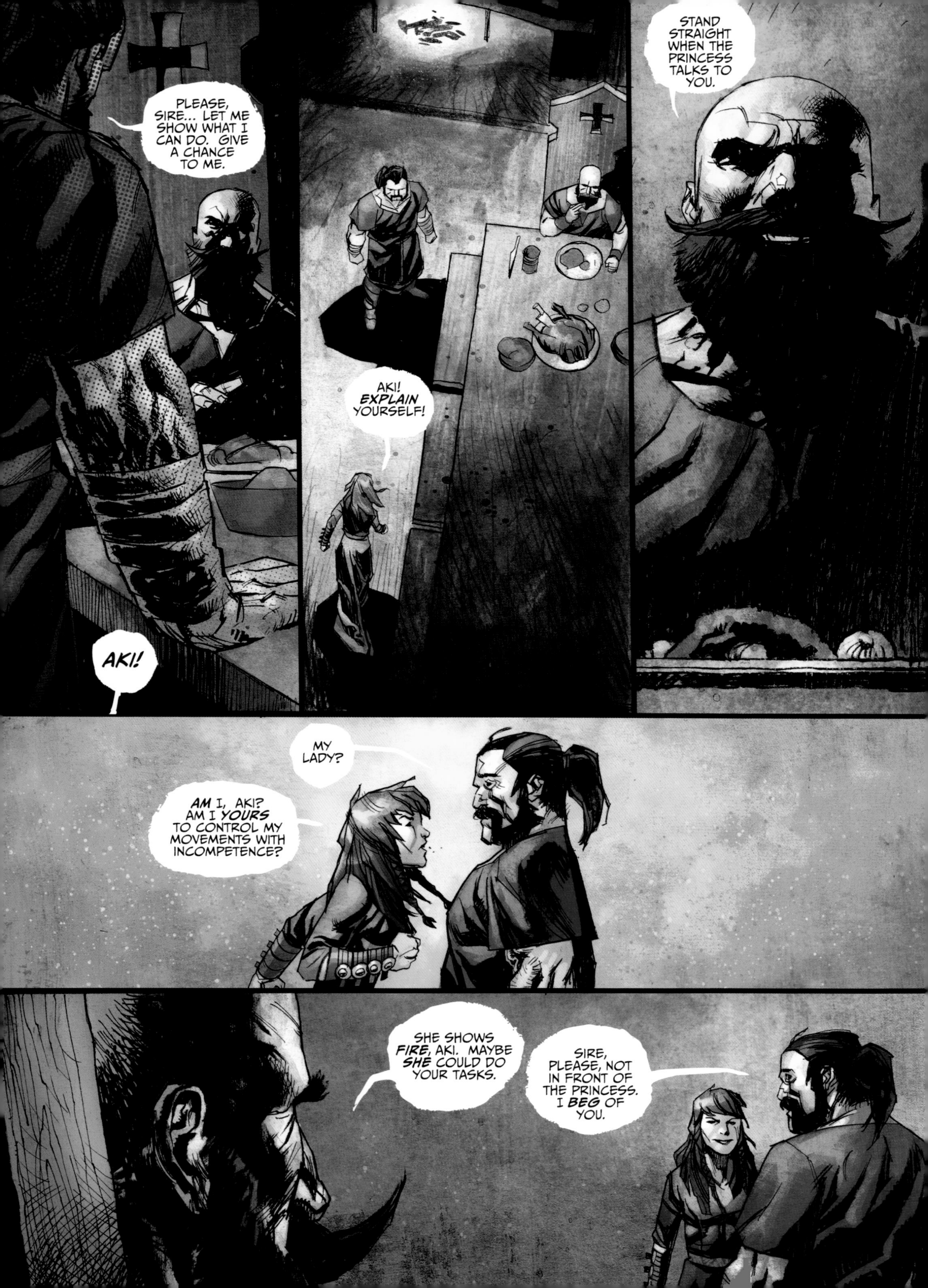
PLEASE, SIRE... LET ME SHOW WHAT I CAN DO. GIVE A CHANCE TO ME.
AKI!
AKI! EXPLAIN YOURSELF!
STAND STRAIGHT WHEN THE PRINCESS TALKS TO YOU.
MY LADY?
AM I, AKI? AM I YOURS TO CONTROL MY MOVEMENTS WITH INCOMPETENCE?
SHE SHOWS FIRE, AKI. MAYBE SHE COULD DO YOUR TASKS.
SIRE, PLEASE, NOT IN FRONT OF THE PRINCESS. I BEG OF YOU.

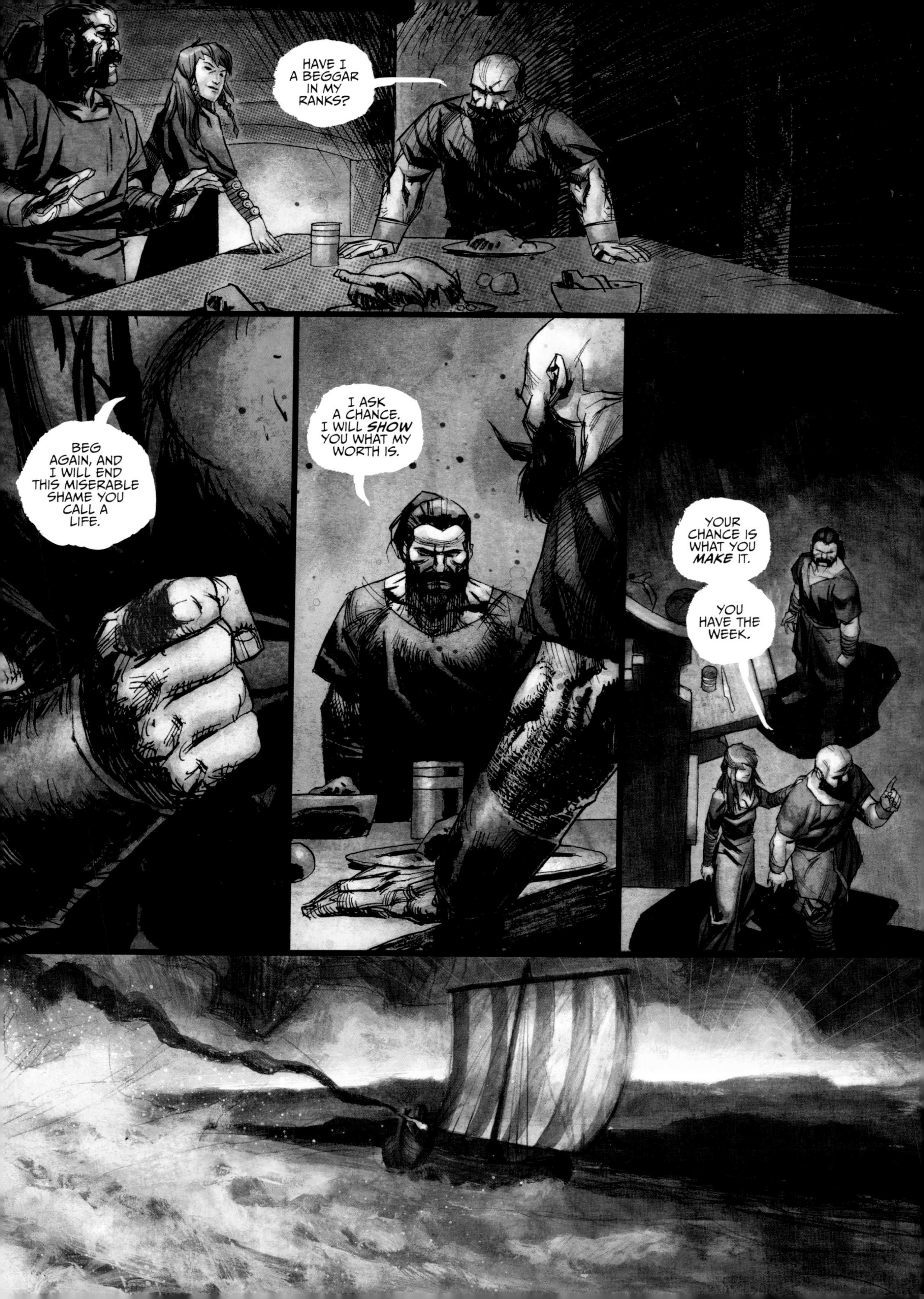
HAVE I A BEGGAR IN MY RANKS?
BEG AGAIN, AND I WILL END THIS MISERABLE SHAME YOU CALL A LIFE.
I ASK A CHANCE. I WILL SHOW YOU WHAT MY WORTH IS.
YOUR CHANCE IS WHAT YOU MAKE IT.
YOU HAVE THE WEEK.

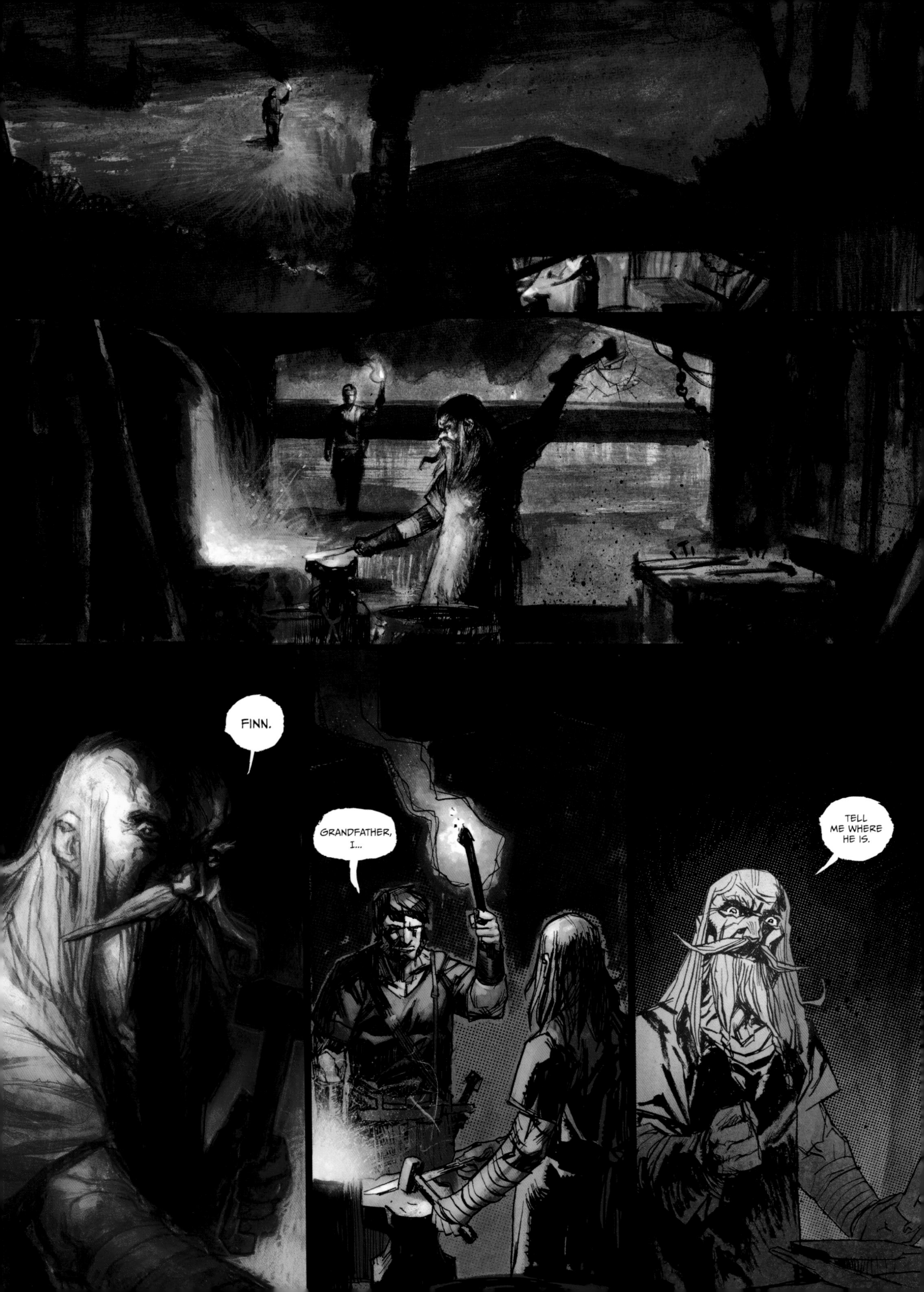
FINN.
GRANDFATHER, I...
TELL ME WHERE HE IS.

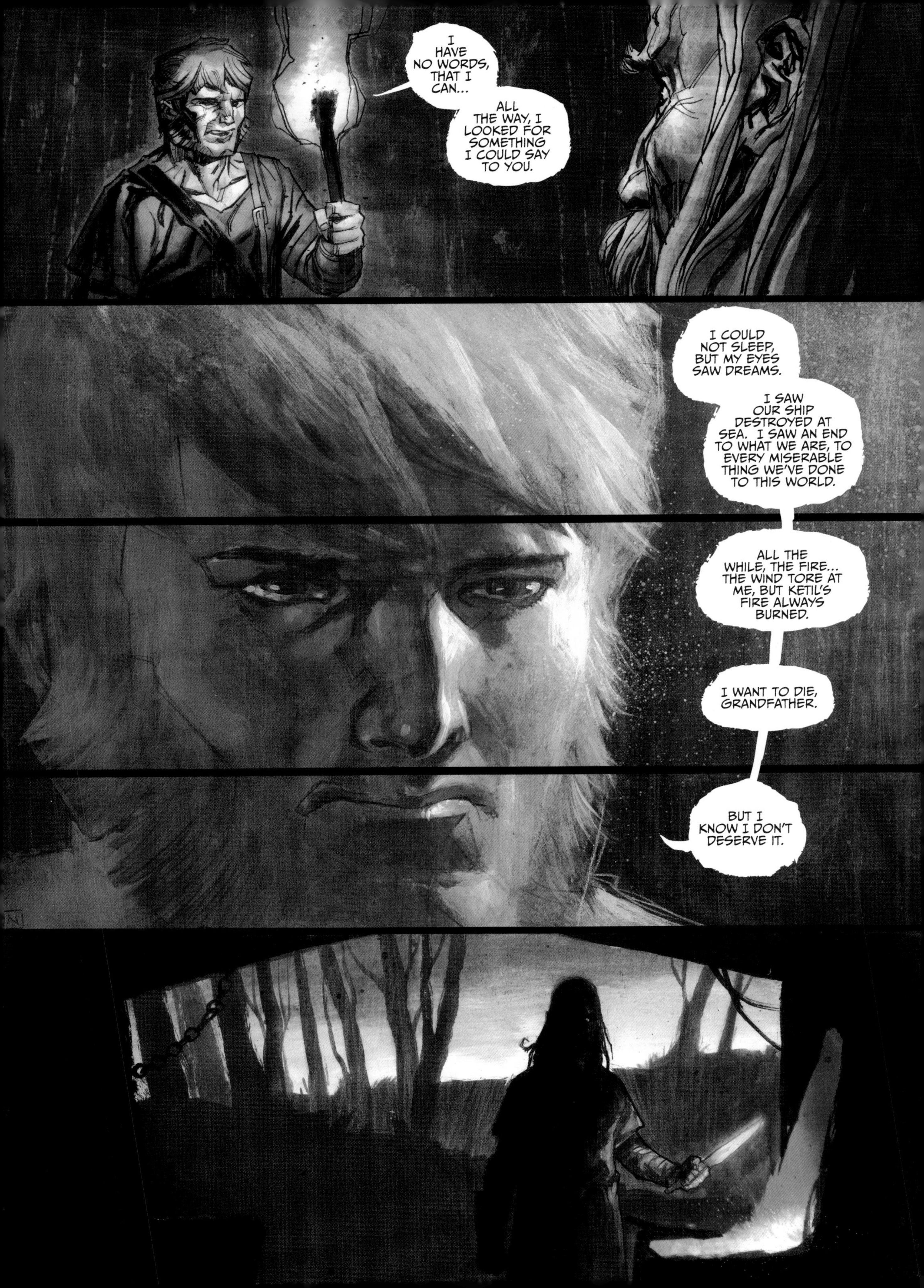
I HAVE NO WORDS, THAT I CAN...
ALL THE WAY, I LOOKED FOR SOMETHING I COULD SAY TO YOU.
I COULD NOT SLEEP, BUT MY EYES SAW DREAMS.
I SAW OUR SHIP DESTROYED AT SEA. I SAW AN END TO WHAT WE ARE, TO EVERY MISERABLE THING WE'VE DONE TO THIS WORLD.
ALL THE WHILE, THE FIRE... THE WIND TORE AT ME, BUT KETIL'S FIRE ALWAYS BURNED.
I WANT TO DIE, GRANDFATHER.
BUT I KNOW I DON'T DESERVE IT.

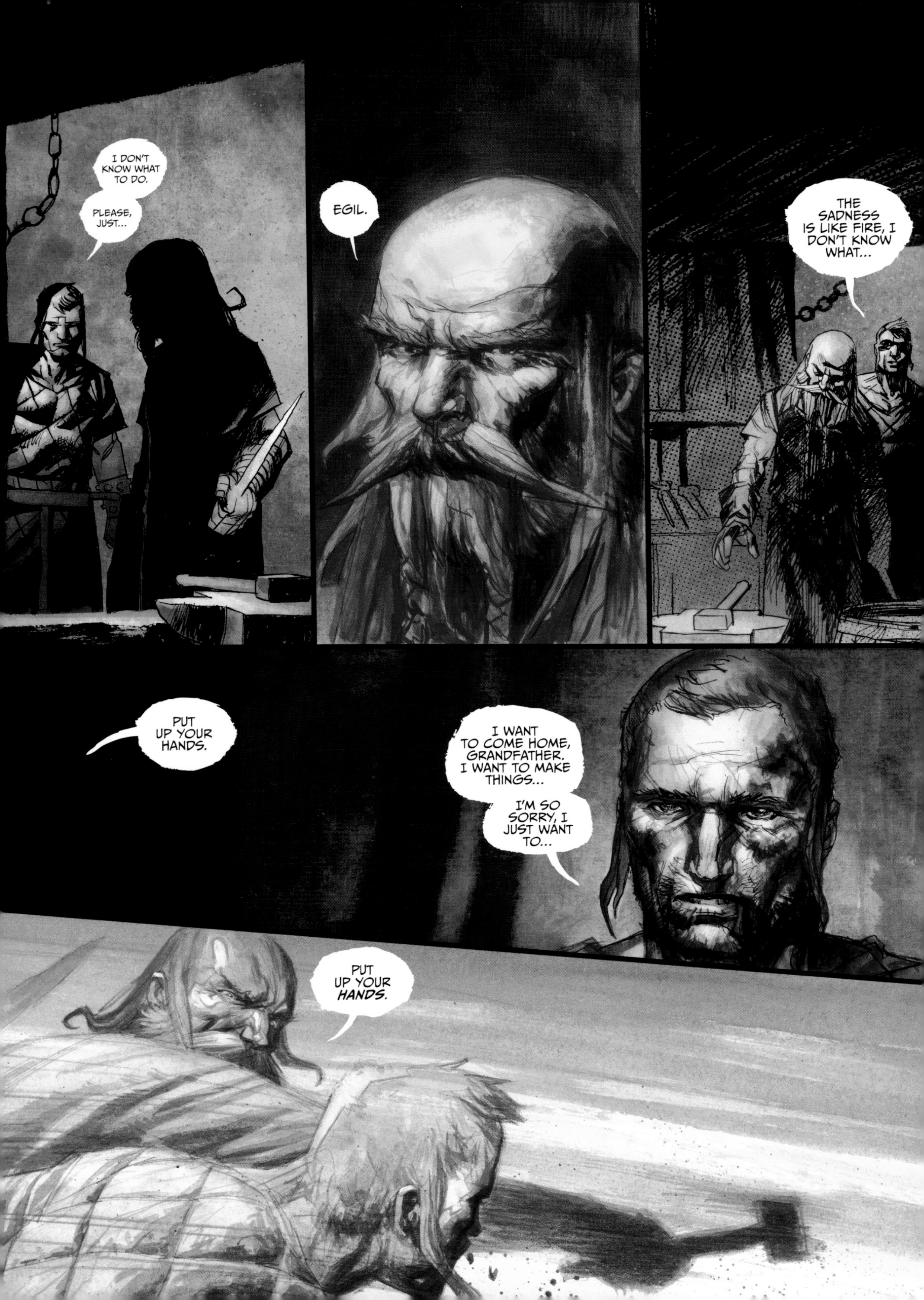

I DON'T KNOW WHAT TO DO.
PLEASE, JUST...
EGIL.
THE SADNESS IS LIKE FIRE, I DON'T KNOW WHAT...
PUT UP YOUR HANDS.
I WANT TO COME HOME, GRANDFATHER. I WANT TO MAKE THINGS...
I'M SO SORRY, I JUST WANT TO...
PUT UP YOUR *HANDS*.

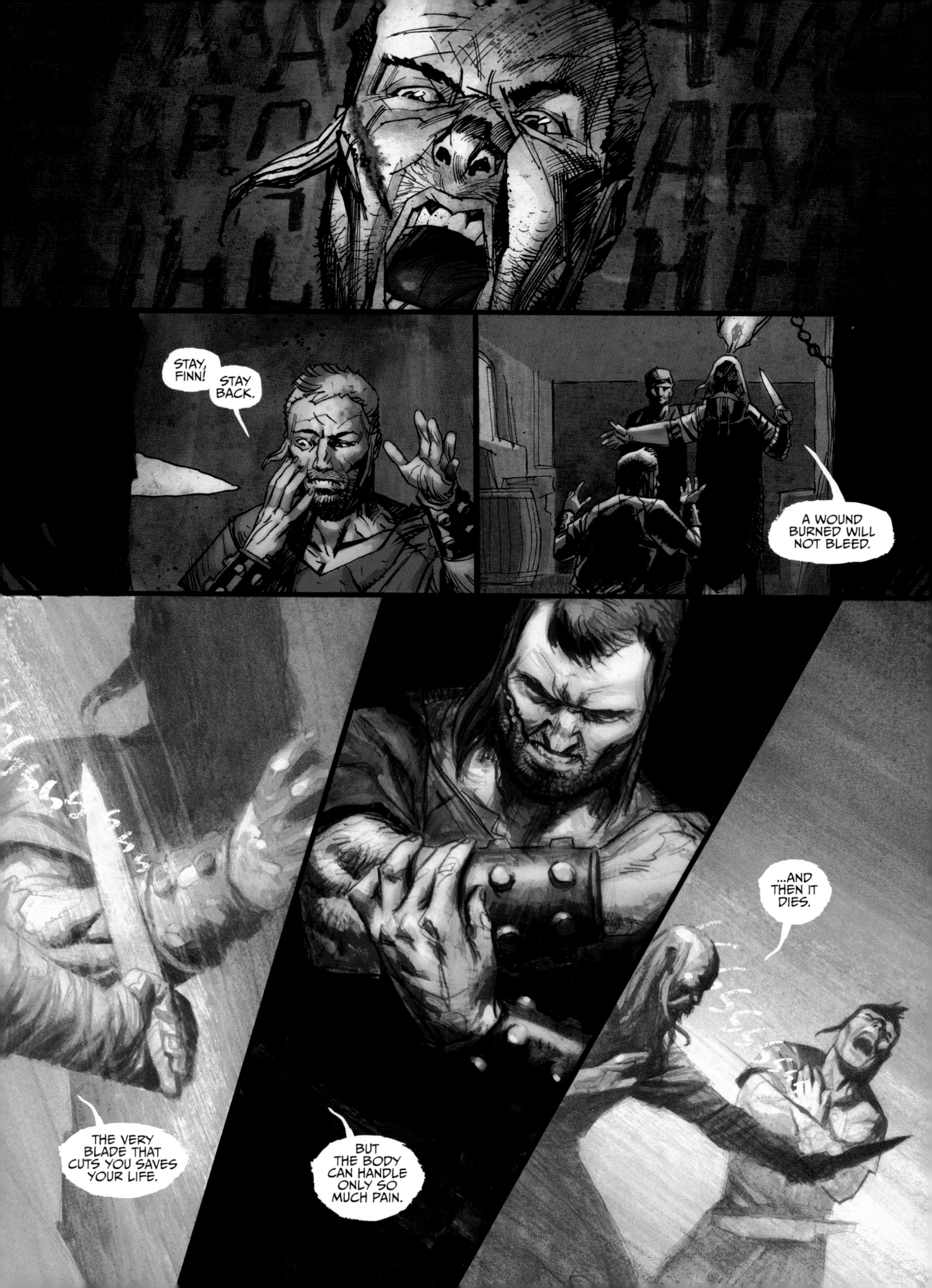
STAY, FINN!
STAY BACK.
A WOUND BURNED WILL NOT BLEED.
THE VERY BLADE THAT CUTS YOU SAVES YOUR LIFE.
BUT THE BODY CAN HANDLE ONLY SO MUCH PAIN.
...AND THEN IT DIES.

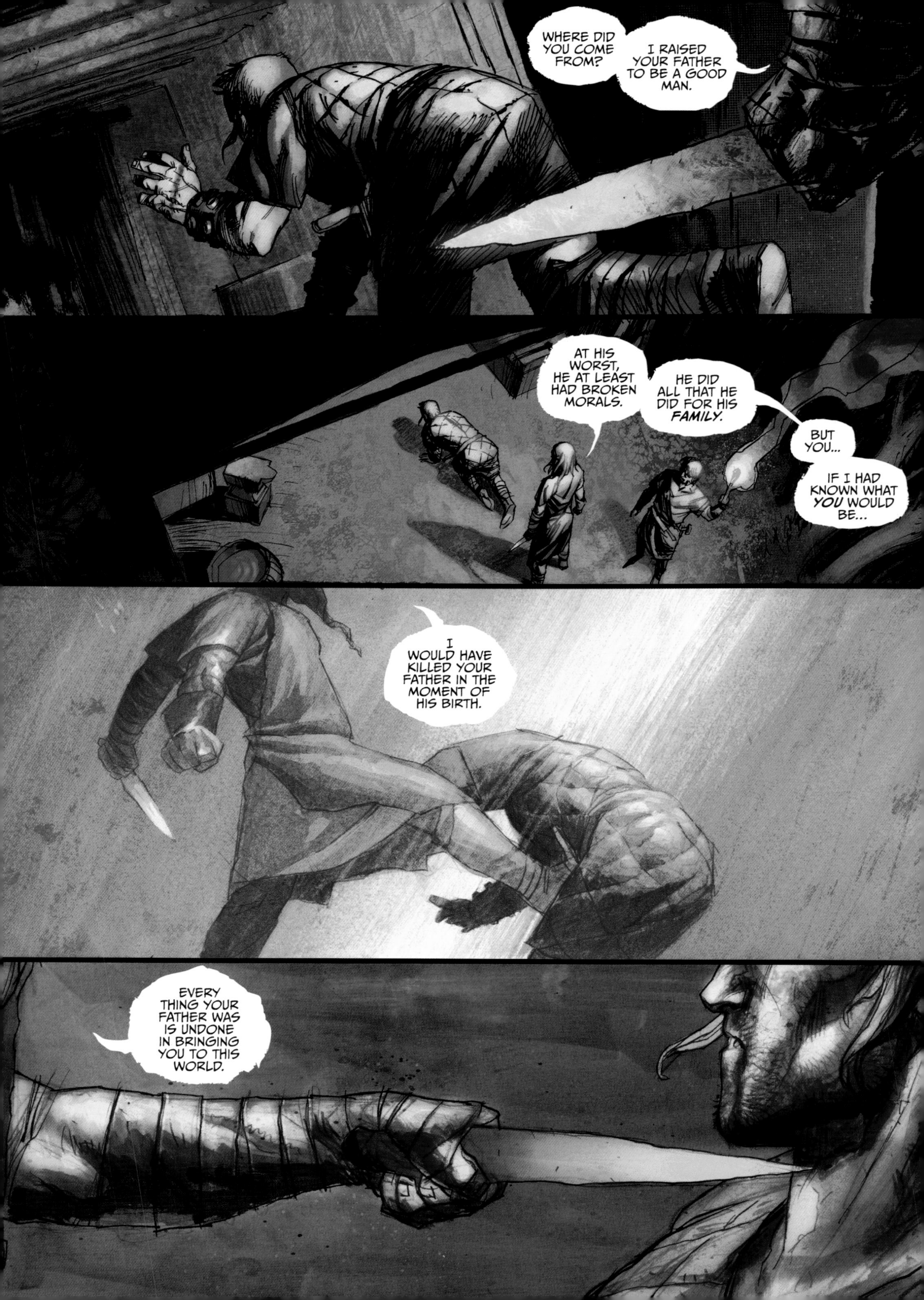
WHERE DID YOU COME FROM?
I RAISED YOUR FATHER TO BE A GOOD MAN.
AT HIS WORST, HE AT LEAST HAD BROKEN MORALS.
HE DID ALL THAT HE DID FOR HIS *FAMILY*.
BUT YOU...
IF I HAD KNOWN WHAT *YOU* WOULD BE...
I WOULD HAVE KILLED YOUR FATHER IN THE MOMENT OF HIS BIRTH.
EVERY THING YOUR FATHER WAS IS UNDONE IN BRINGING YOU TO THIS WORLD.

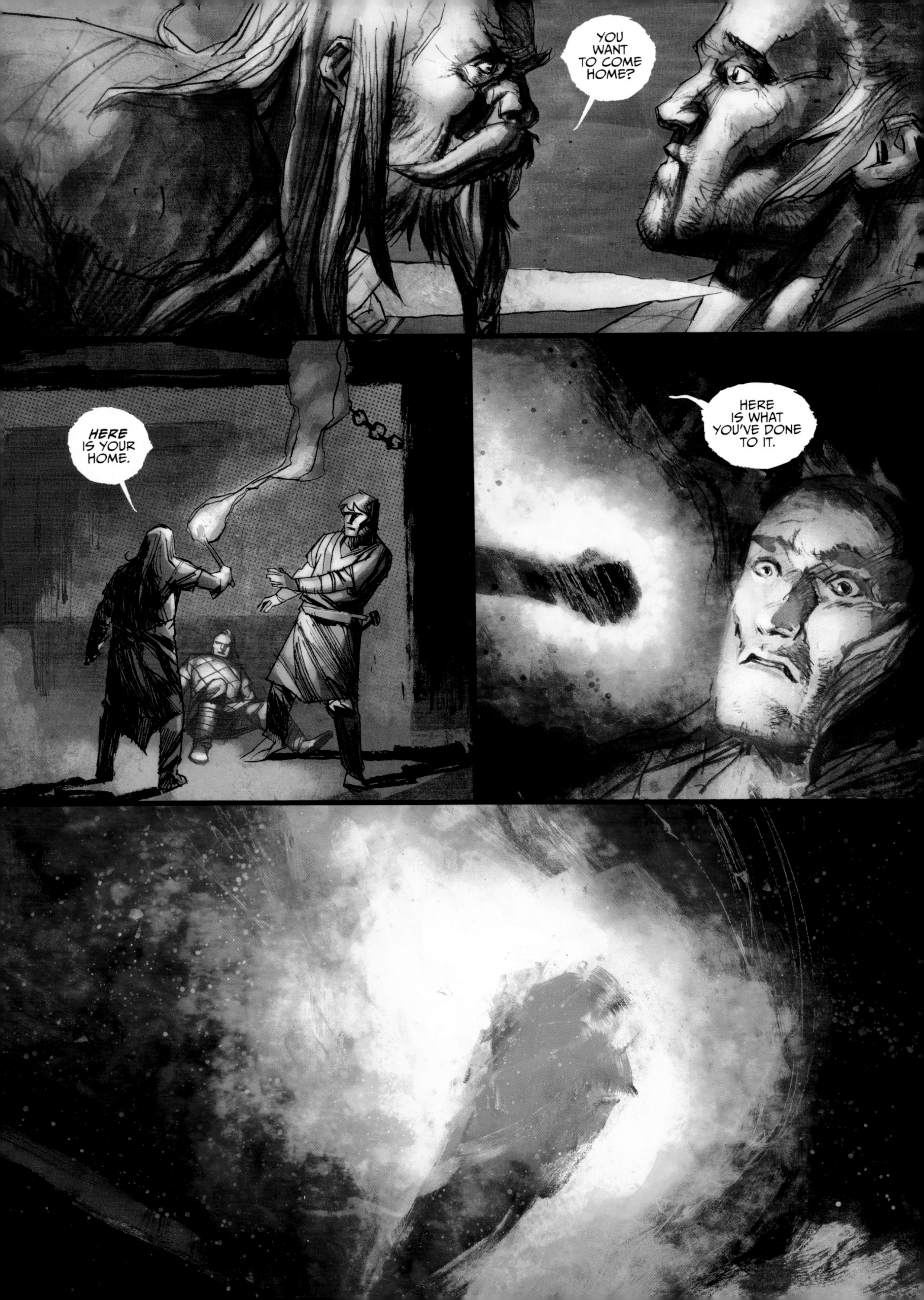
YOU WANT TO COME HOME?
HERE IS YOUR HOME.
HERE IS WHAT YOU'VE DONE TO IT.

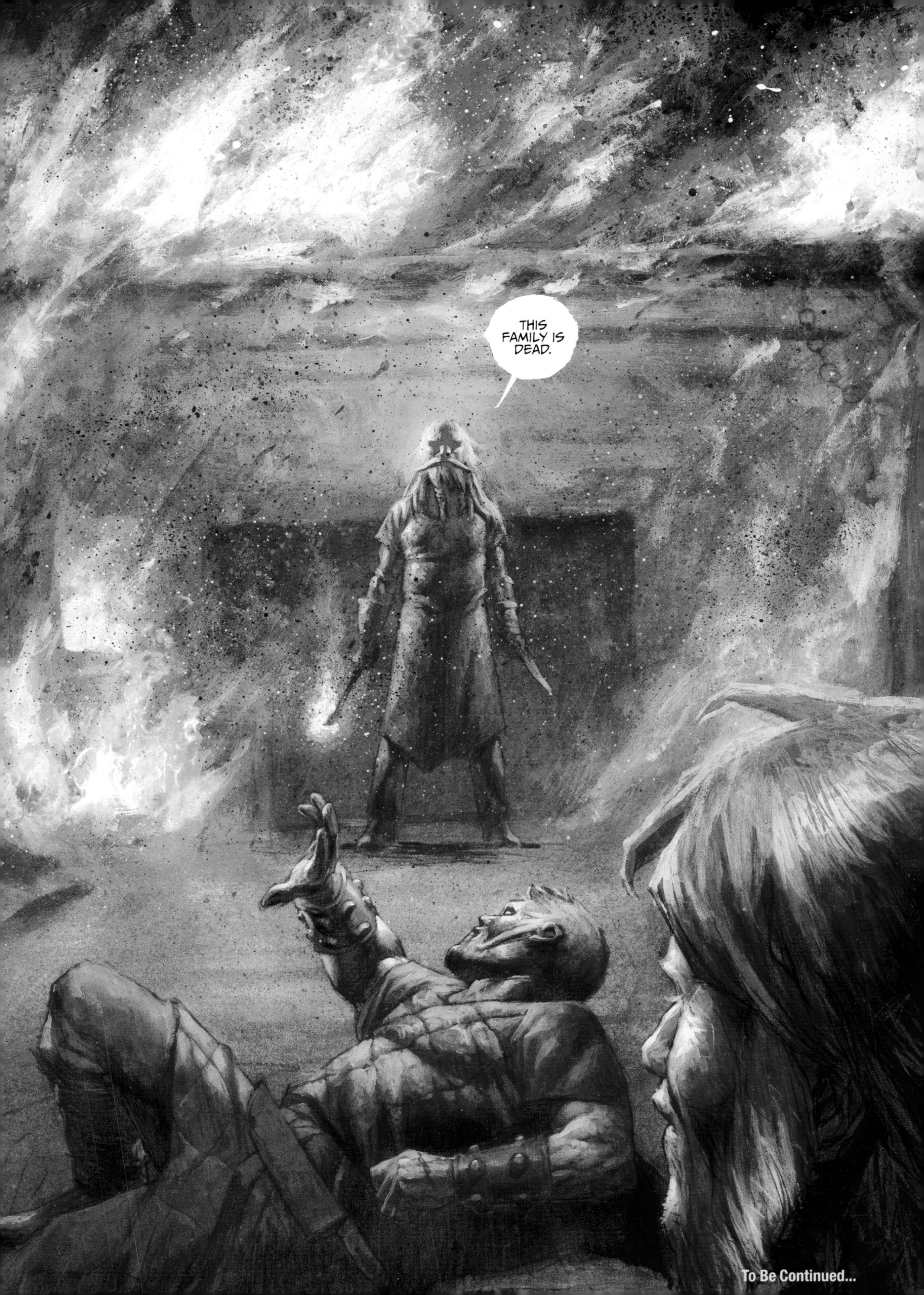
THIS FAMILY IS DEAD.
To Be Continued...

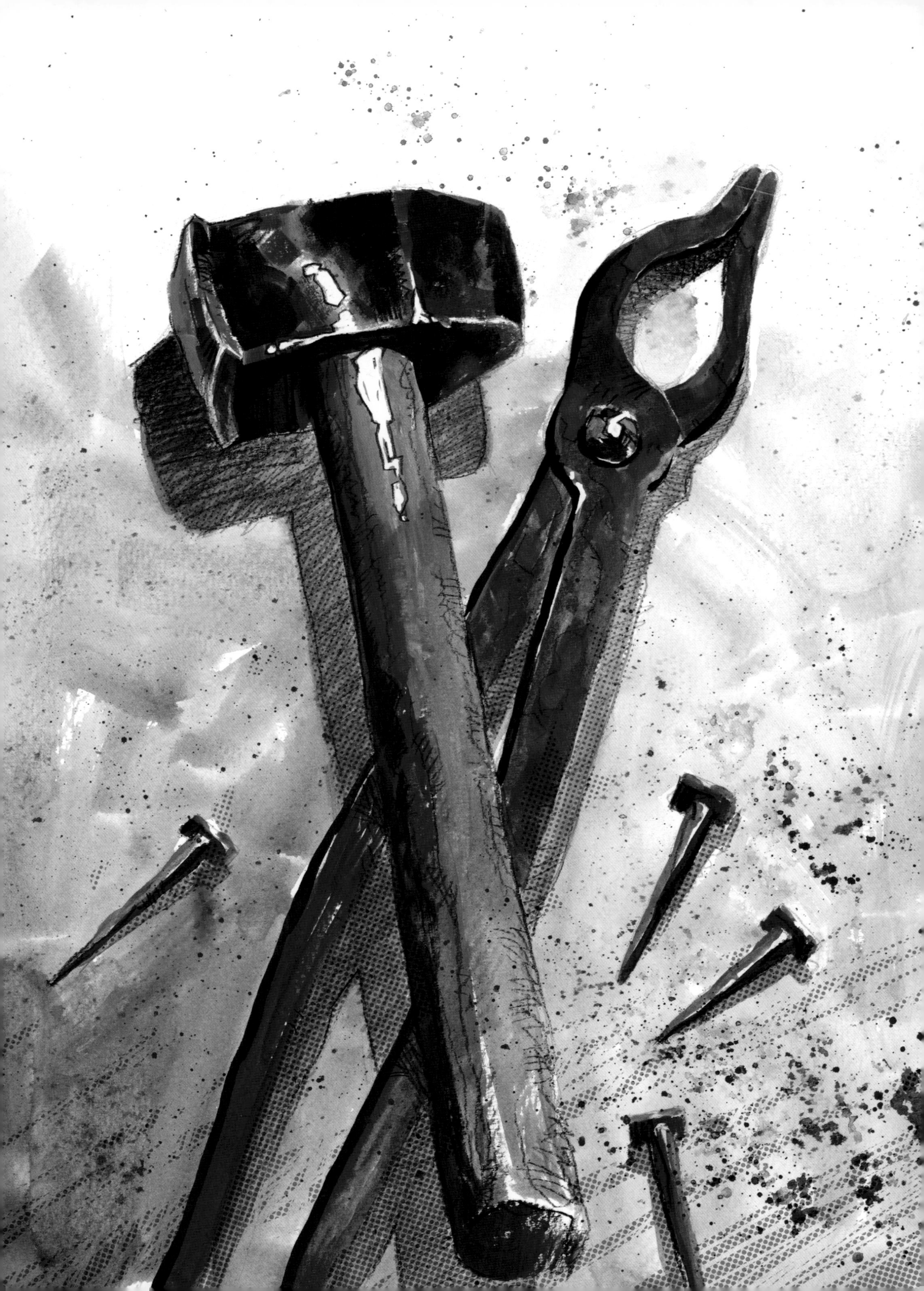

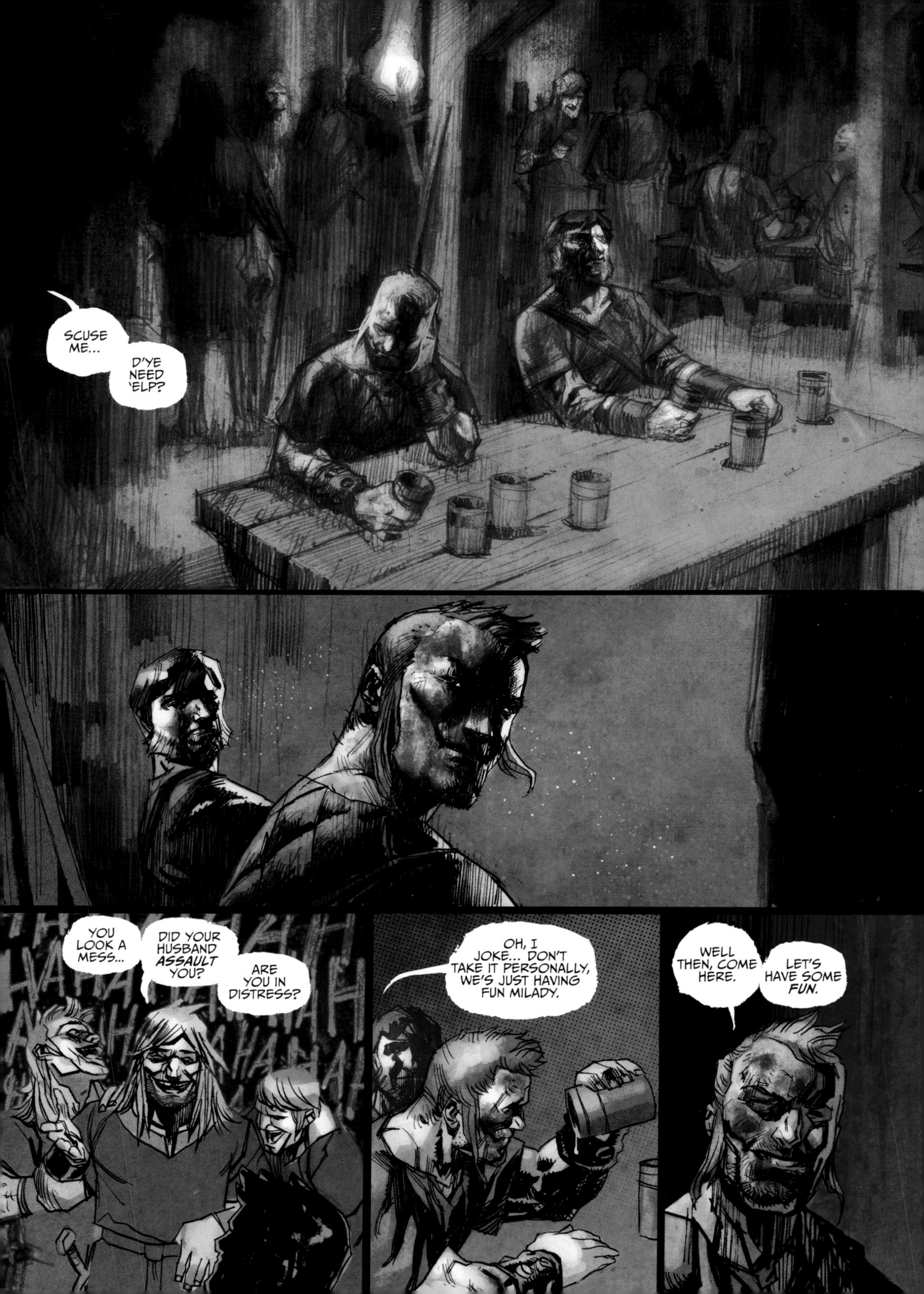
SCUSE ME...
D'YE NEED 'ELP?
YOU LOOK A MESS...
DID YOUR HUSBAND ASSAULT YOU?
ARE YOU IN DISTRESS?
OH, I JOKE... DON'T TAKE IT PERSONALLY, WE'S JUST HAVING FUN MILADY.
WELL THEN, COME HERE.
LET'S HAVE SOME FUN.

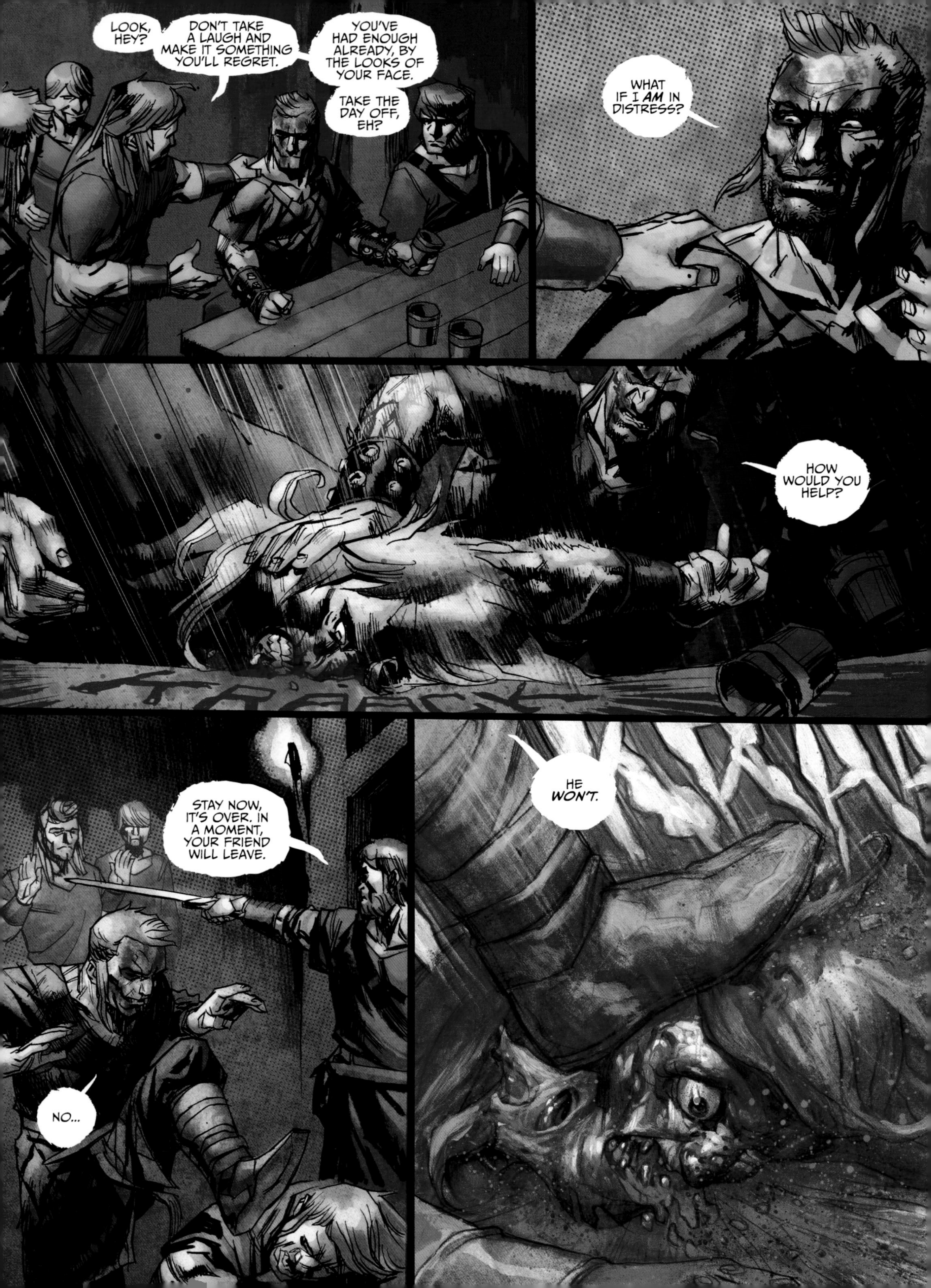
LOOK, HEY?
DON'T TAKE A LAUGH AND MAKE IT SOMETHING YOU'LL REGRET.
YOU'VE HAD ENOUGH ALREADY, BY THE LOOKS OF YOUR FACE.
TAKE THE DAY OFF, EH?
WHAT IF I *AM* IN DISTRESS?
HOW WOULD YOU HELP?
STAY NOW, IT'S OVER. IN A MOMENT, YOUR FRIEND WILL LEAVE.
NO...
HE *WON'T*.

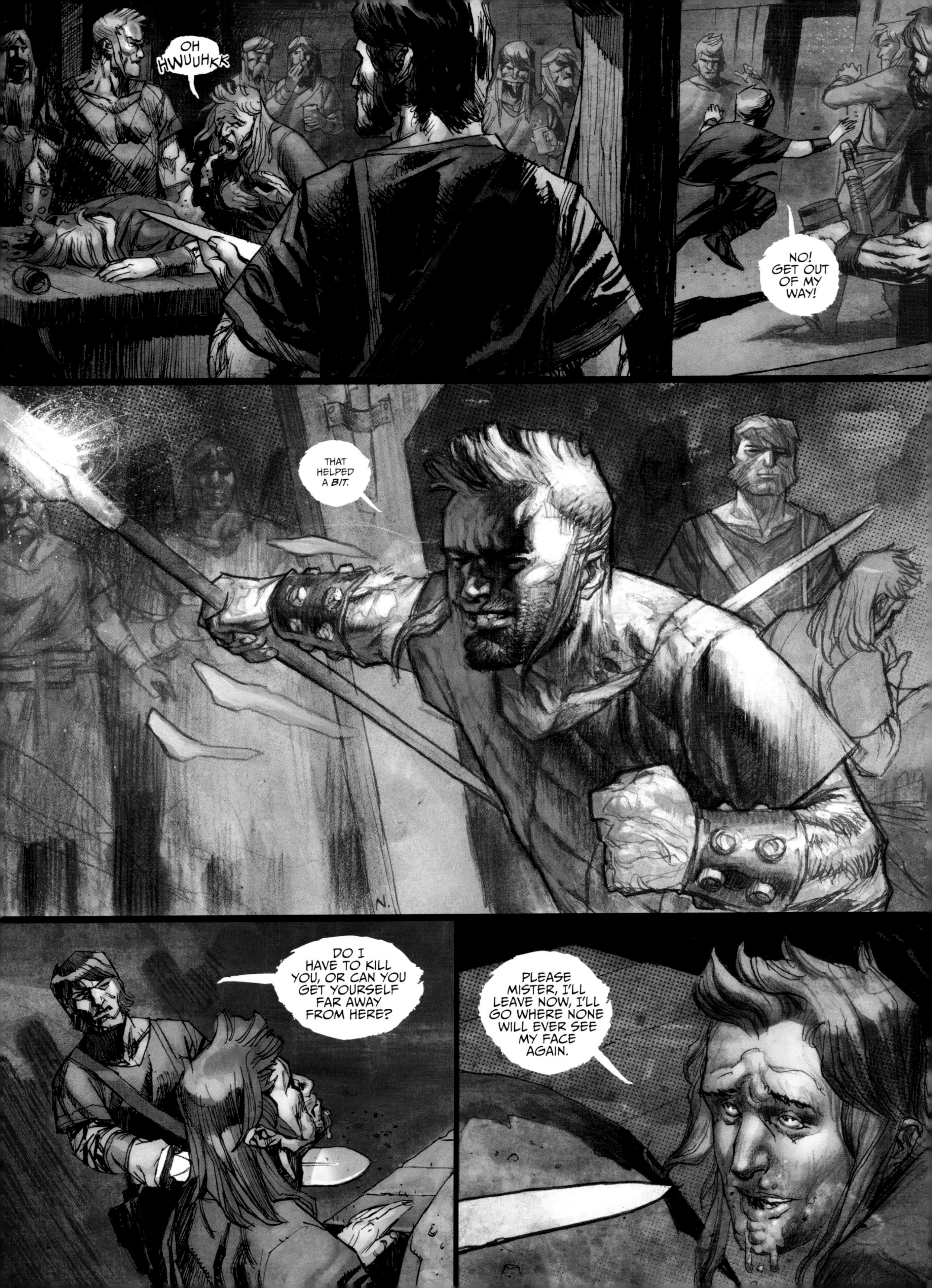
OH HWUUHKK
NO! GET OUT OF MY WAY!
THAT HELPED A BIT.
DO I HAVE TO KILL YOU, OR CAN YOU GET YOURSELF FAR AWAY FROM HERE?
PLEASE MISTER, I'LL LEAVE NOW, I'LL GO WHERE NONE WILL EVER SEE MY FACE AGAIN.

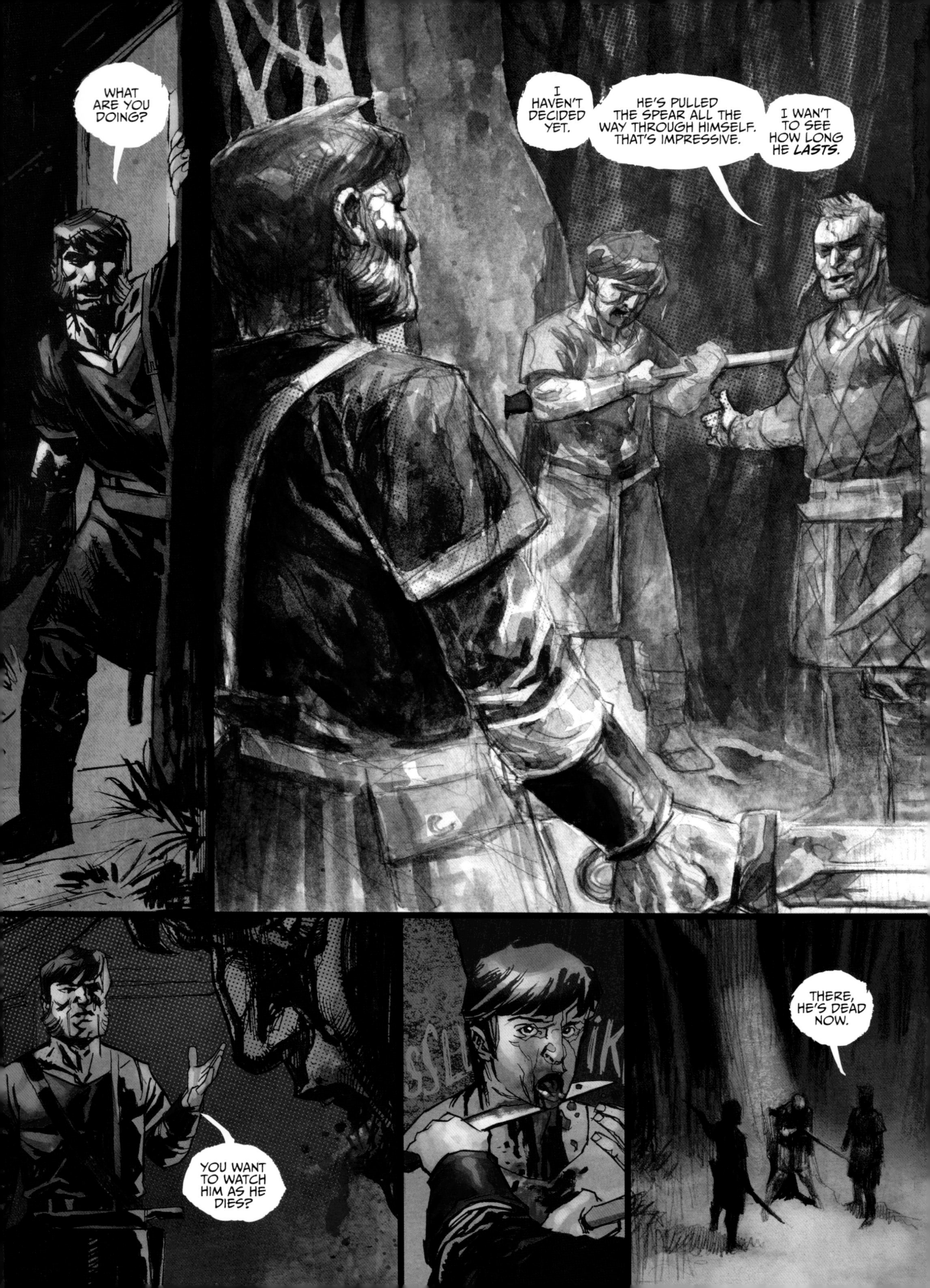
WHAT ARE YOU DOING?
I HAVEN'T DECIDED YET.
HE'S PULLED THE SPEAR ALL THE WAY THROUGH HIMSELF. THAT'S IMPRESSIVE.
I WAN'T TO SEE HOW LONG HE *LASTS*.
YOU WANT TO WATCH HIM AS HE DIES?
THERE, HE'S DEAD NOW.

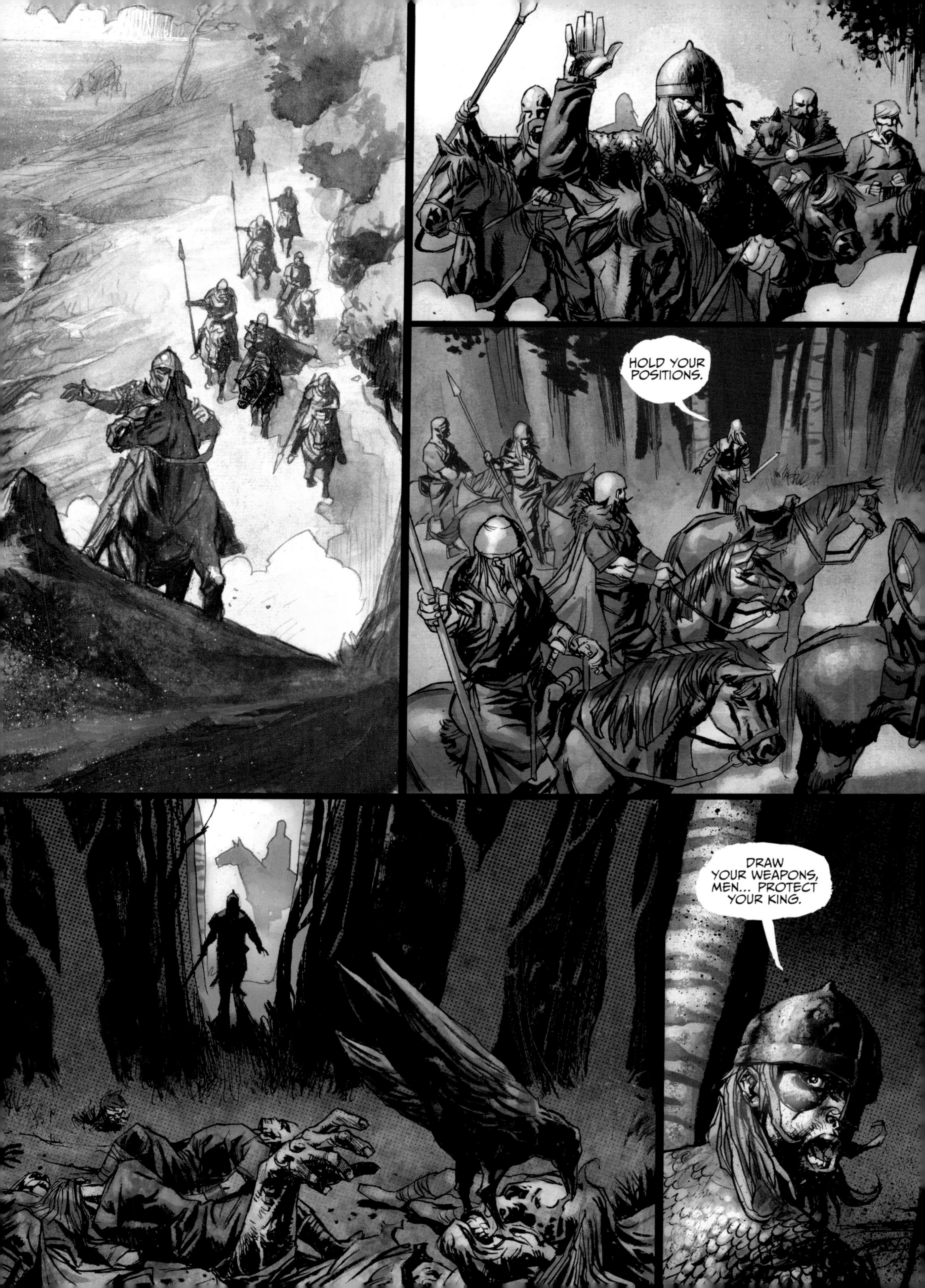
HOLD YOUR POSITIONS.
DRAW YOUR WEAPONS, MEN... PROTECT YOUR KING.

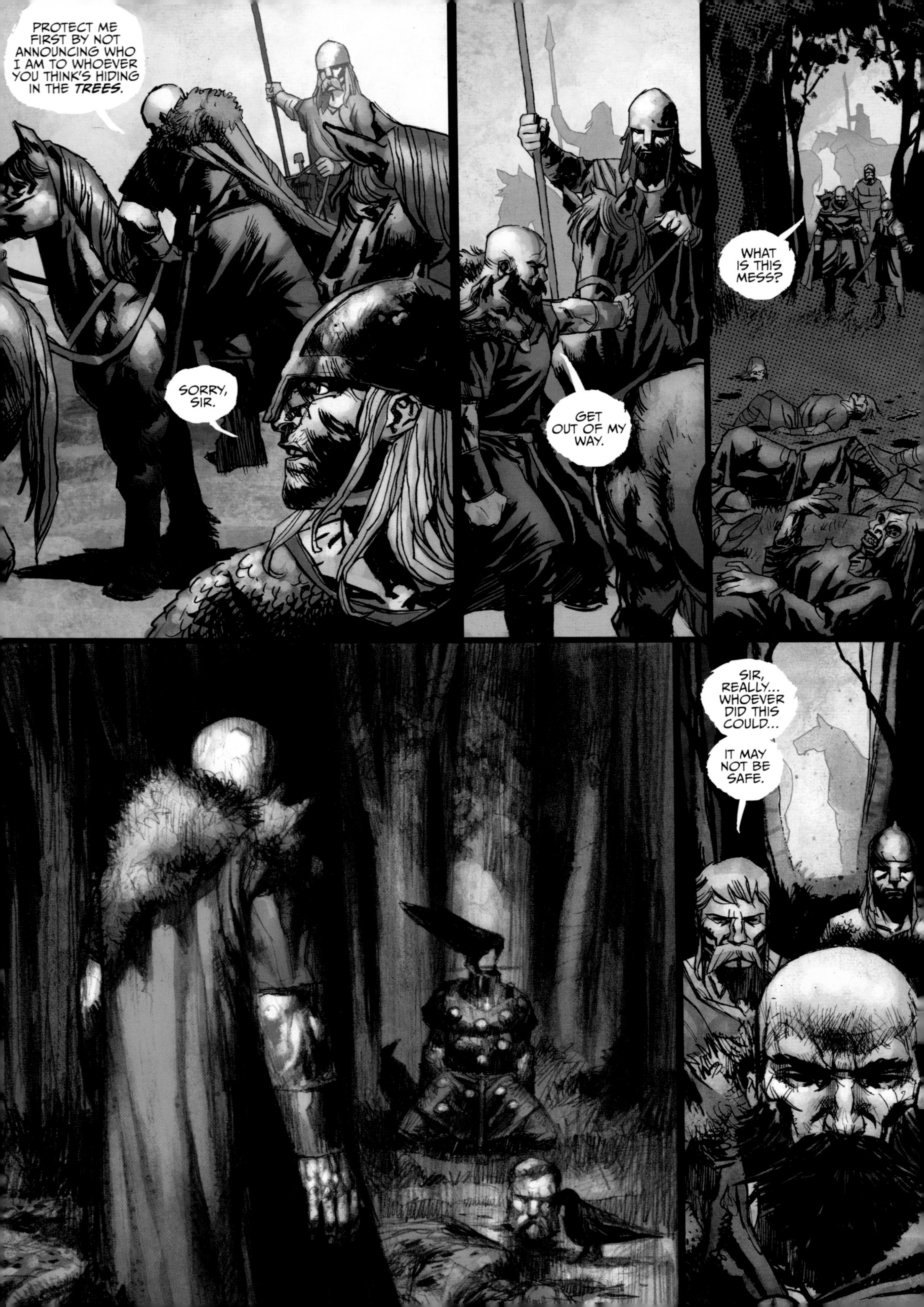
PROTECT ME FIRST BY NOT ANNOUNCING WHO I AM TO WHOEVER YOU THINK'S HIDING IN THE *TREES*.
SORRY, SIR.
GET OUT OF MY WAY.
WHAT IS THIS MESS?
SIR, REALLY... WHOEVER DID THIS COULD...
IT MAY NOT BE SAFE.

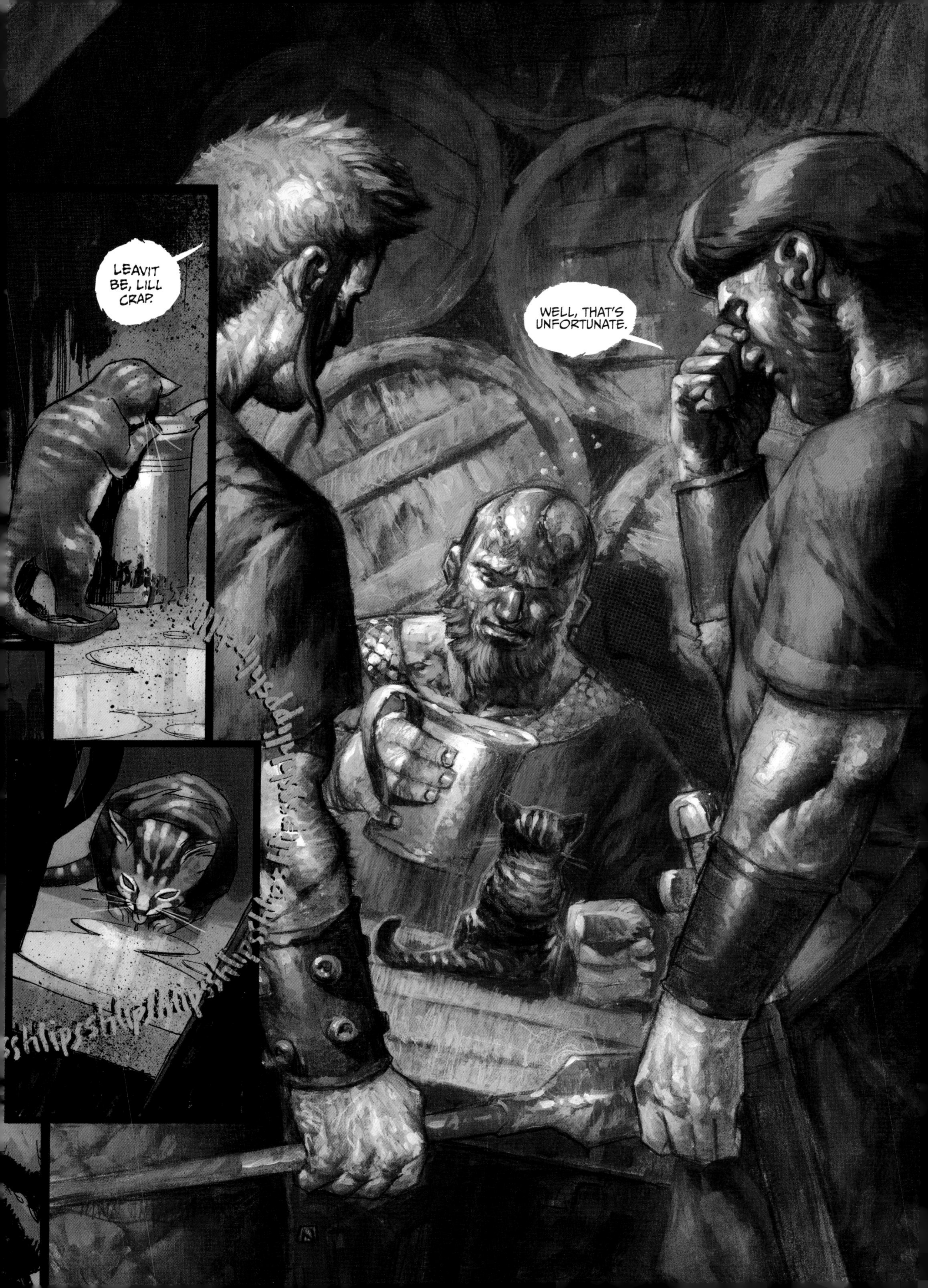
LEAVIT BE, LILL CRAP.
WELL, THAT'S UNFORTUNATE.

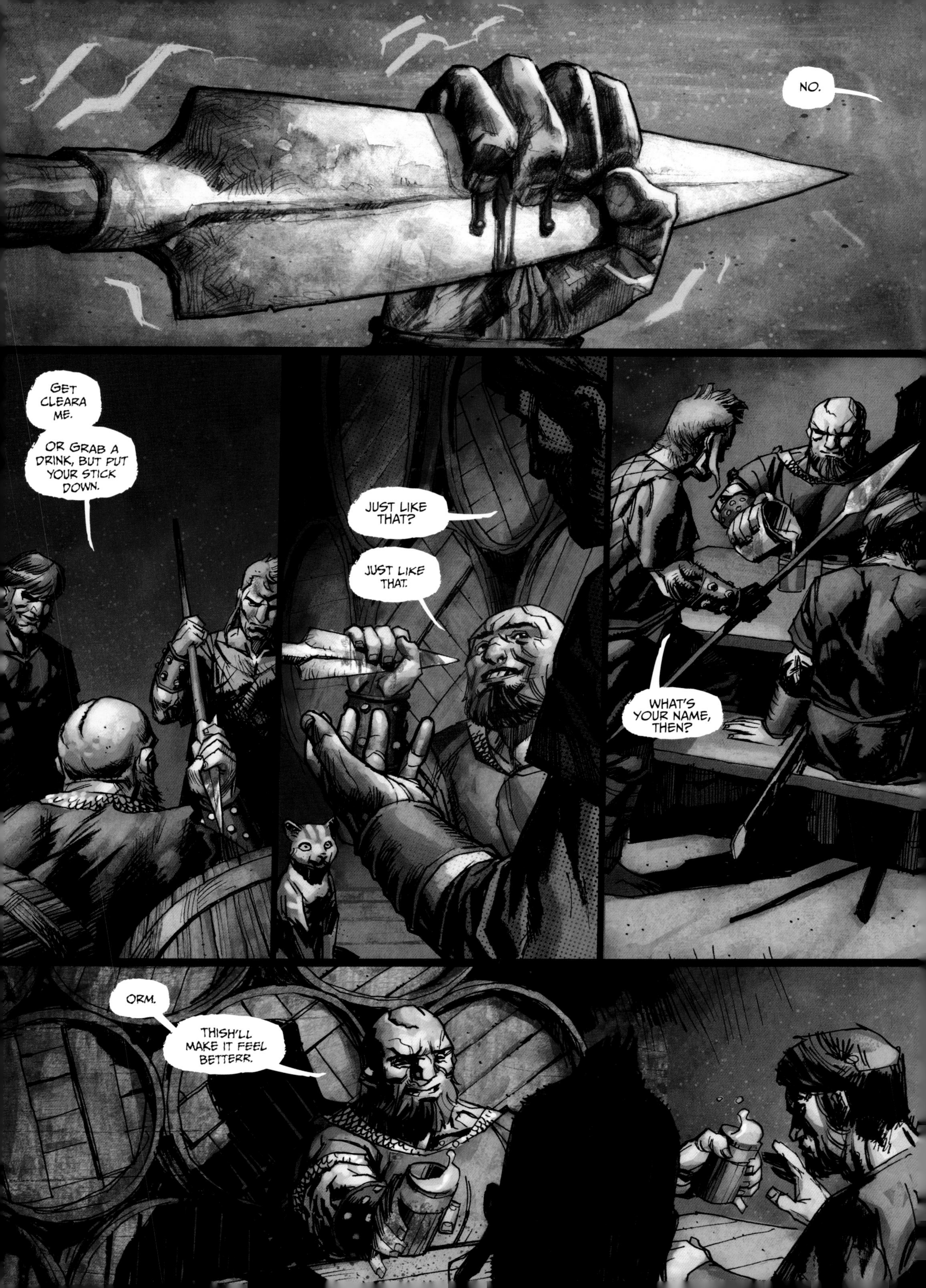
NO.
GET CLEARA ME.
OR GRAB A DRINK, BUT PUT YOUR STICK DOWN.
JUST LIKE THAT?
JUST LIKE THAT.
WHAT'S YOUR NAME, THEN?
ORM.
THISH'LL MAKE IT FEEL BETTERR.

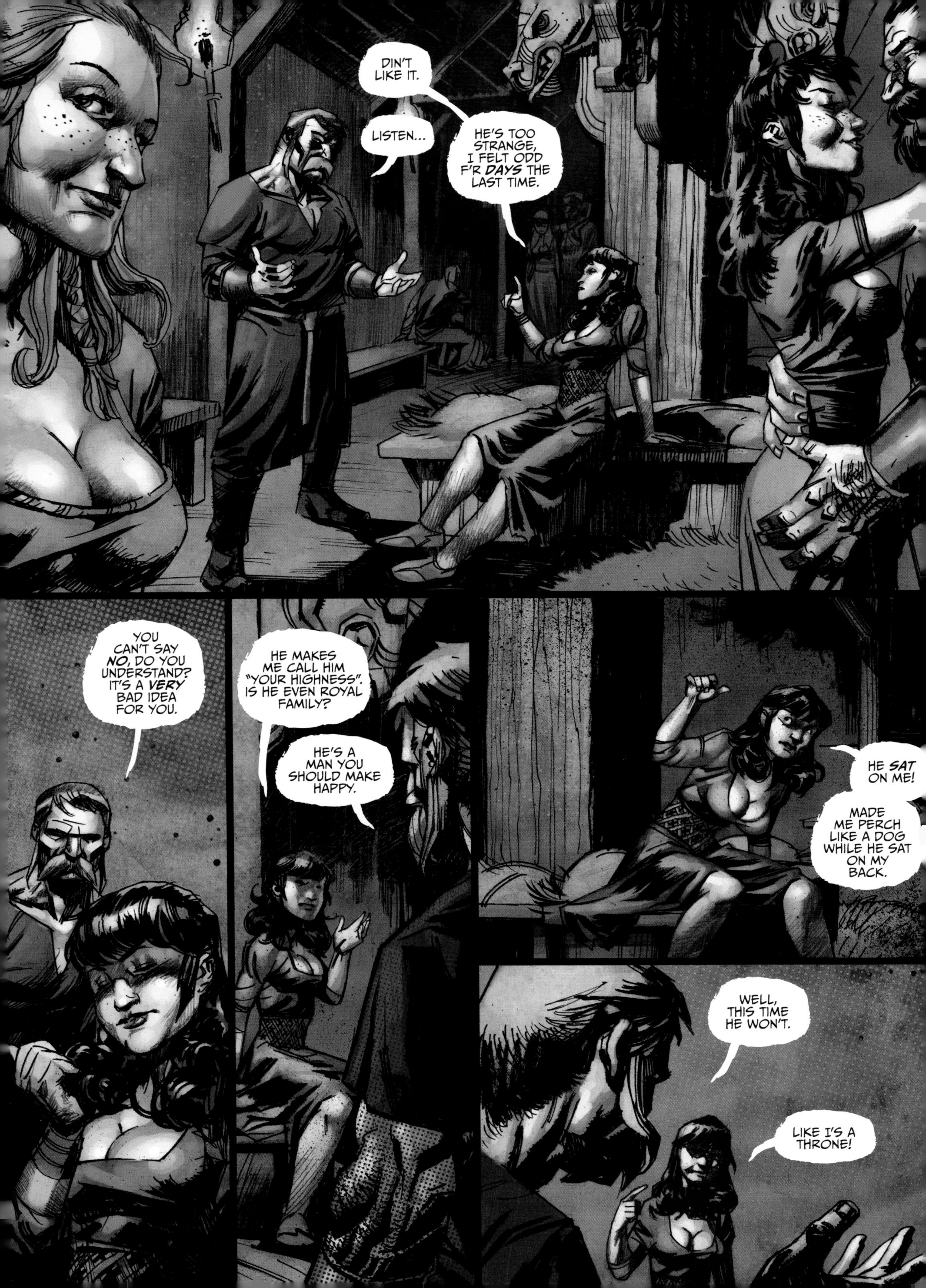
DIN'T LIKE IT.
LISTEN...
HE'S TOO STRANGE, I FELT ODD F'R DAYS THE LAST TIME.
YOU CAN'T SAY NO, DO YOU UNDERSTAND? IT'S A VERY BAD IDEA FOR YOU.
HE MAKES ME CALL HIM "YOUR HIGHNESS". IS HE EVEN ROYAL FAMILY?
HE'S A MAN YOU SHOULD MAKE HAPPY.
HE SAT ON ME!
MADE ME PERCH LIKE A DOG WHILE HE SAT ON MY BACK.
WELL, THIS TIME HE WON'T.
LIKE I'S A THRONE!

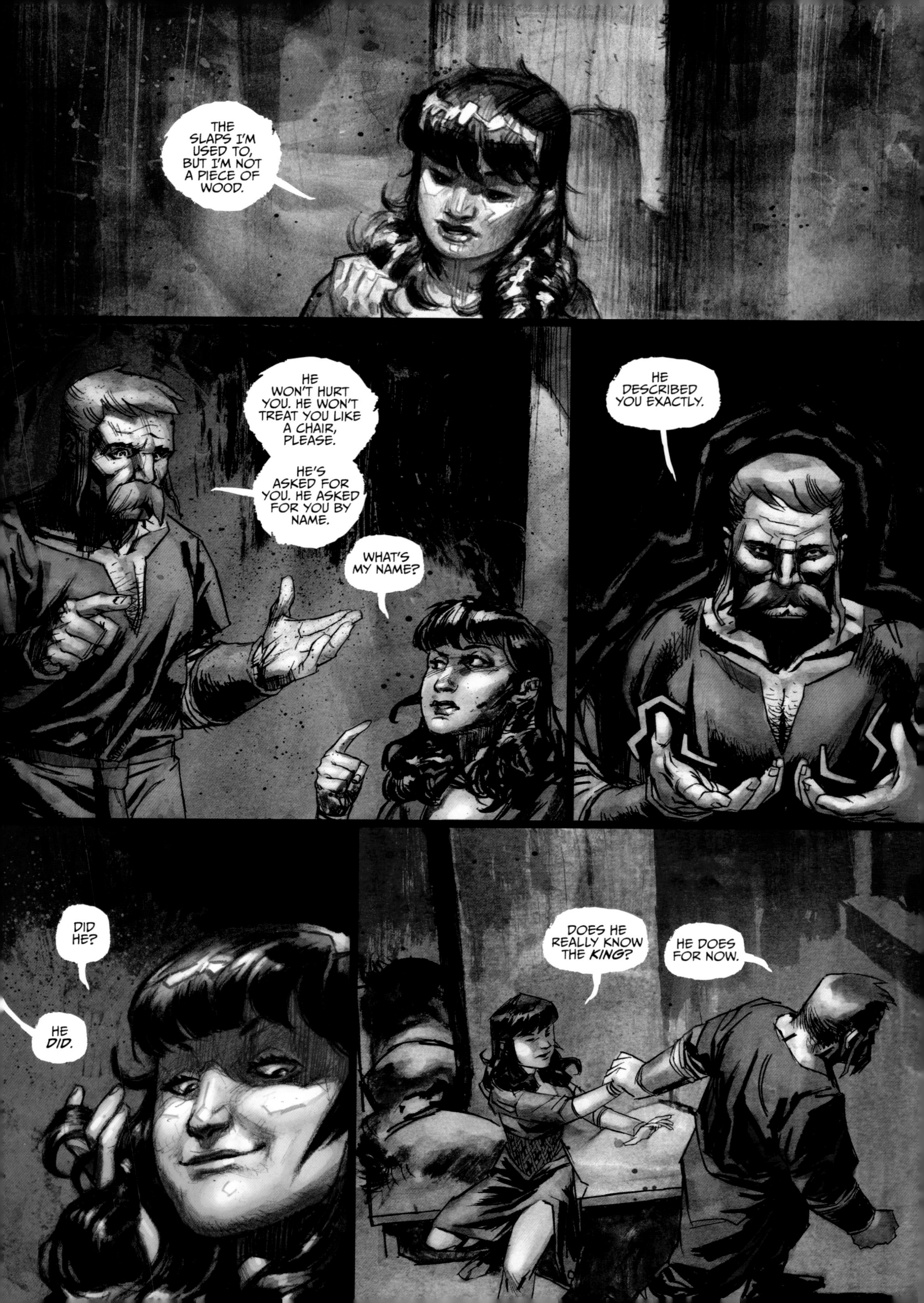
THE SLAPS I'M USED TO, BUT I'M NOT A PIECE OF WOOD.
HE WON'T HURT YOU. HE WON'T TREAT YOU LIKE A CHAIR, PLEASE.
HE'S ASKED FOR YOU. HE ASKED FOR YOU BY NAME.
WHAT'S MY NAME?
HE DESCRIBED YOU EXACTLY.
DID HE?
HE *DID*.
DOES HE REALLY KNOW THE *KING*?
HE DOES FOR NOW.

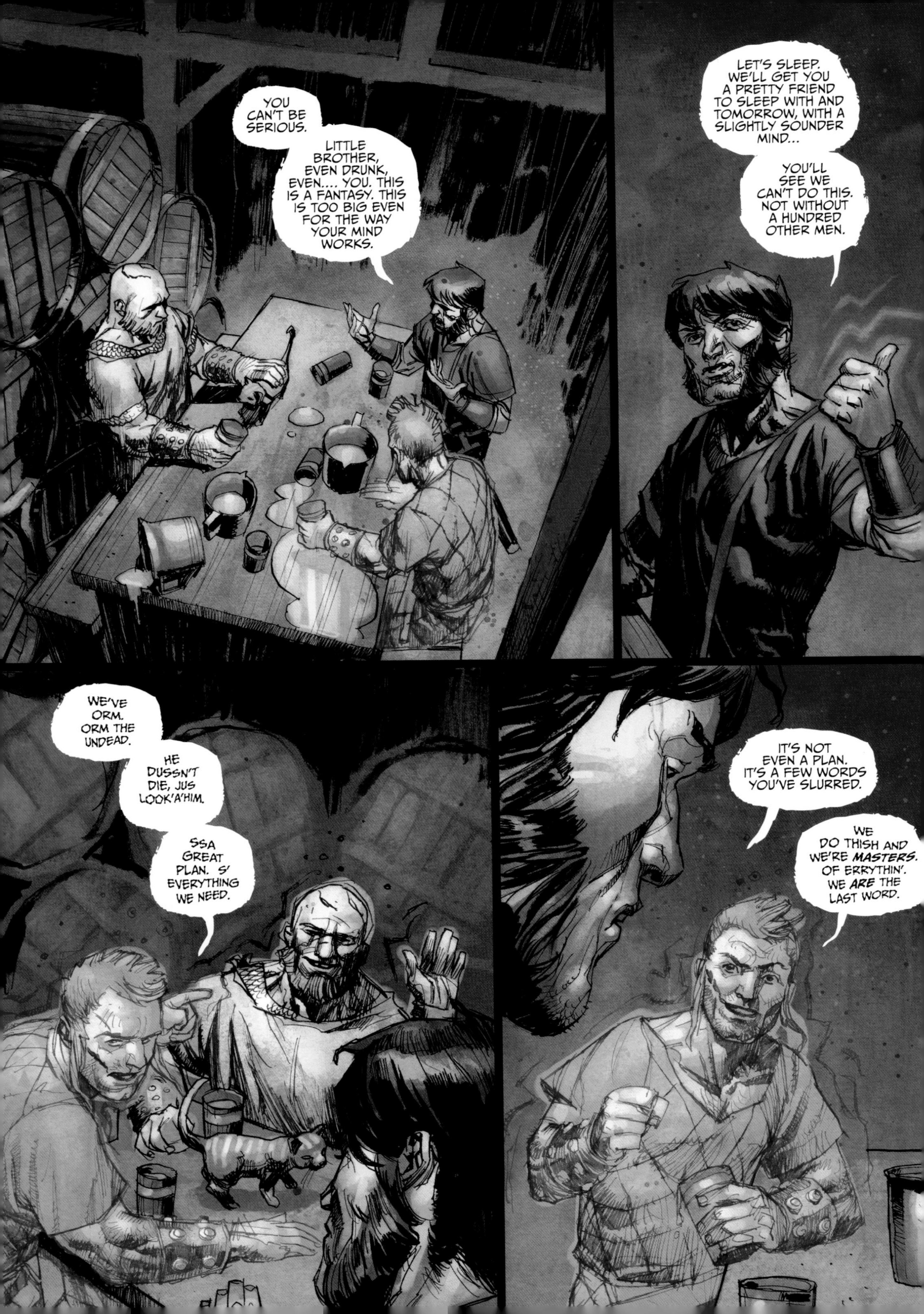
YOU CAN'T BE SERIOUS.
LITTLE BROTHER, EVEN DRUNK, EVEN.... YOU. THIS IS A FANTASY. THIS IS TOO BIG EVEN FOR THE WAY YOUR MIND WORKS.
LET'S SLEEP. WE'LL GET YOU A PRETTY FRIEND TO SLEEP WITH AND TOMORROW, WITH A SLIGHTLY SOUNDER MIND...
YOU'LL SEE WE CAN'T DO THIS. NOT WITHOUT A HUNDRED OTHER MEN.
WE'VE ORM. ORM THE UNDEAD.
HE DUSSN'T DIE, JUS LOOK'A'HIM.
SSA GREAT PLAN. S' EVERYTHING WE NEED.
IT'S NOT EVEN A PLAN. IT'S A FEW WORDS YOU'VE SLURRED.
WE DO THISH AND WE'RE *MASTERS*. OF ERRYTHIN'. WE *ARE* THE LAST WORD.

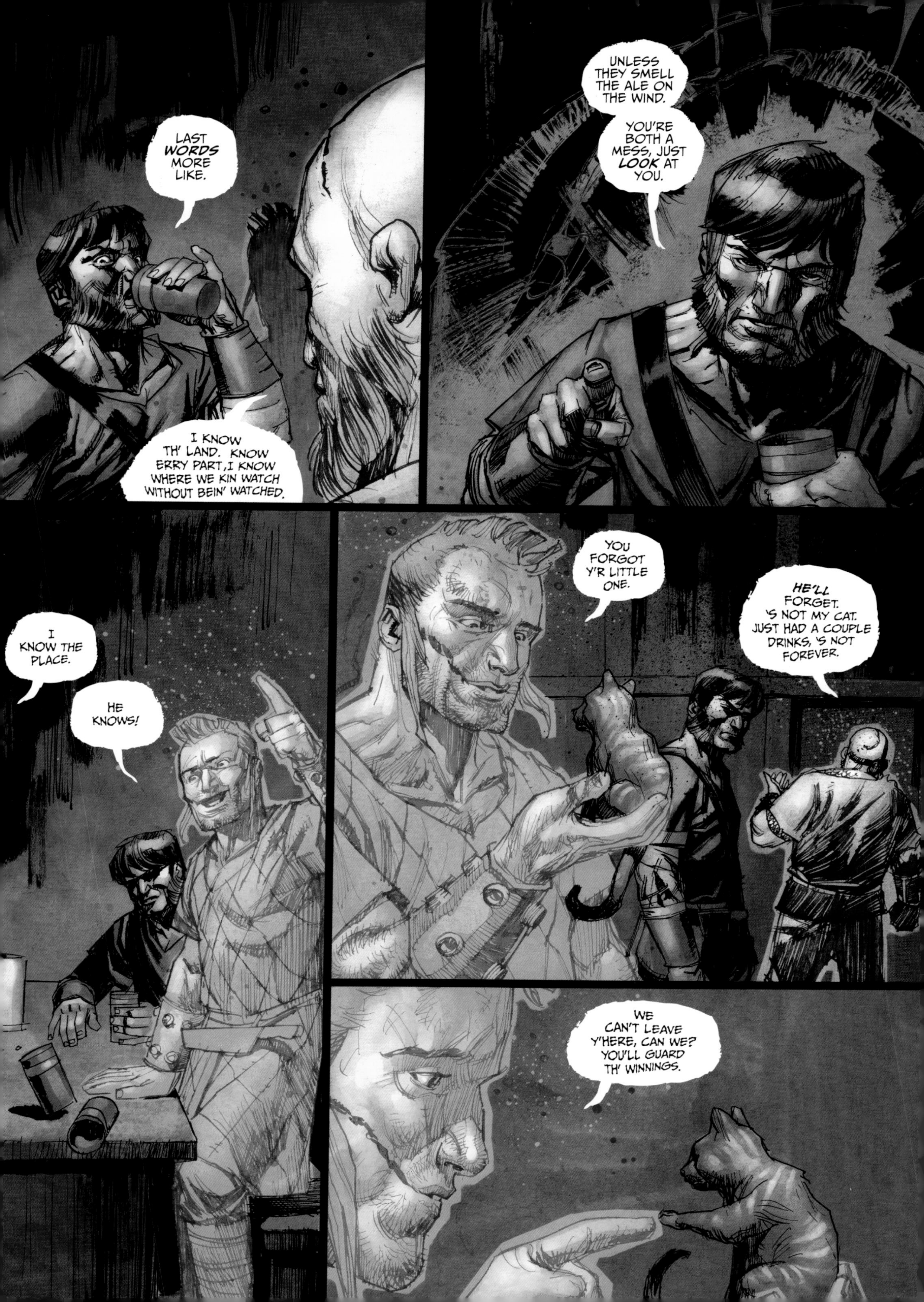
LAST WORDS MORE LIKE.
I KNOW TH' LAND. KNOW ERRY PART, I KNOW WHERE WE KIN WATCH WITHOUT BEIN' WATCHED.
UNLESS THEY SMELL THE ALE ON THE WIND.
YOU'RE BOTH A MESS, JUST LOOK AT YOU.
I KNOW THE PLACE.
HE KNOWS!
YOU FORGOT Y'R LITTLE ONE.
HE'LL FORGET. 'S NOT MY CAT. JUST HAD A COUPLE DRINKS, 'S NOT FOREVER.
WE CAN'T LEAVE Y'HERE, CAN WE? YOU'LL GUARD TH' WINNINGS.

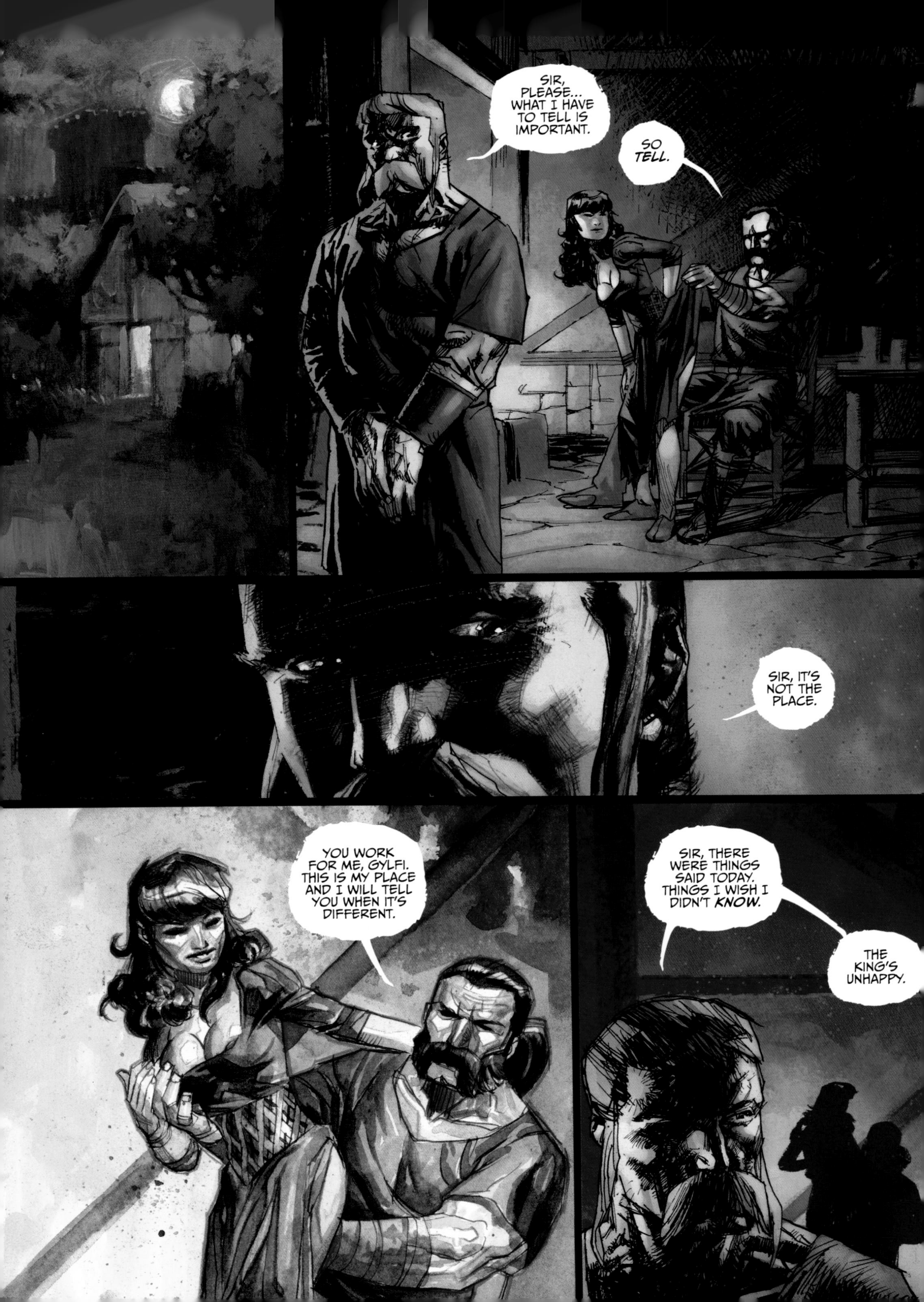
SIR, PLEASE... WHAT I HAVE TO TELL IS IMPORTANT.
SO *TELL*.
SIR, IT'S NOT THE PLACE.
YOU WORK FOR ME, GYLFI. THIS IS MY PLACE AND I WILL TELL YOU WHEN IT'S DIFFERENT.
SIR, THERE WERE THINGS SAID TODAY. THINGS I WISH I DIDN'T *KNOW*.
THE KING'S UNHAPPY.

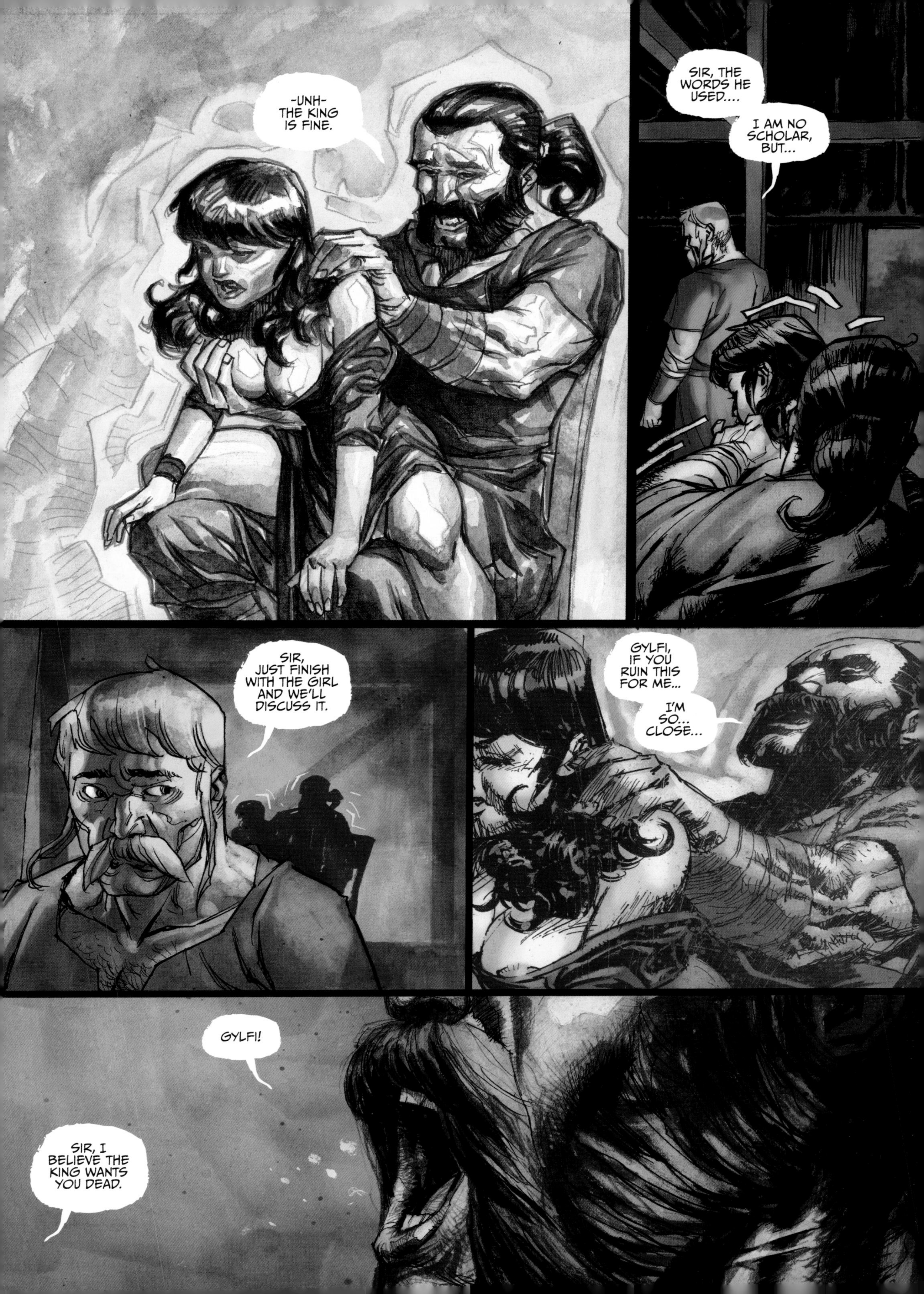
-UNH-
THE KING
IS FINE.
SIR, THE
WORDS HE
USED....
I AM NO
SCHOLAR,
BUT...
SIR,
JUST FINISH
WITH THE GIRL
AND WE'LL
DISCUSS IT.
GYLFI,
IF YOU
RUIN THIS
FOR ME...
I'M
SO...
CLOSE...
GYLFI!
SIR, I
BELIEVE THE
KING WANTS
YOU DEAD.

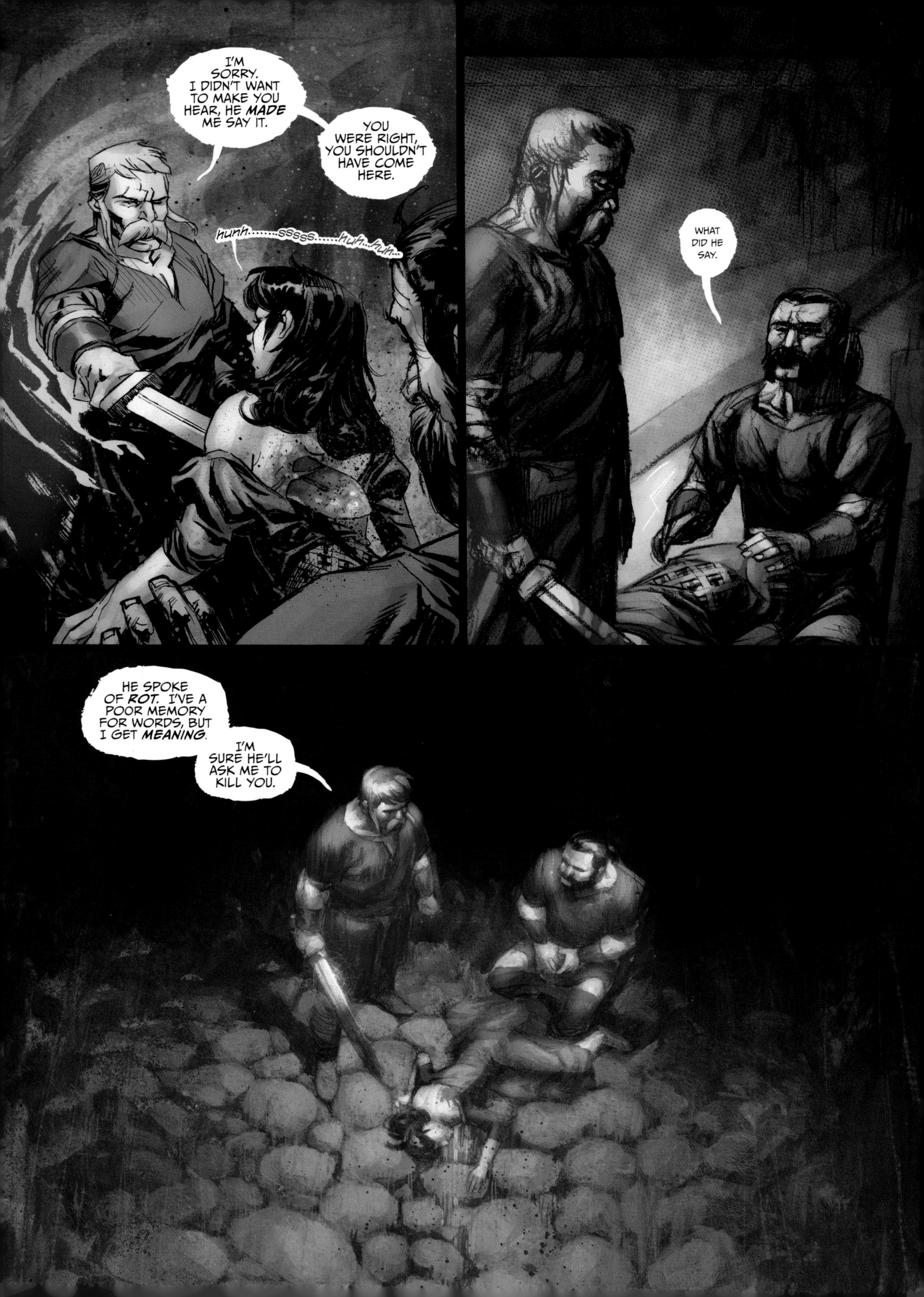
I'M SORRY. I DIDN'T WANT TO MAKE YOU HEAR, HE MADE ME SAY IT.
YOU WERE RIGHT, YOU SHOULDN'T HAVE COME HERE.
hunh.......sssss.......huh...huh...
WHAT DID HE SAY.
HE SPOKE OF ROT. I'VE A POOR MEMORY FOR WORDS, BUT I GET MEANING.
I'M SURE HE'LL ASK ME TO KILL YOU.

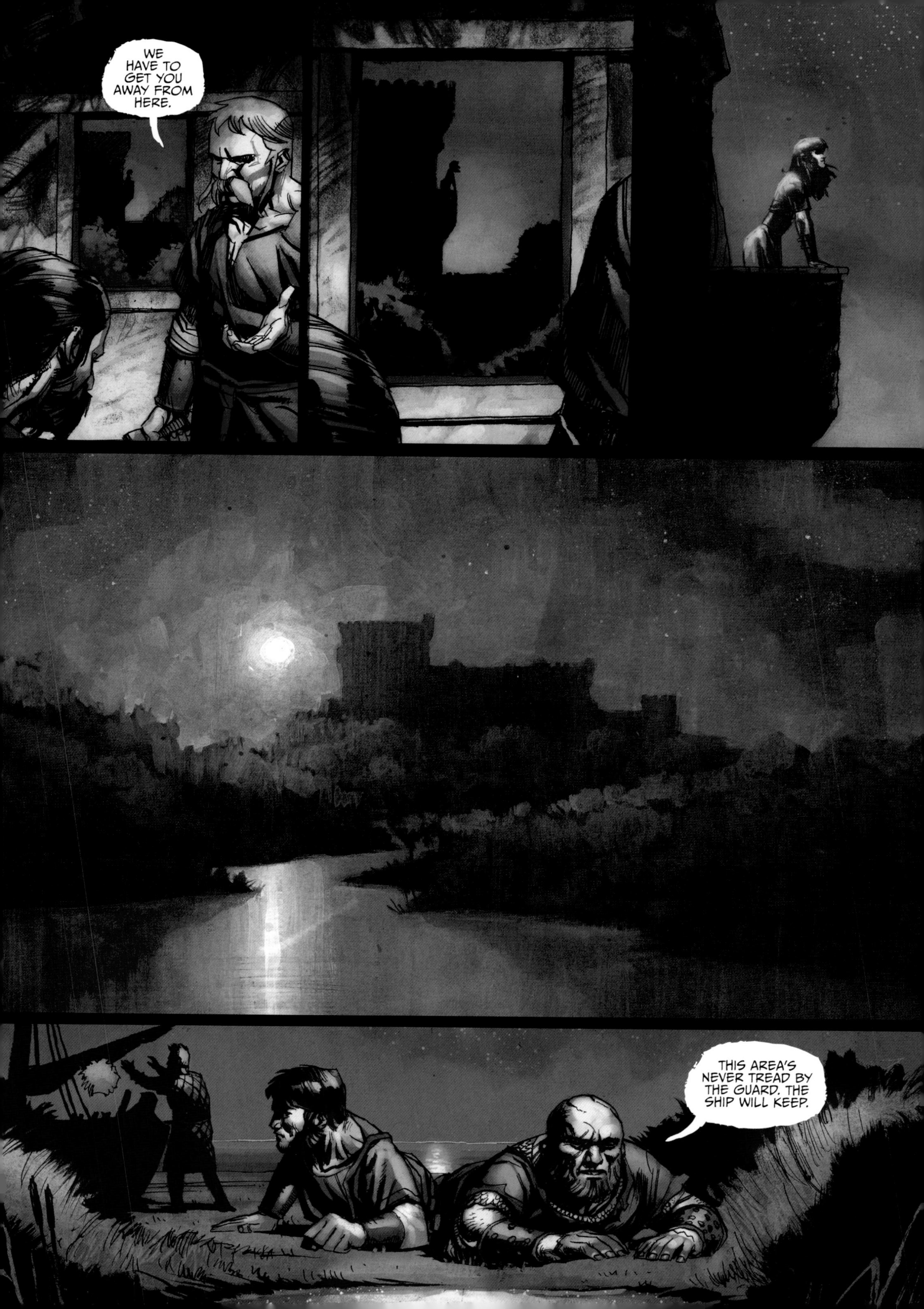
WE HAVE TO GET YOU AWAY FROM HERE.
THIS AREA'S NEVER TREAD BY THE GUARD. THE SHIP WILL KEEP.

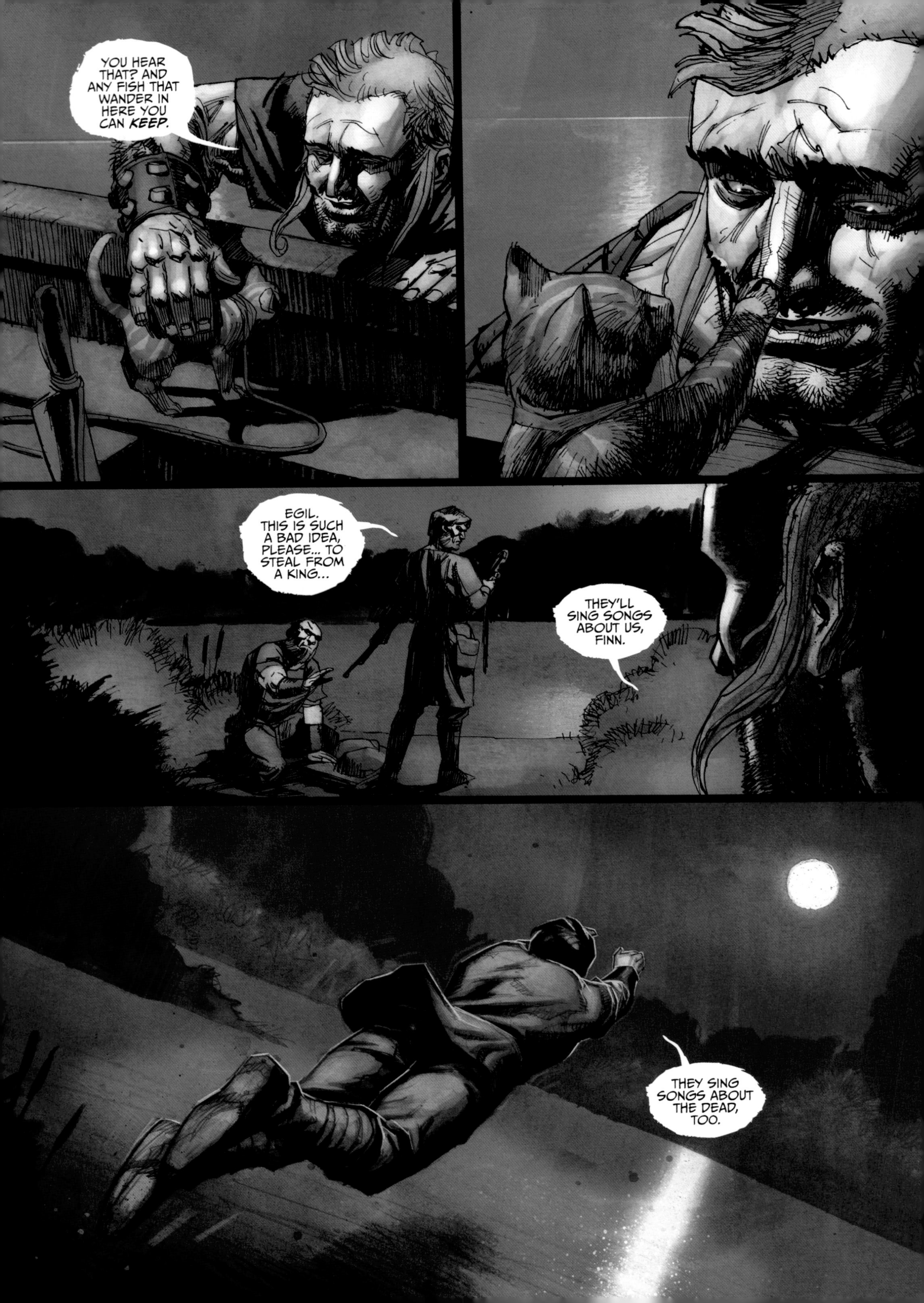
YOU HEAR THAT? AND ANY FISH THAT WANDER IN HERE YOU CAN *KEEP*.
EGIL. THIS IS SUCH A BAD IDEA, PLEASE... TO STEAL FROM A KING...
THEY'LL SING SONGS ABOUT US, FINN.
THEY SING SONGS ABOUT THE DEAD, TOO.

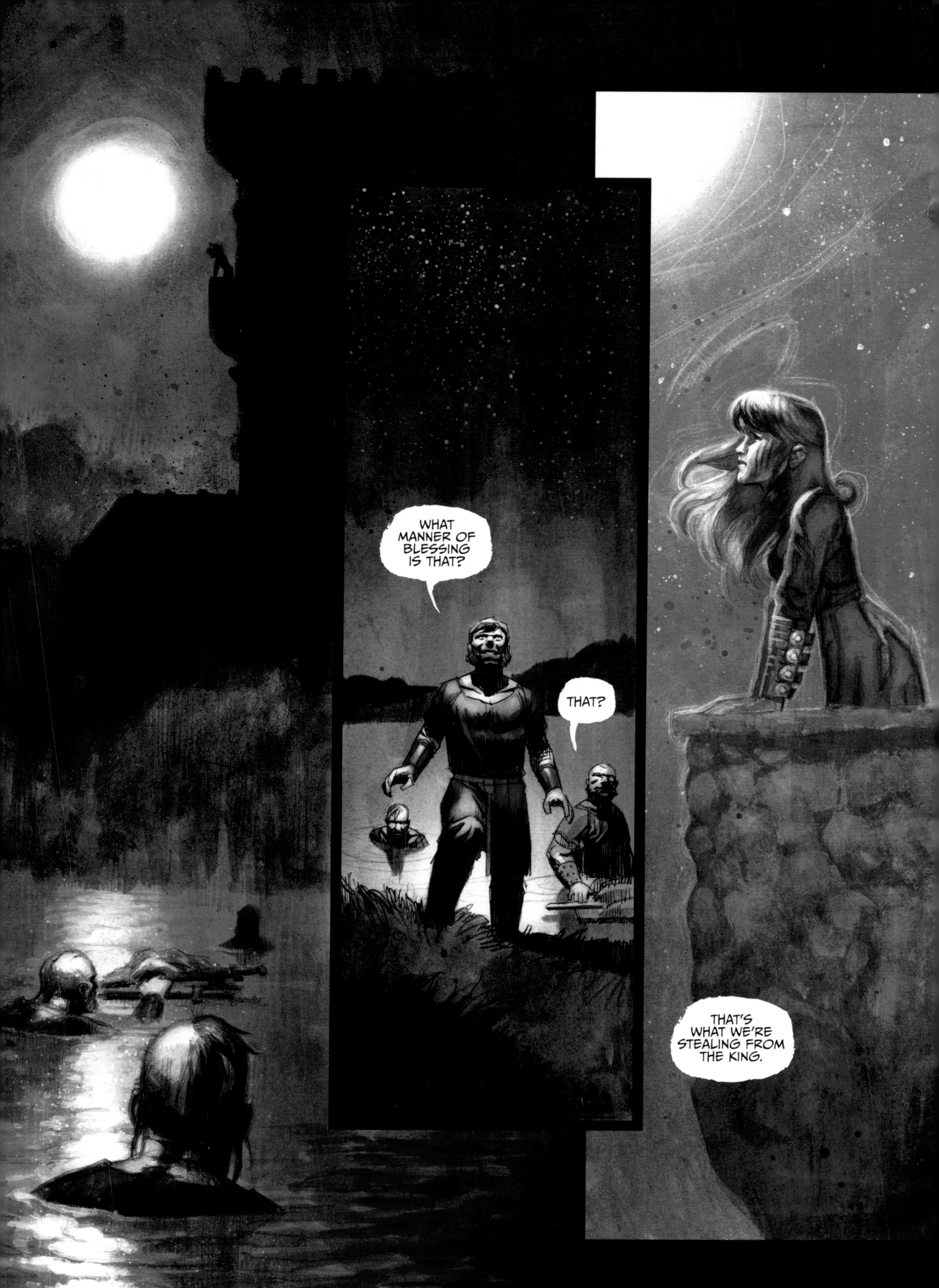
WHAT MANNER OF BLESSING IS THAT?
THAT?
THAT'S WHAT WE'RE STEALING FROM THE KING.

To Be Continued...

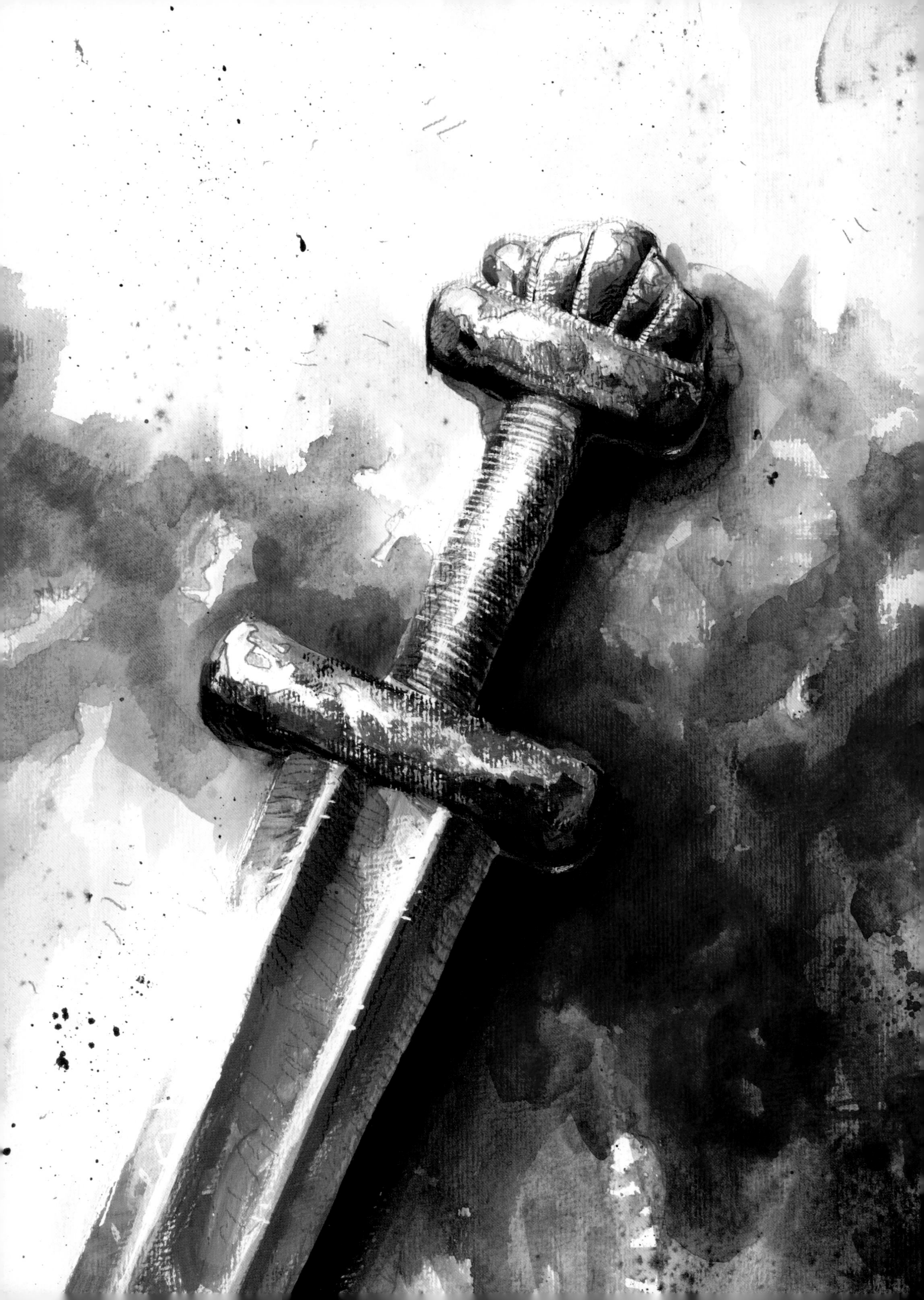

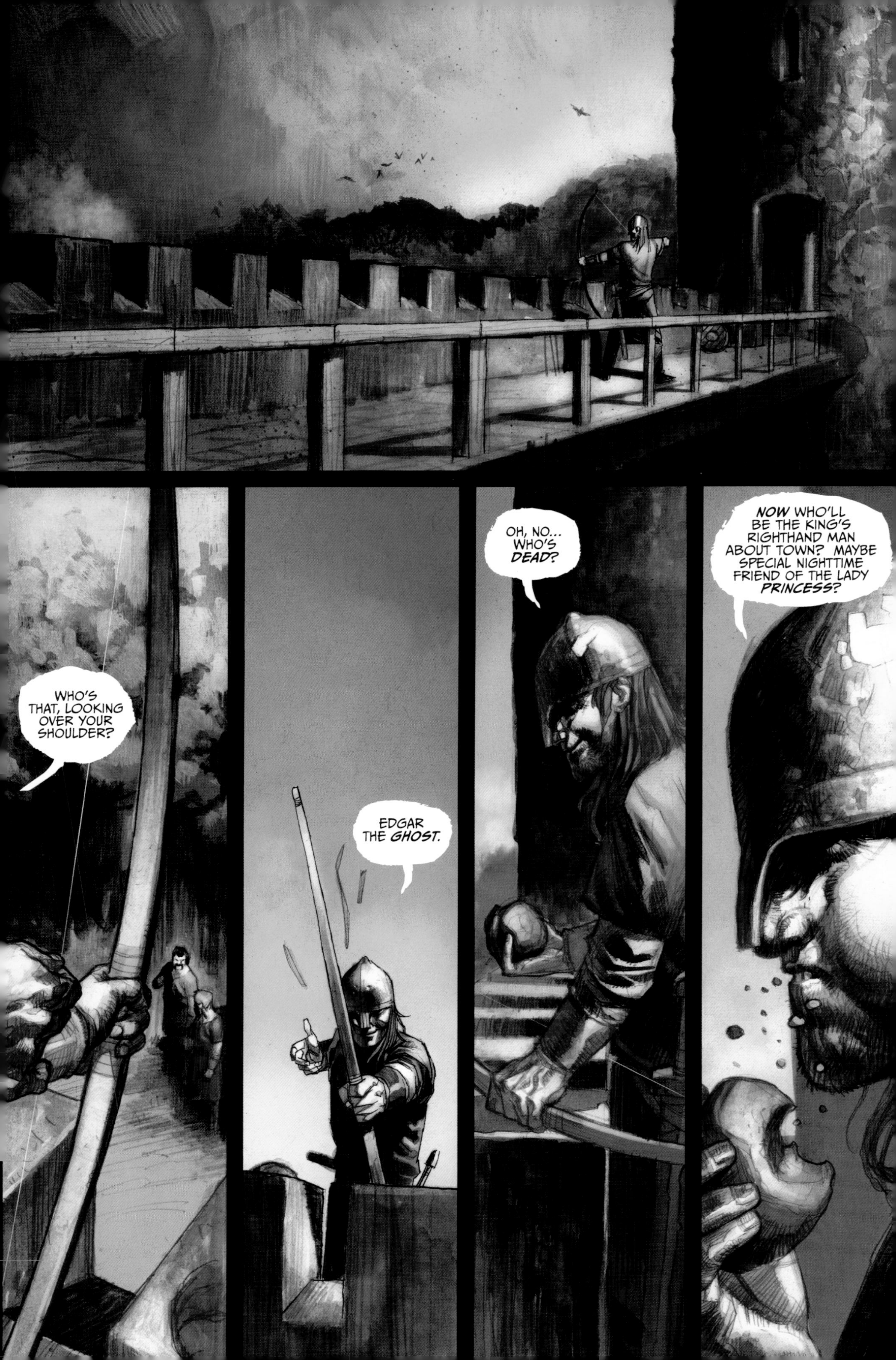
WHO'S THAT, LOOKING OVER YOUR SHOULDER?
EDGAR THE GHOST.
OH, NO... WHO'S DEAD?
NOW WHO'LL BE THE KING'S RIGHTHAND MAN ABOUT TOWN? MAYBE SPECIAL NIGHTTIME FRIEND OF THE LADY PRINCESS?

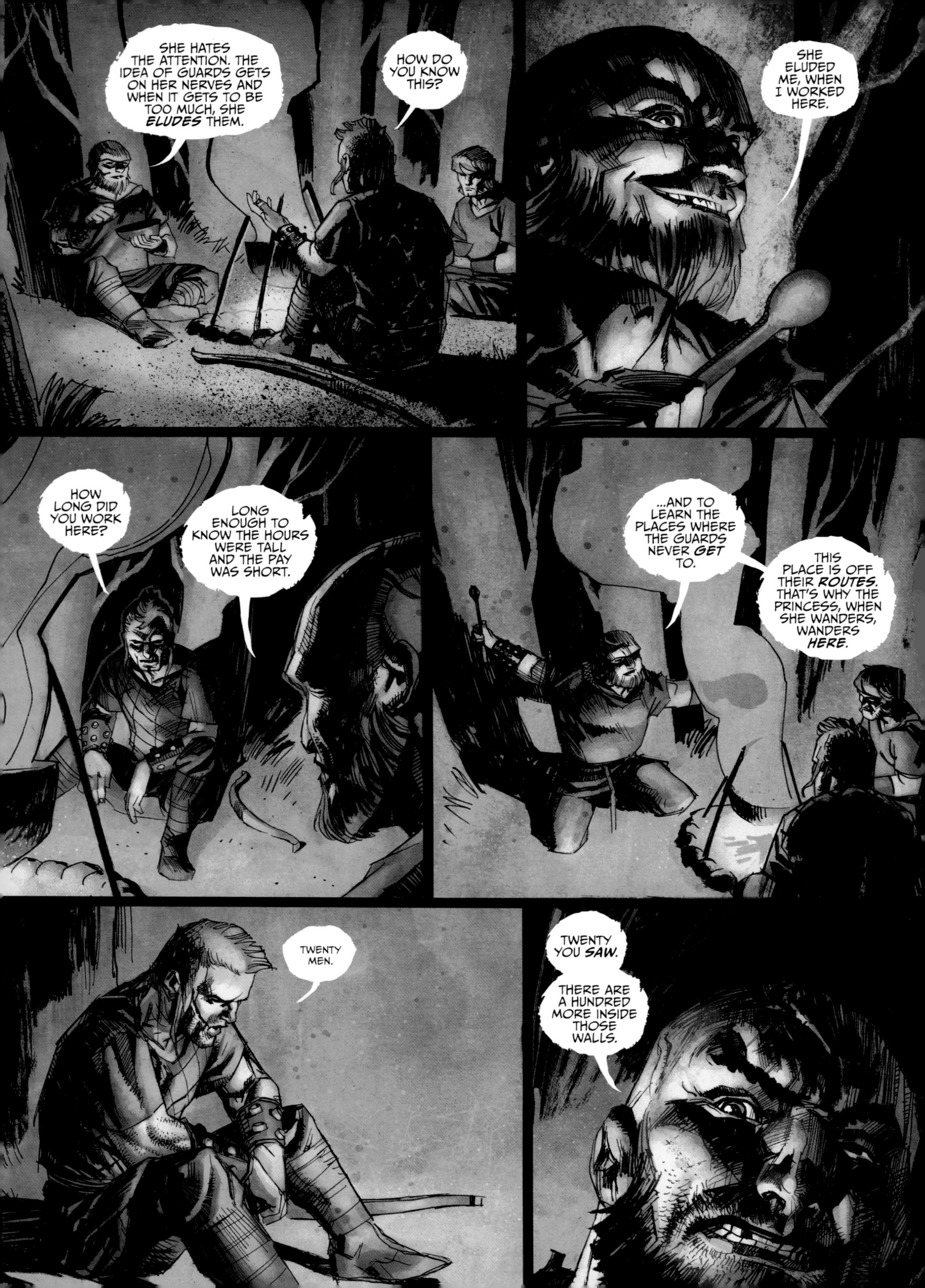
SHE HATES THE ATTENTION. THE IDEA OF GUARDS GETS ON HER NERVES AND WHEN IT GETS TO BE TOO MUCH, SHE *ELUDES* THEM.
HOW DO YOU KNOW THIS?
SHE ELUDED ME, WHEN I WORKED HERE.
HOW LONG DID YOU WORK HERE?
LONG ENOUGH TO KNOW THE HOURS WERE TALL AND THE PAY WAS SHORT.
...AND TO LEARN THE PLACES WHERE THE GUARDS NEVER *GET* TO.
THIS PLACE IS OFF THEIR *ROUTES.* THAT'S WHY THE PRINCESS, WHEN SHE WANDERS, WANDERS *HERE.*
TWENTY MEN.
TWENTY YOU *SAW.*
THERE ARE A HUNDRED MORE INSIDE THOSE WALLS.

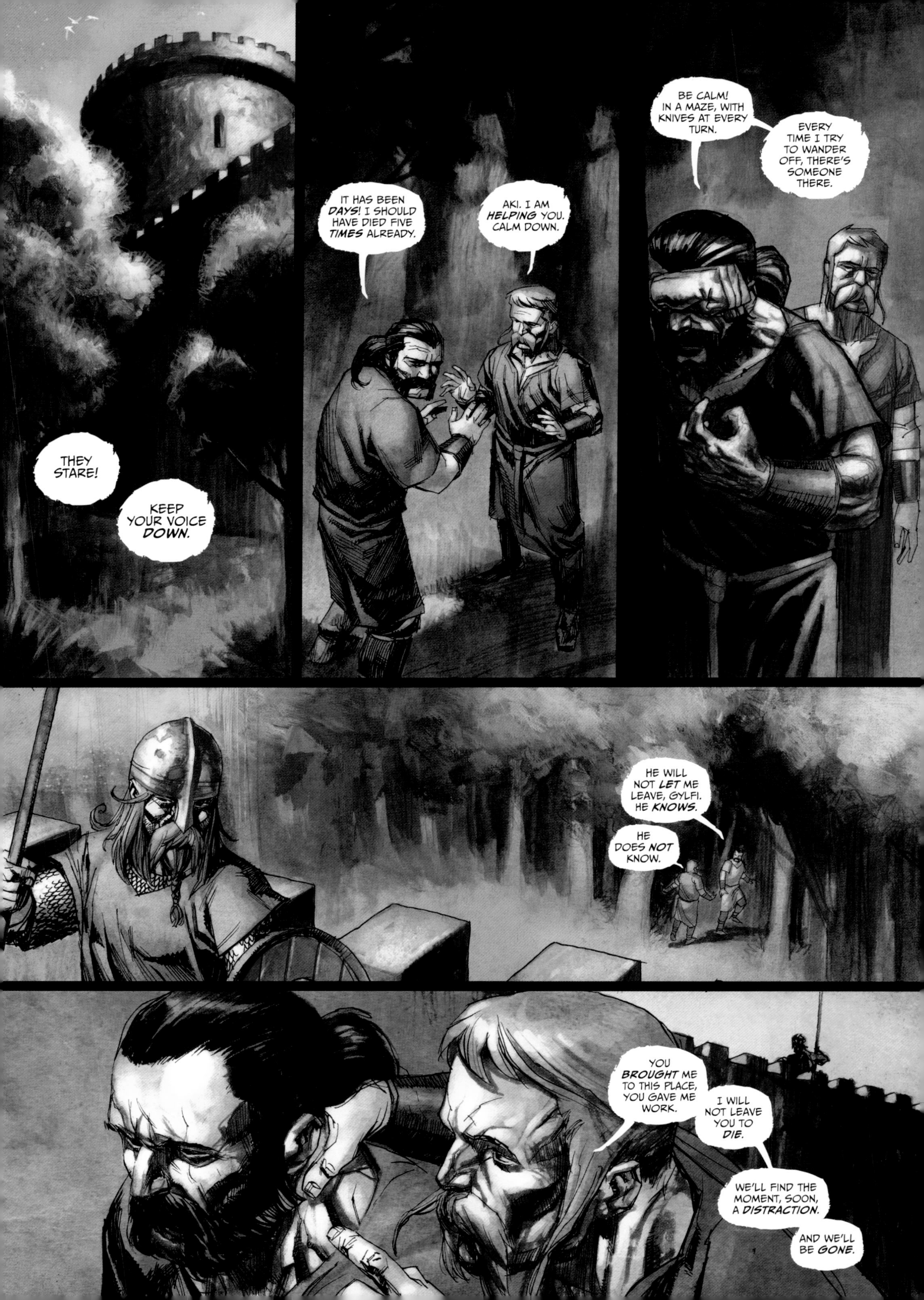
THEY STARE!
KEEP YOUR VOICE DOWN.
IT HAS BEEN DAYS! I SHOULD HAVE DIED FIVE TIMES ALREADY.
AKI. I AM HELPING YOU. CALM DOWN.
BE CALM! IN A MAZE, WITH KNIVES AT EVERY TURN.
EVERY TIME I TRY TO WANDER OFF, THERE'S SOMEONE THERE.
HE WILL NOT LET ME LEAVE, GYLFI. HE KNOWS.
HE DOES NOT KNOW.
YOU BROUGHT ME TO THIS PLACE, YOU GAVE ME WORK.
I WILL NOT LEAVE YOU TO DIE.
WE'LL FIND THE MOMENT, SOON, A DISTRACTION.
AND WE'LL BE GONE.

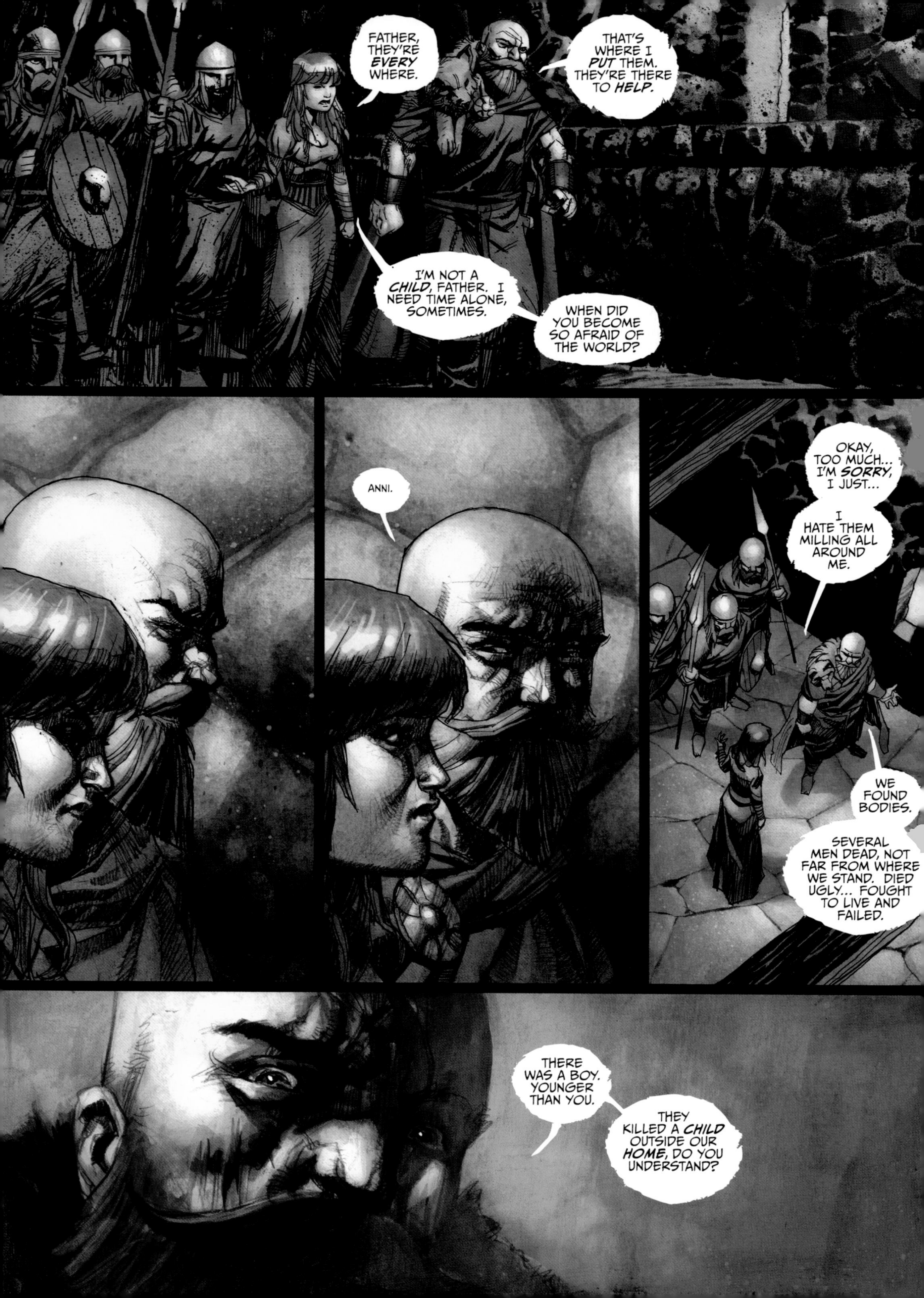
FATHER, THEY'RE *EVERY* WHERE.
THAT'S WHERE I *PUT* THEM. THEY'RE THERE TO *HELP*.
I'M NOT A *CHILD*, FATHER. I NEED TIME ALONE, SOMETIMES.
WHEN DID YOU BECOME SO AFRAID OF THE WORLD?
ANNI.
OKAY, TOO MUCH... I'M *SORRY*, I JUST...
I HATE THEM MILLING ALL AROUND ME.
WE FOUND BODIES.
SEVERAL MEN DEAD, NOT FAR FROM WHERE WE STAND. DIED UGLY... FOUGHT TO LIVE AND FAILED.
THERE WAS A BOY. YOUNGER THAN YOU.
THEY KILLED A *CHILD* OUTSIDE OUR *HOME*, DO YOU UNDERSTAND?

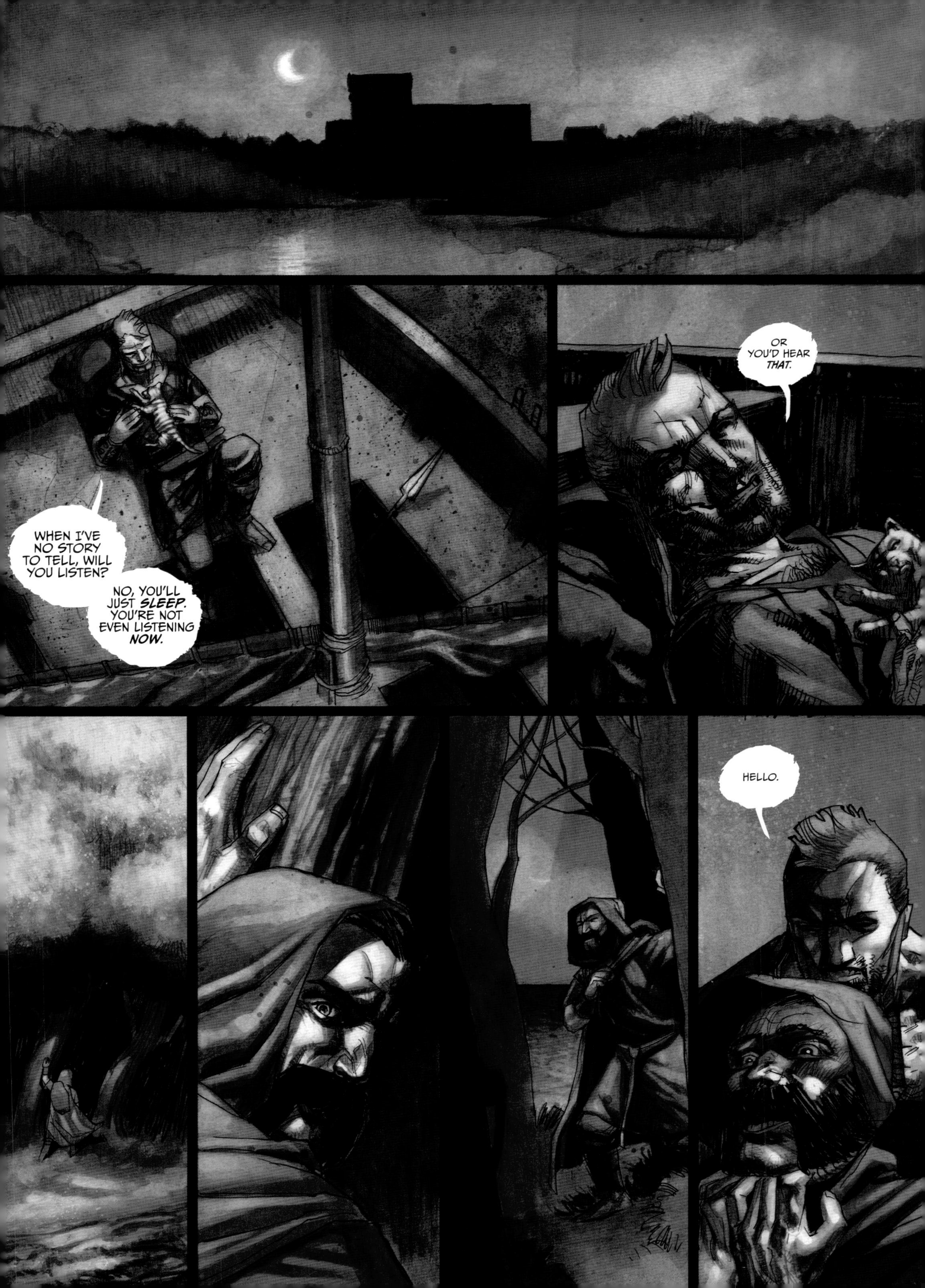
WHEN I'VE NO STORY TO TELL, WILL YOU LISTEN?
NO, YOU'LL JUST SLEEP. YOU'RE NOT EVEN LISTENING NOW.
OR YOU'D HEAR THAT.
HELLO.

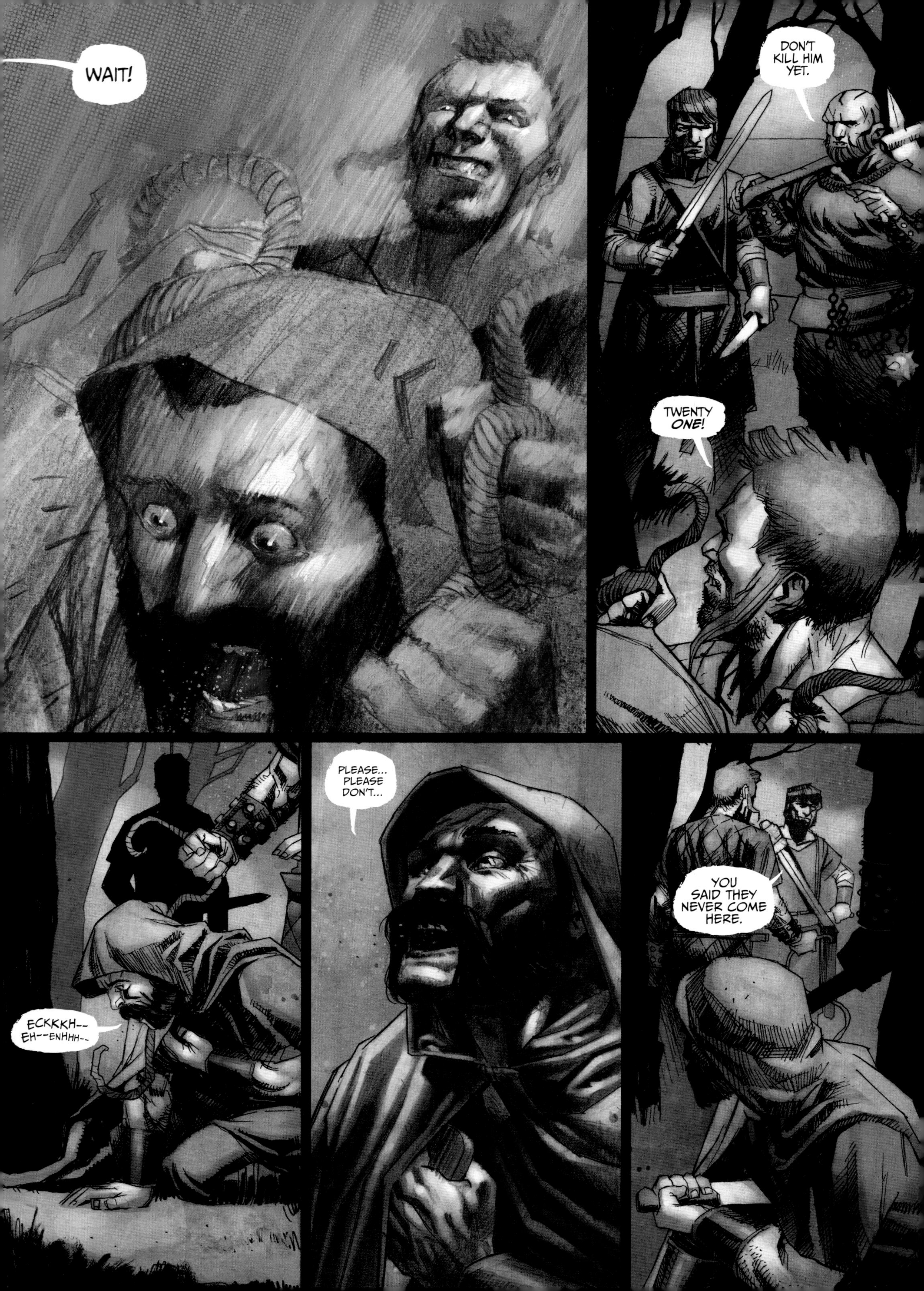
WAIT!
DON'T KILL HIM YET.
TWENTY ONE!
ECKKKH-- EH--ENHHH--
PLEASE... PLEASE DON'T...
YOU SAID THEY NEVER COME HERE.

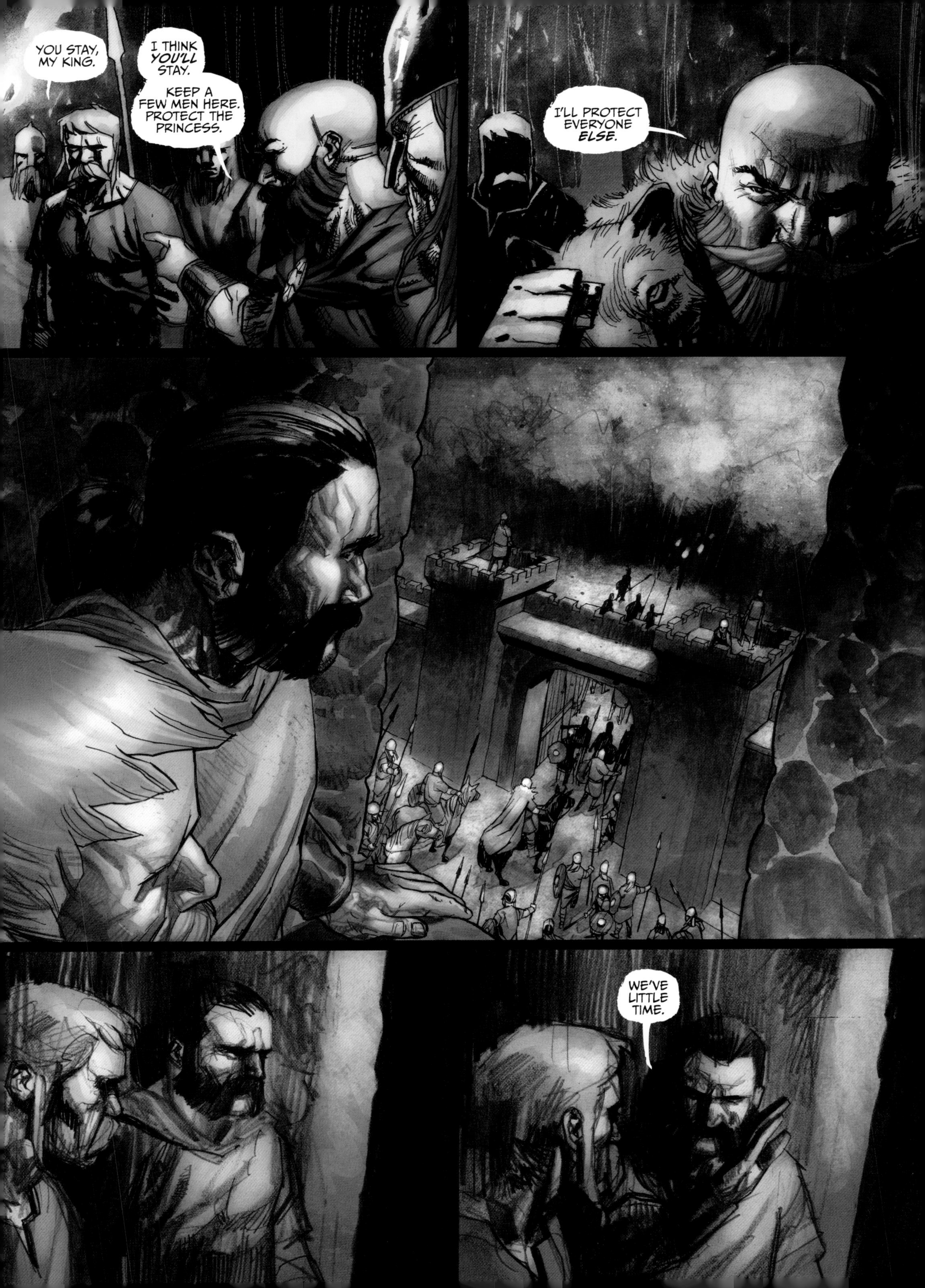
YOU STAY, MY KING.
I THINK *YOU'LL* STAY.
KEEP A FEW MEN HERE. PROTECT THE PRINCESS.
I'LL PROTECT EVERYONE *ELSE*.
WE'VE LITTLE TIME.

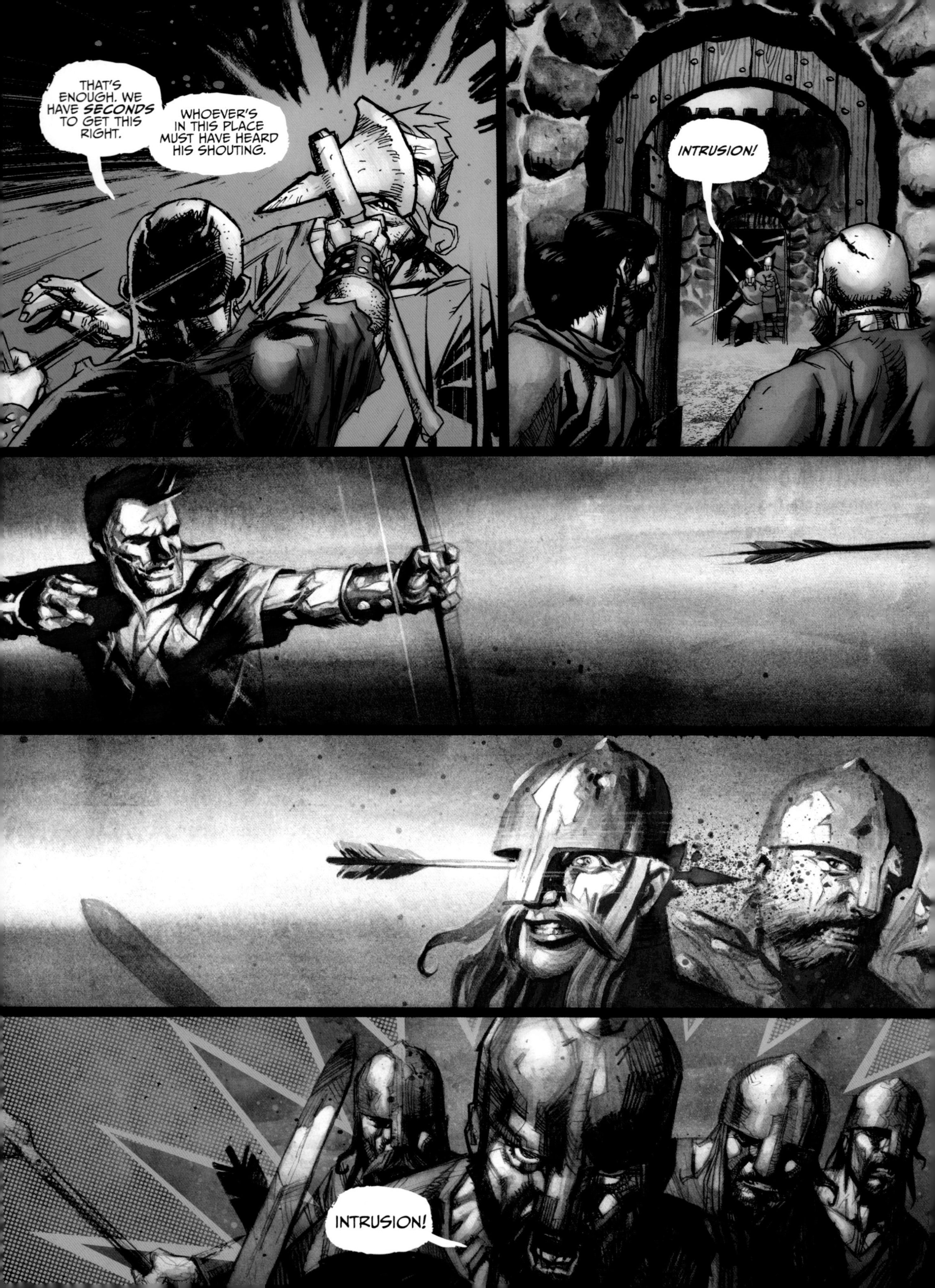
THAT'S ENOUGH. WE HAVE SECONDS TO GET THIS RIGHT.
WHOEVER'S IN THIS PLACE MUST HAVE HEARD HIS SHOUTING.
INTRUSION!
INTRUSION!

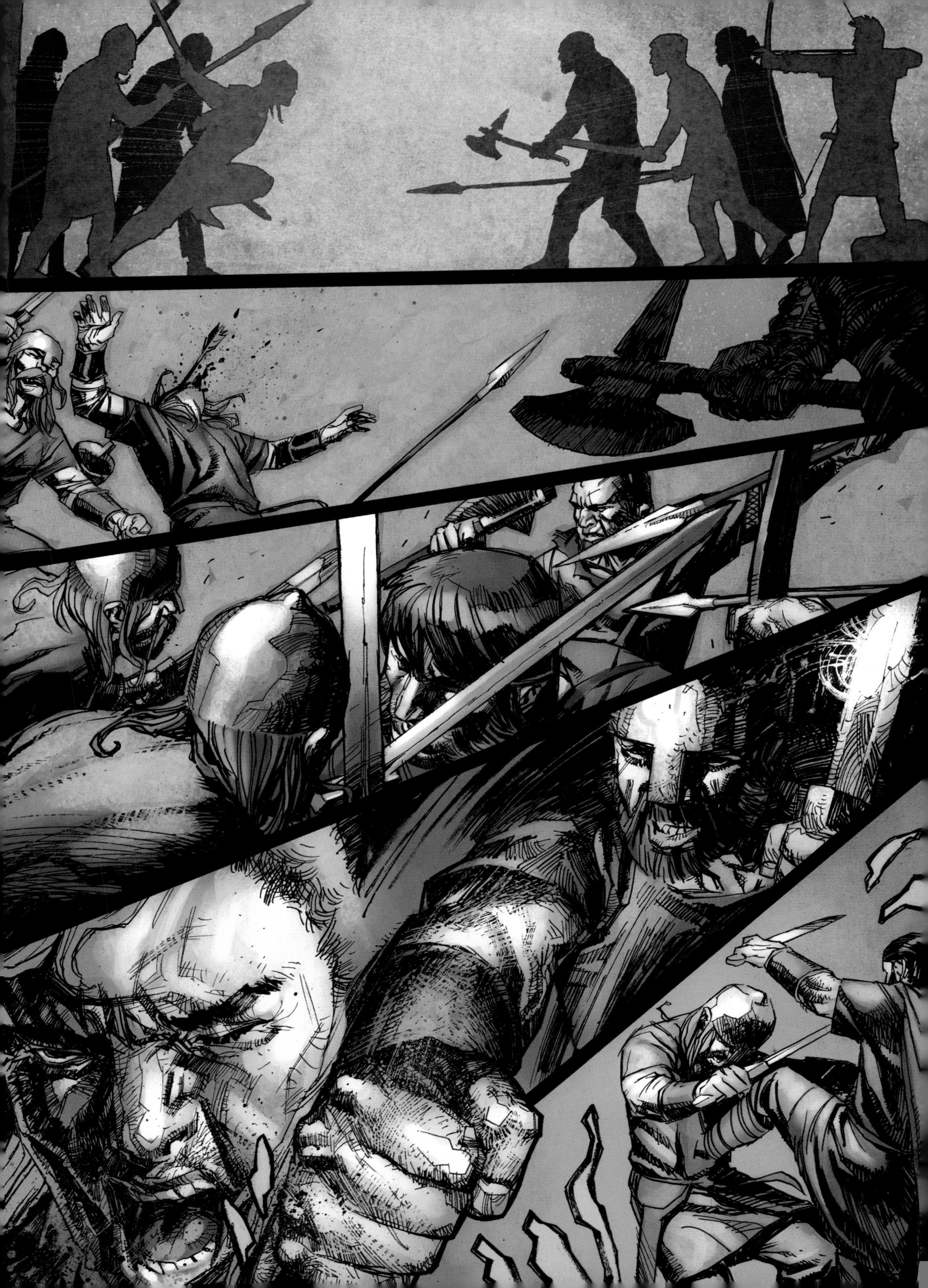

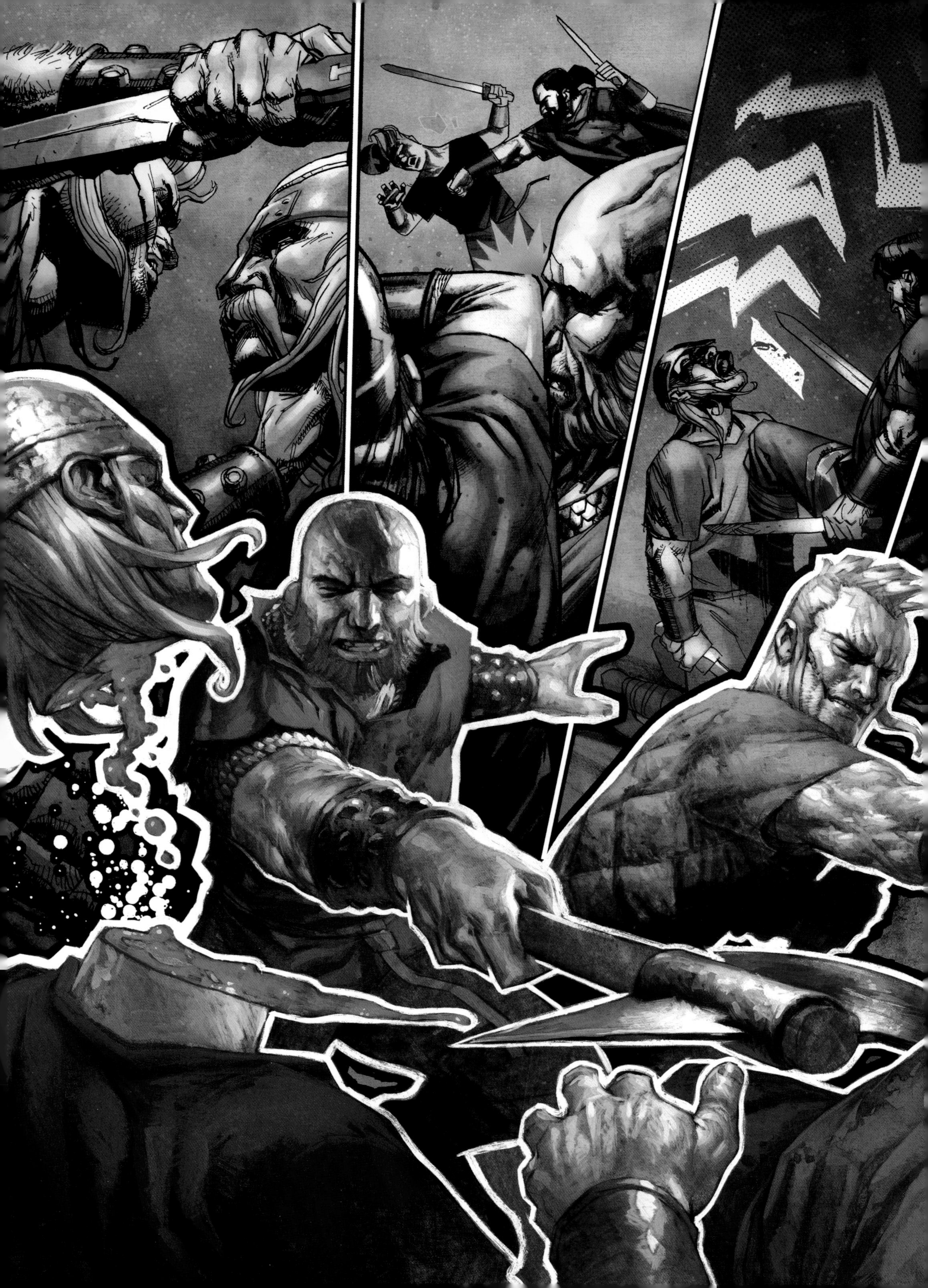

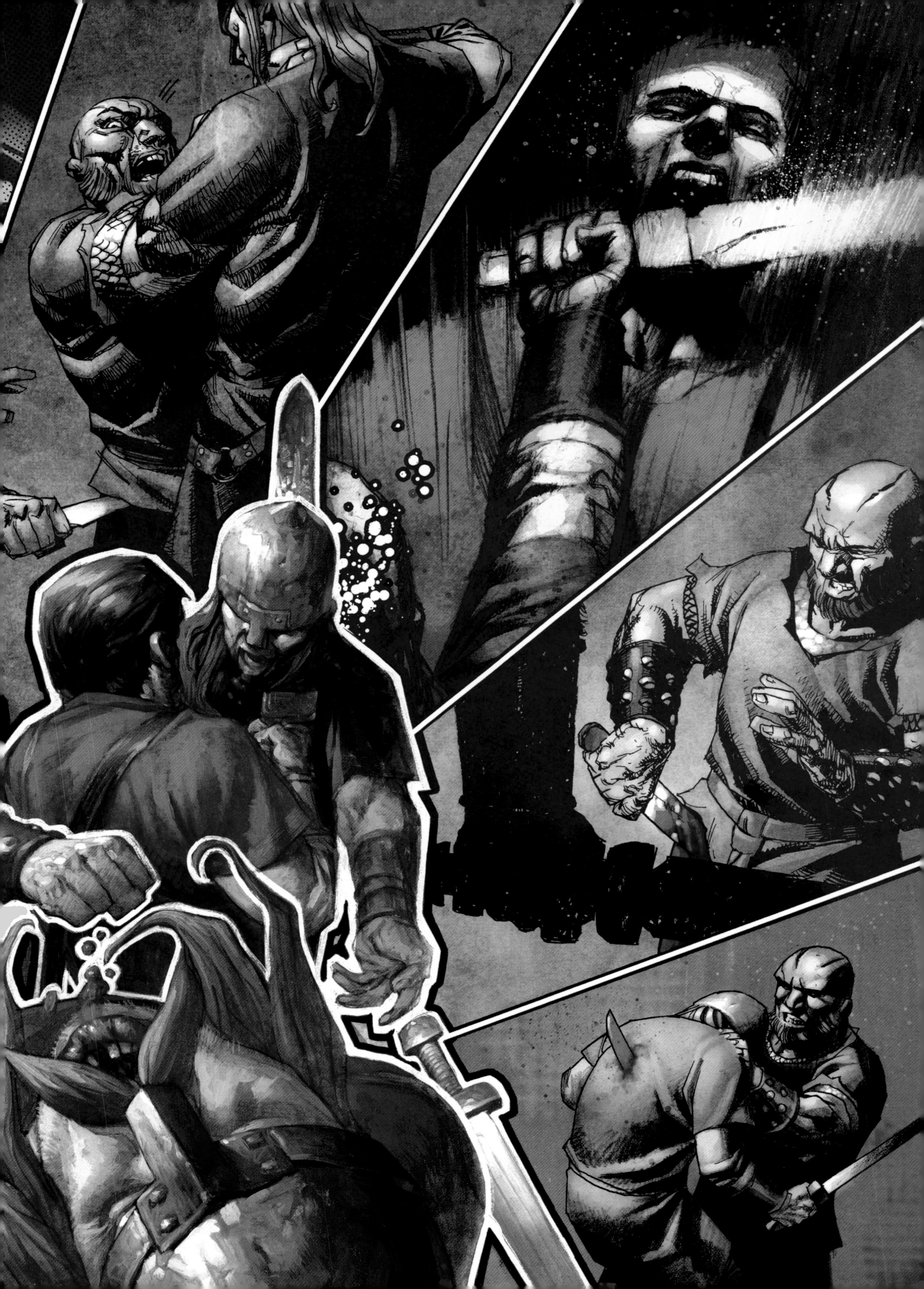

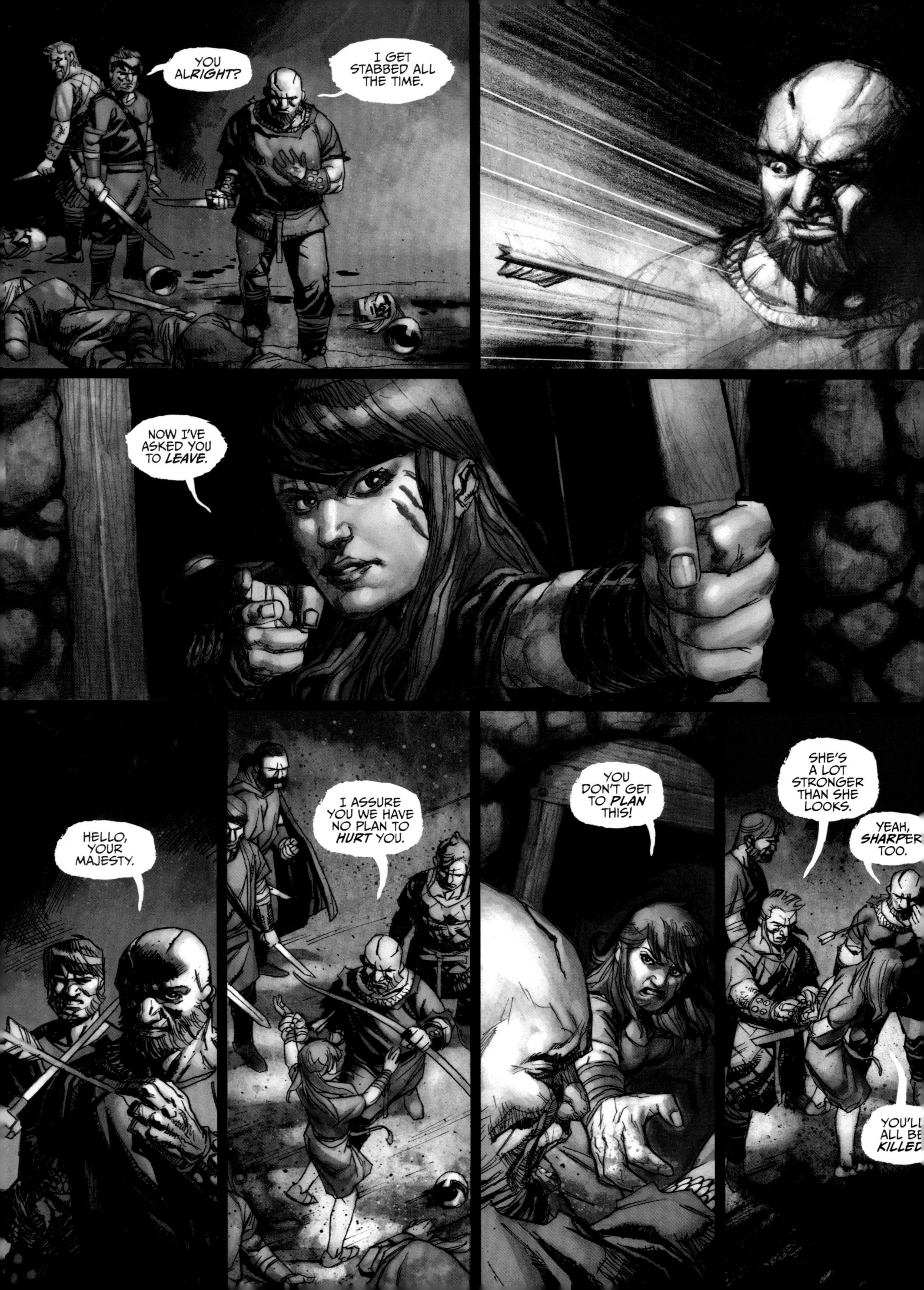
YOU ALRIGHT?
I GET STABBED ALL THE TIME.
NOW I'VE ASKED YOU TO LEAVE.
HELLO, YOUR MAJESTY.
I ASSURE YOU WE HAVE NO PLAN TO HURT YOU.
YOU DON'T GET TO PLAN THIS!
SHE'S A LOT STRONGER THAN SHE LOOKS.
YEAH, SHARPER TOO.
YOU'LL ALL BE KILLED

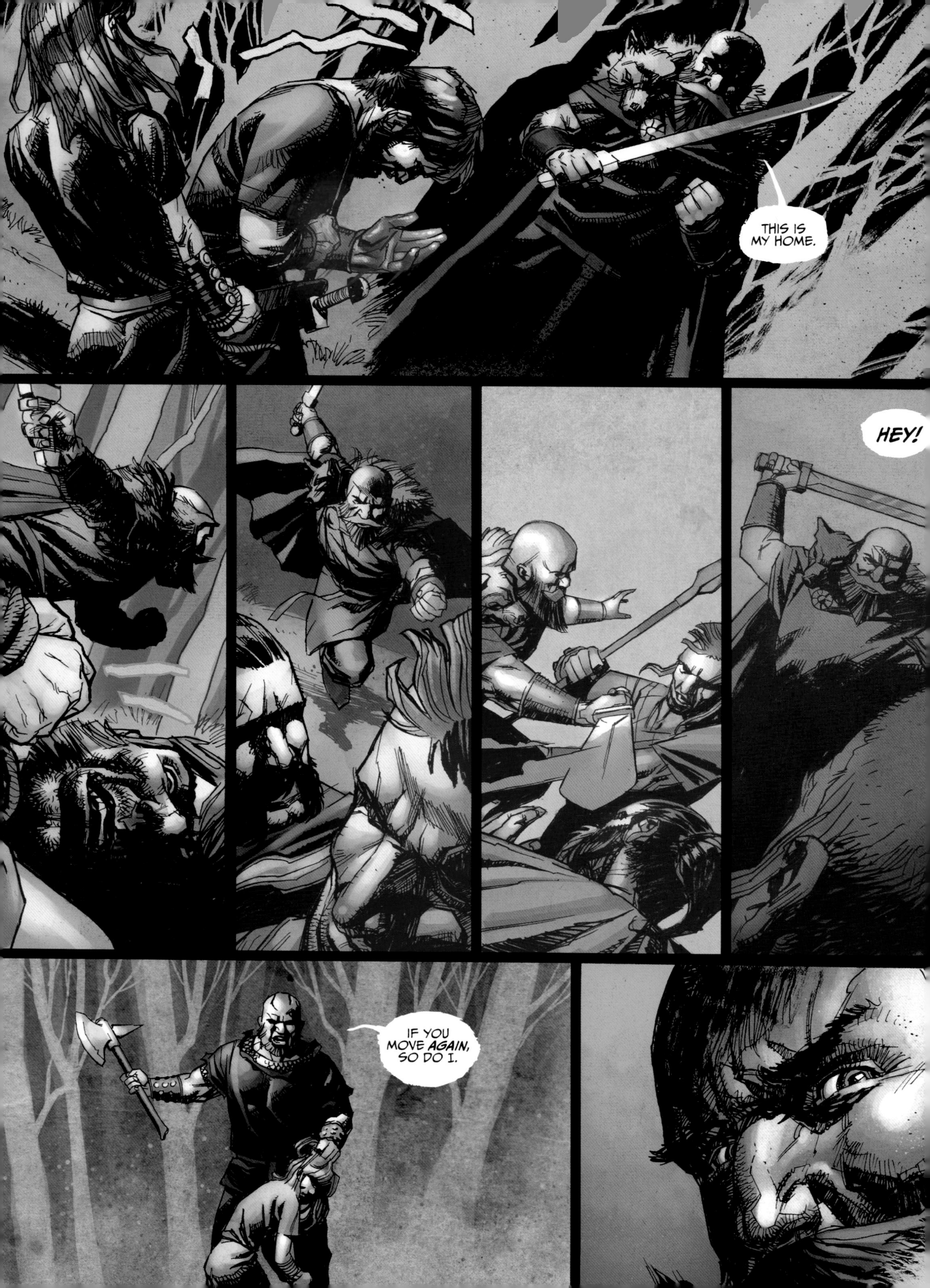
THIS IS
MY HOME.
HEY!
IF YOU
MOVE AGAIN,
SO DO I.

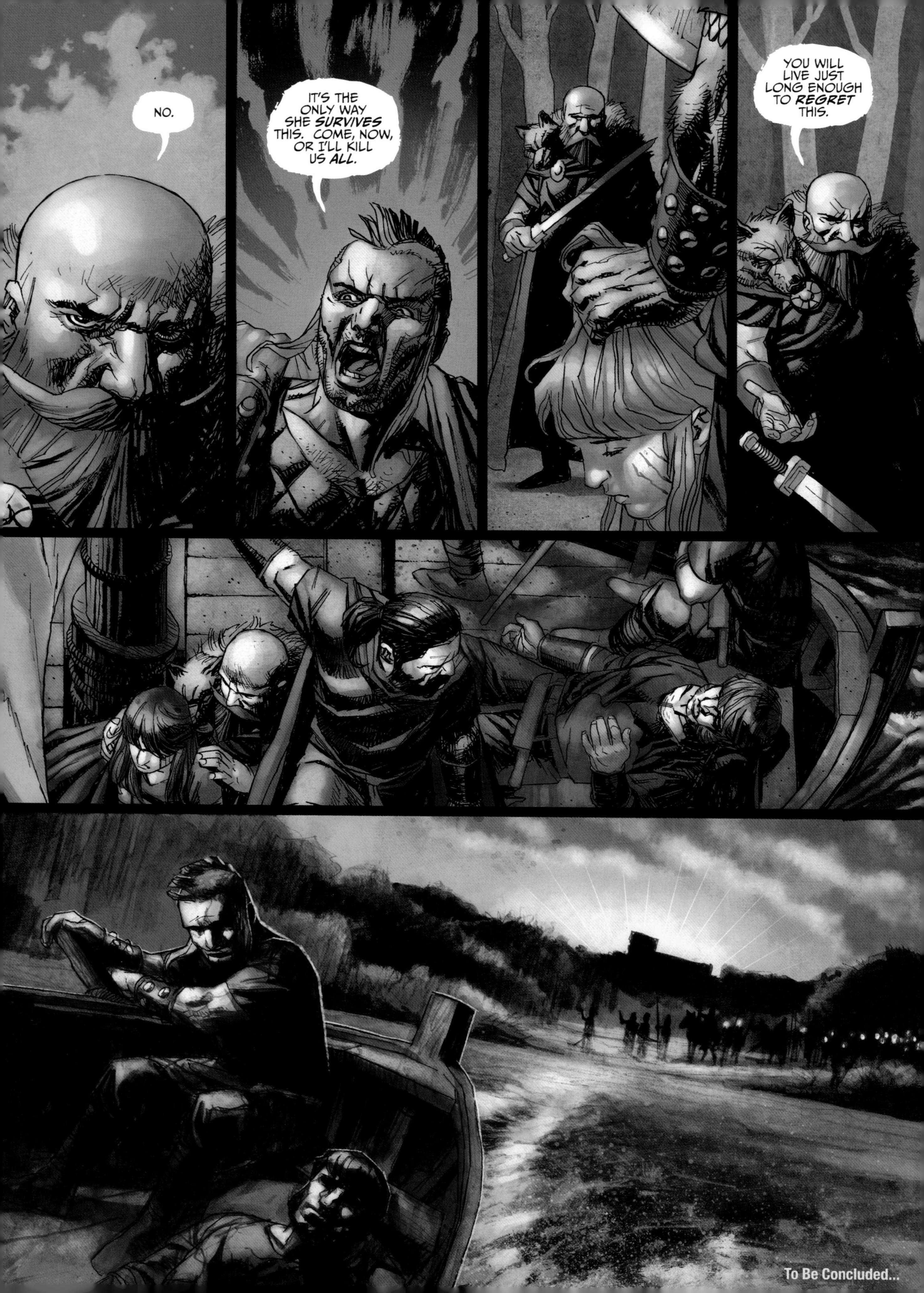
NO.
IT'S THE ONLY WAY SHE SURVIVES THIS. COME, NOW, OR I'LL KILL US ALL.
YOU WILL LIVE JUST LONG ENOUGH TO REGRET THIS.
To Be Concluded...

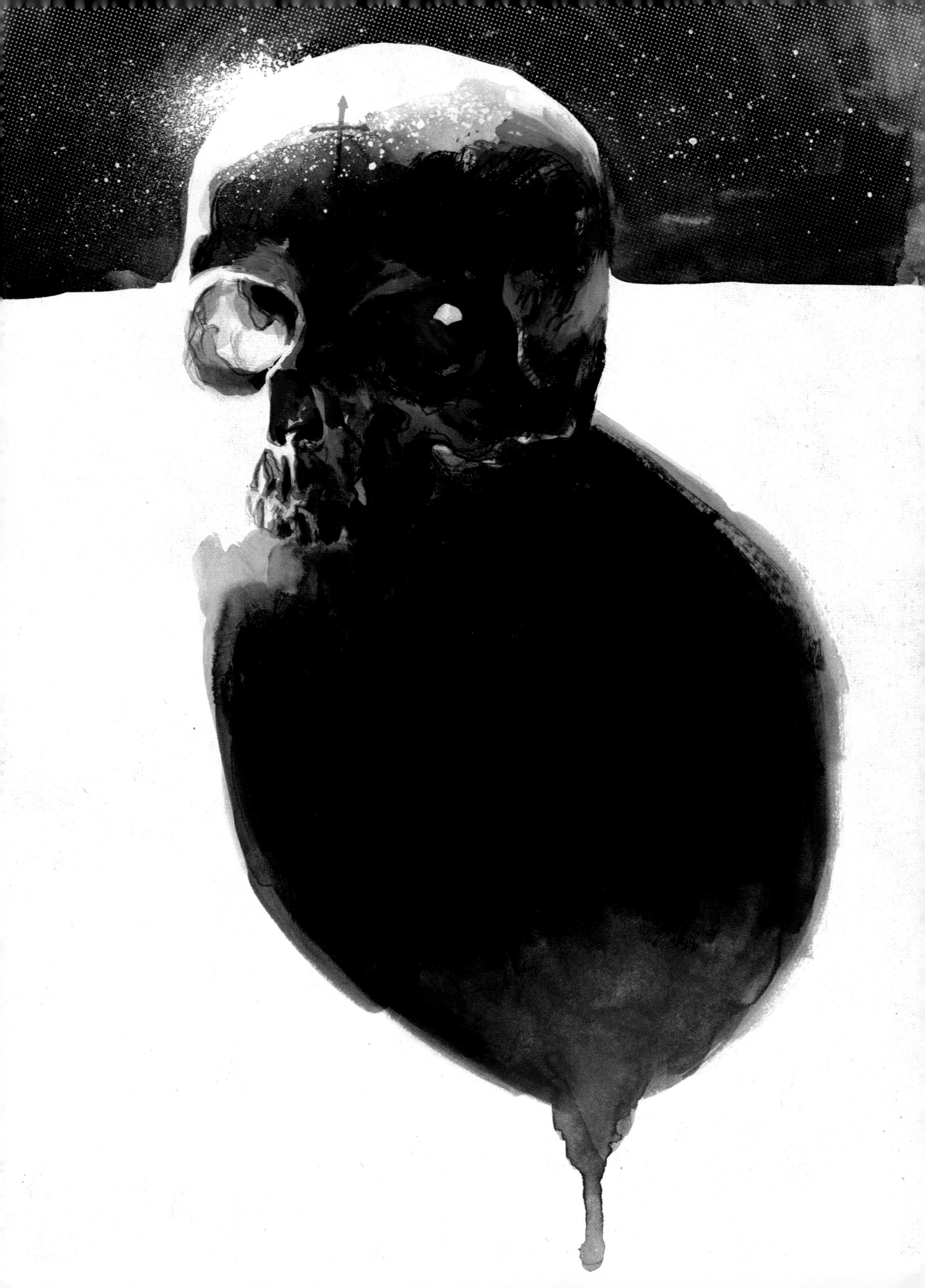

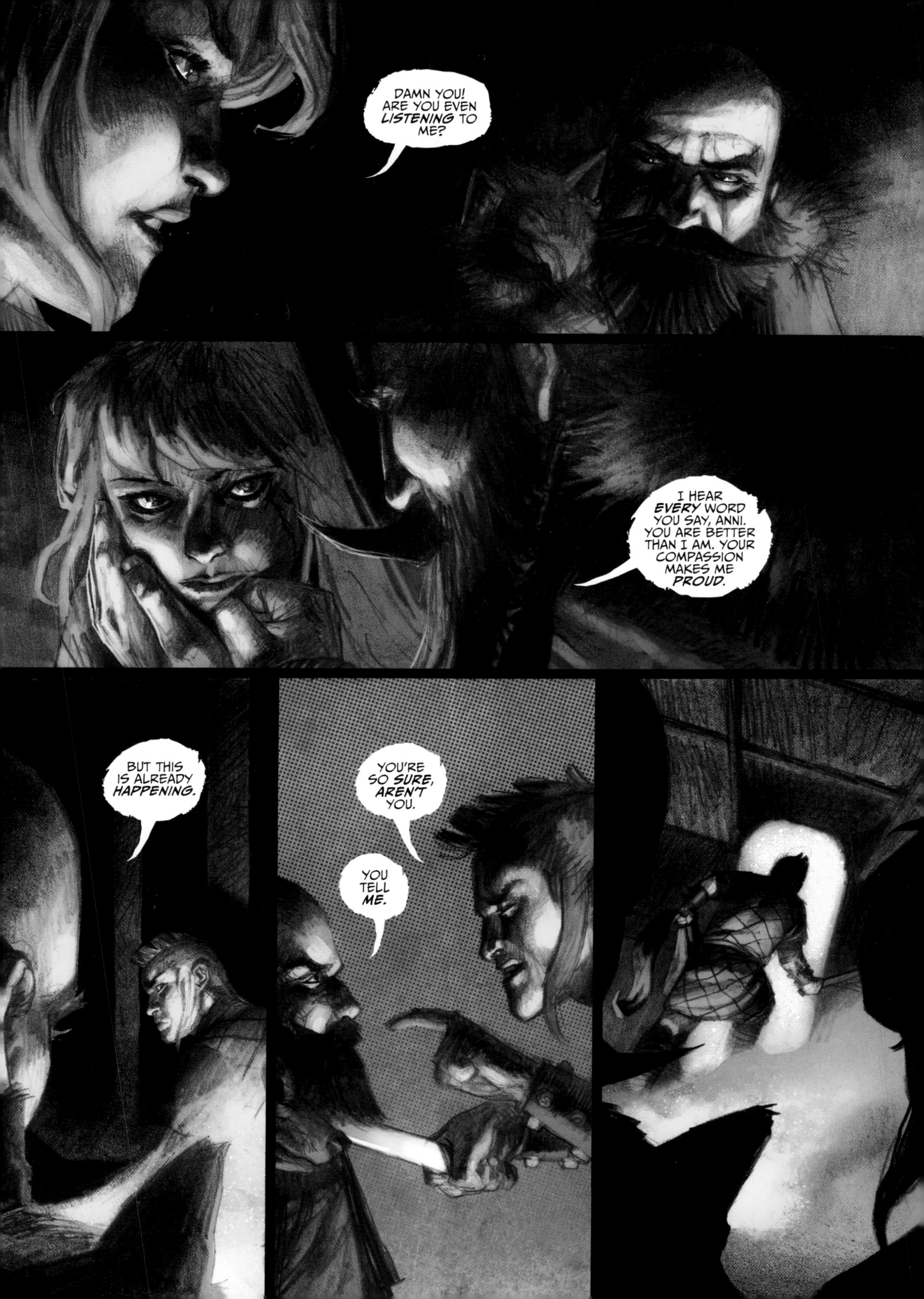
DAMN YOU! ARE YOU EVEN LISTENING TO ME?
I HEAR EVERY WORD YOU SAY, ANNI. YOU ARE BETTER THAN I AM. YOUR COMPASSION MAKES ME PROUD.
BUT THIS IS ALREADY HAPPENING.
YOU'RE SO SURE, AREN'T YOU.
YOU TELL ME.

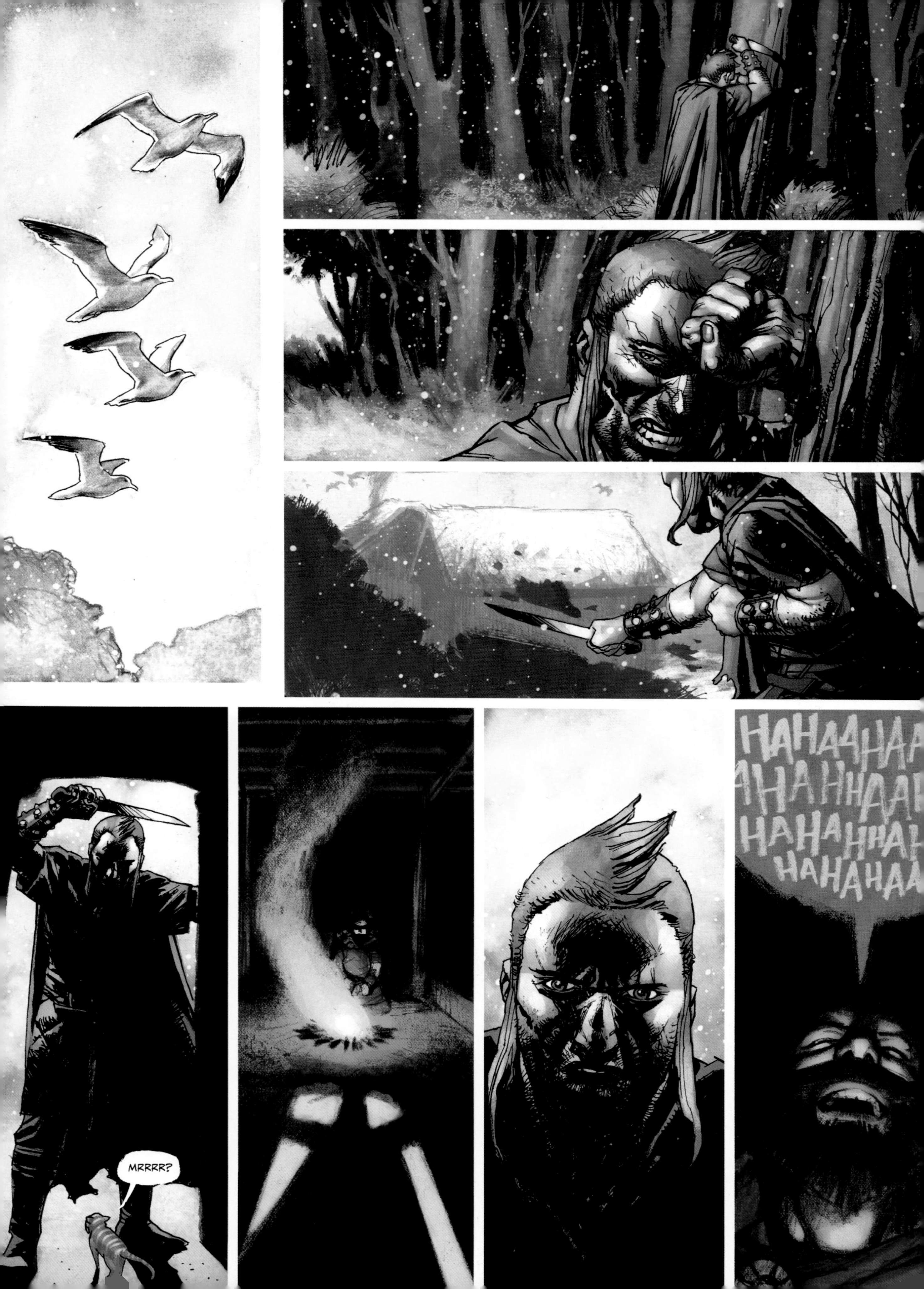
MRRRR?
HAHAHAHA
AHAHHAA
HAHAHHAH
HAHAHAA

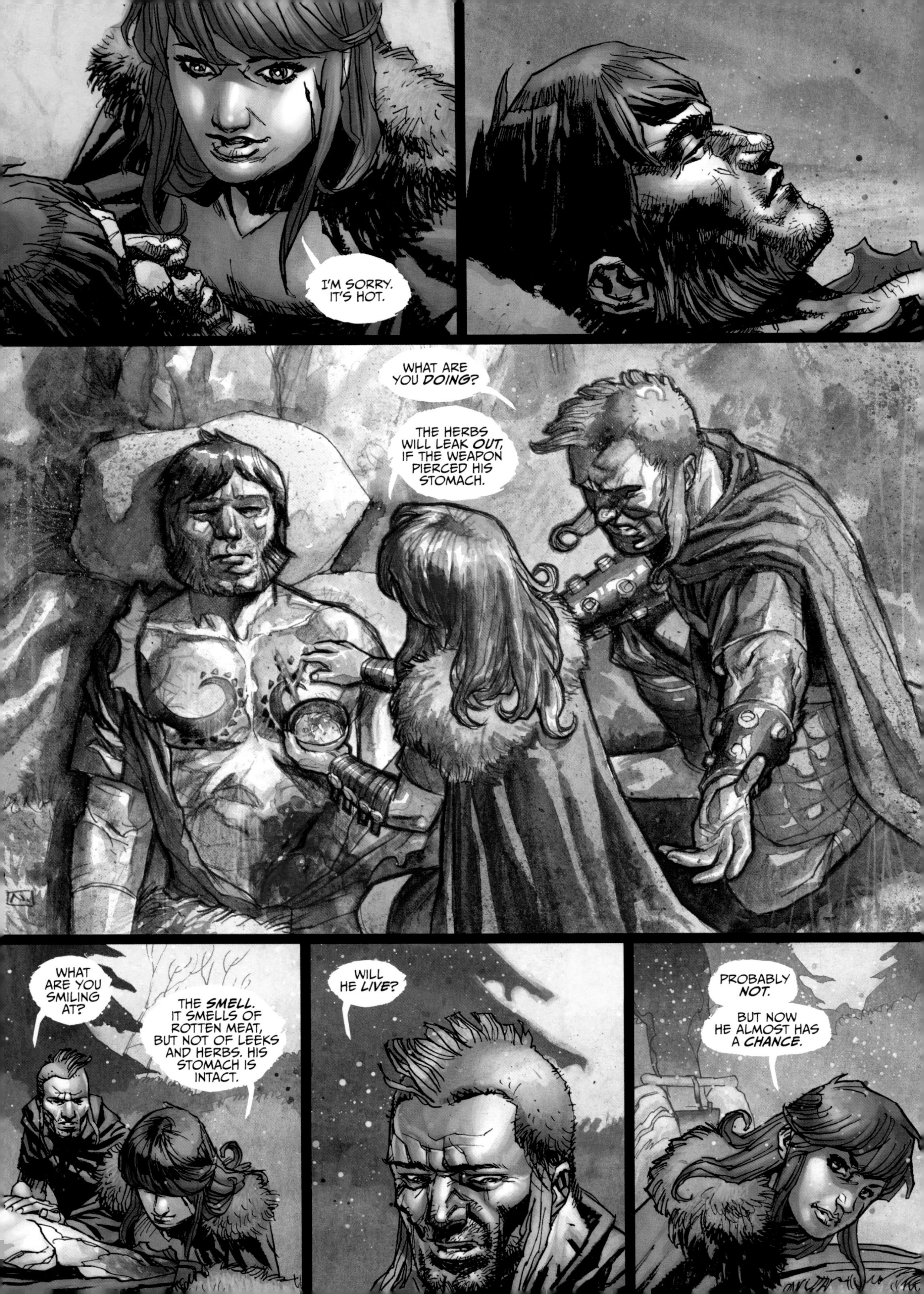
I'M SORRY. IT'S HOT.
WHAT ARE YOU *DOING*?
THE HERBS WILL LEAK *OUT*, IF THE WEAPON PIERCED HIS STOMACH.
WHAT ARE YOU SMILING AT?
THE *SMELL*. IT SMELLS OF ROTTEN MEAT, BUT NOT OF LEEKS AND HERBS. HIS STOMACH IS INTACT.
WILL HE *LIVE*?
PROBABLY *NOT*.
BUT NOW HE ALMOST HAS A *CHANCE*.

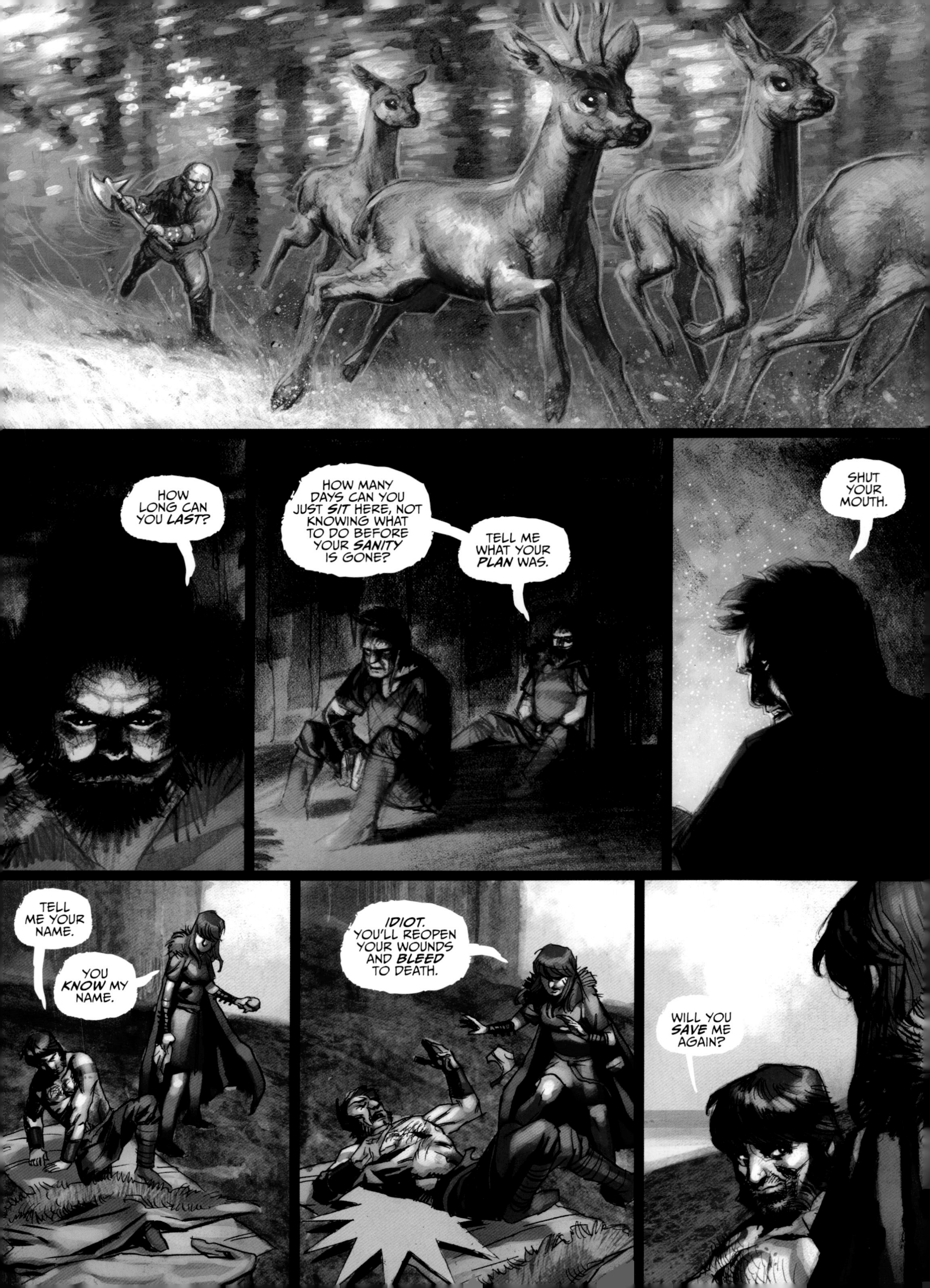
HOW LONG CAN YOU LAST?
HOW MANY DAYS CAN YOU JUST SIT HERE, NOT KNOWING WHAT TO DO BEFORE YOUR SANITY IS GONE?
TELL ME WHAT YOUR PLAN WAS.
SHUT YOUR MOUTH.
TELL ME YOUR NAME.
YOU KNOW MY NAME.
IDIOT. YOU'LL REOPEN YOUR WOUNDS AND BLEED TO DEATH.
WILL YOU SAVE ME AGAIN?

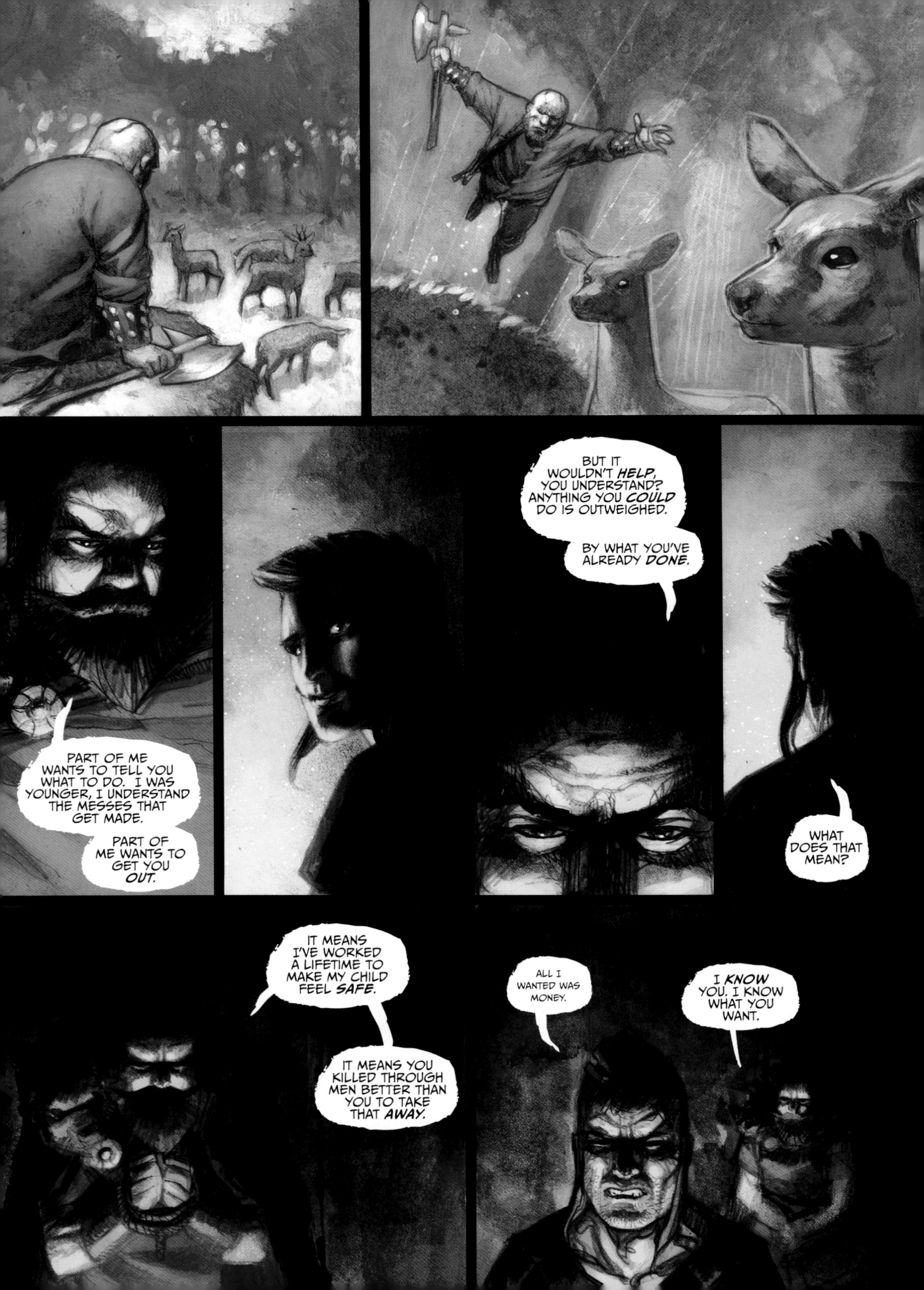
PART OF ME WANTS TO TELL YOU WHAT TO DO. I WAS YOUNGER, I UNDERSTAND THE MESSES THAT GET MADE.
PART OF ME WANTS TO GET YOU OUT.
BUT IT WOULDN'T HELP, YOU UNDERSTAND? ANYTHING YOU COULD DO IS OUTWEIGHED.
BY WHAT YOU'VE ALREADY DONE.
WHAT DOES THAT MEAN?
IT MEANS I'VE WORKED A LIFETIME TO MAKE MY CHILD FEEL SAFE.
IT MEANS YOU KILLED THROUGH MEN BETTER THAN YOU TO TAKE THAT AWAY.
ALL I WANTED WAS MONEY.
I KNOW YOU. I KNOW WHAT YOU WANT.

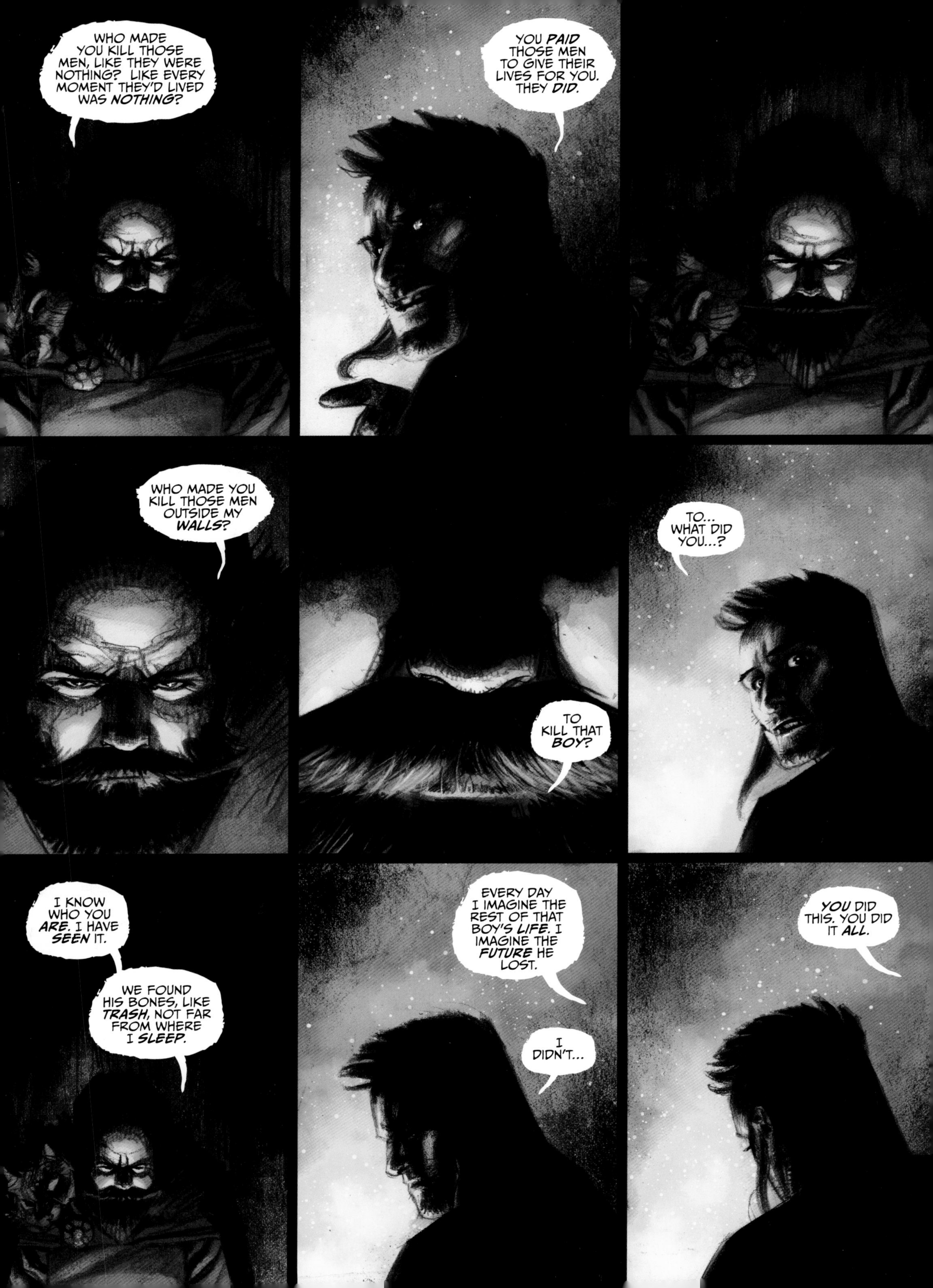

WHO MADE YOU KILL THOSE MEN, LIKE THEY WERE NOTHING? LIKE EVERY MOMENT THEY'D LIVED WAS NOTHING?
YOU PAID THOSE MEN TO GIVE THEIR LIVES FOR YOU. THEY DID.
WHO MADE YOU KILL THOSE MEN OUTSIDE MY WALLS?
TO KILL THAT BOY?
TO... WHAT DID YOU...?
I KNOW WHO YOU ARE. I HAVE SEEN IT.
WE FOUND HIS BONES, LIKE TRASH, NOT FAR FROM WHERE I SLEEP.
EVERY DAY I IMAGINE THE REST OF THAT BOY'S LIFE. I IMAGINE THE FUTURE HE LOST.
I DIDN'T...
YOU DID THIS. YOU DID IT ALL.

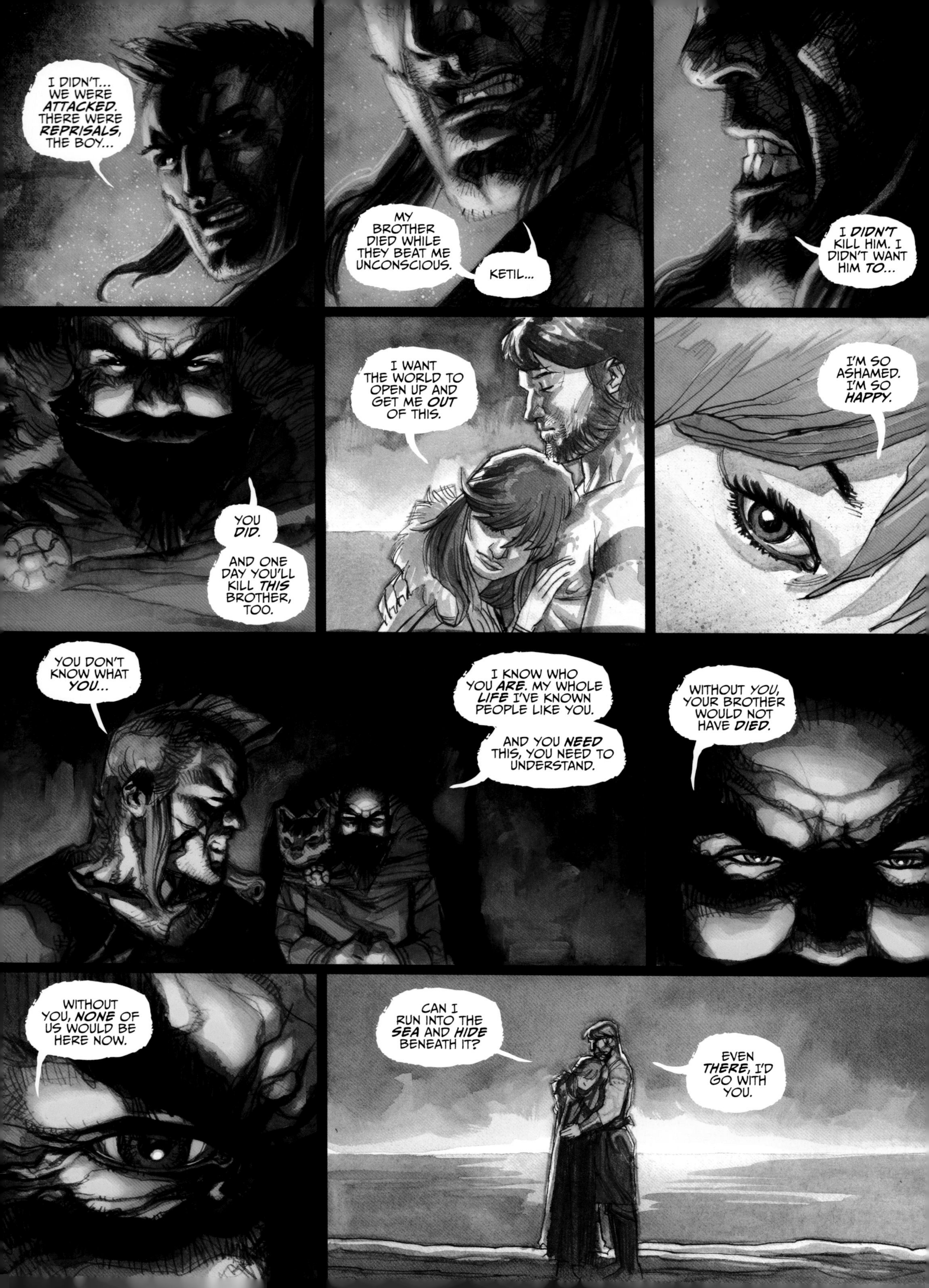
I DIDN'T... WE WERE ATTACKED. THERE WERE REPRISALS, THE BOY...
MY BROTHER DIED WHILE THEY BEAT ME UNCONSCIOUS.
KETIL...
I DIDN'T KILL HIM. I DIDN'T WANT HIM TO...
YOU DID.
AND ONE DAY YOU'LL KILL THIS BROTHER, TOO.
I WANT THE WORLD TO OPEN UP AND GET ME OUT OF THIS.
I'M SO ASHAMED. I'M SO HAPPY.
YOU DON'T KNOW WHAT YOU...
I KNOW WHO YOU ARE. MY WHOLE LIFE I'VE KNOWN PEOPLE LIKE YOU.
AND YOU NEED THIS, YOU NEED TO UNDERSTAND.
WITHOUT YOU, YOUR BROTHER WOULD NOT HAVE DIED.
WITHOUT YOU, NONE OF US WOULD BE HERE NOW.
CAN I RUN INTO THE SEA AND HIDE BENEATH IT?
EVEN THERE, I'D GO WITH YOU.

End Season One.

ORIGINAL SERIES COVERS

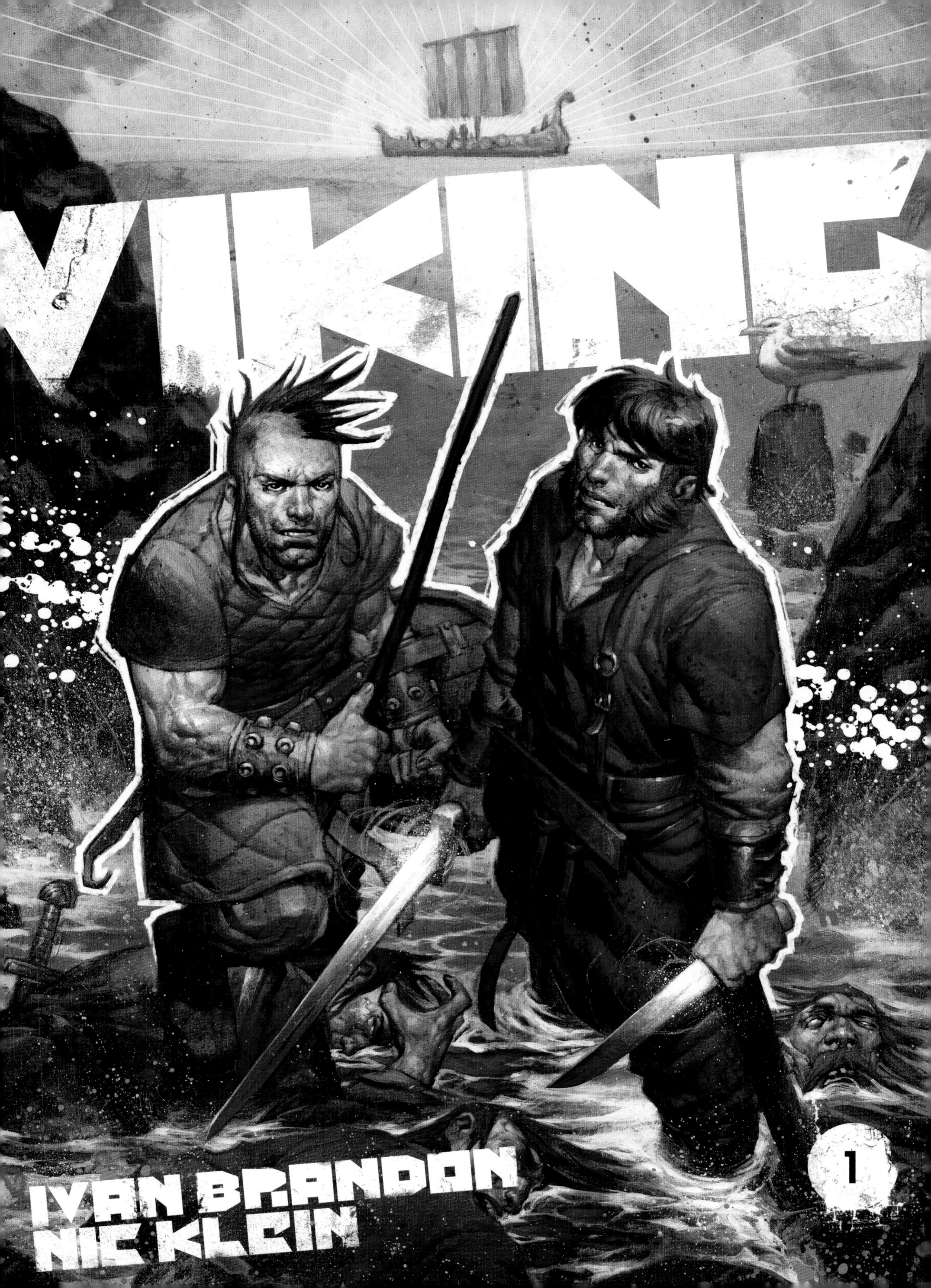

VIKING
IVAN BRANDON
NIC KLEIN
1

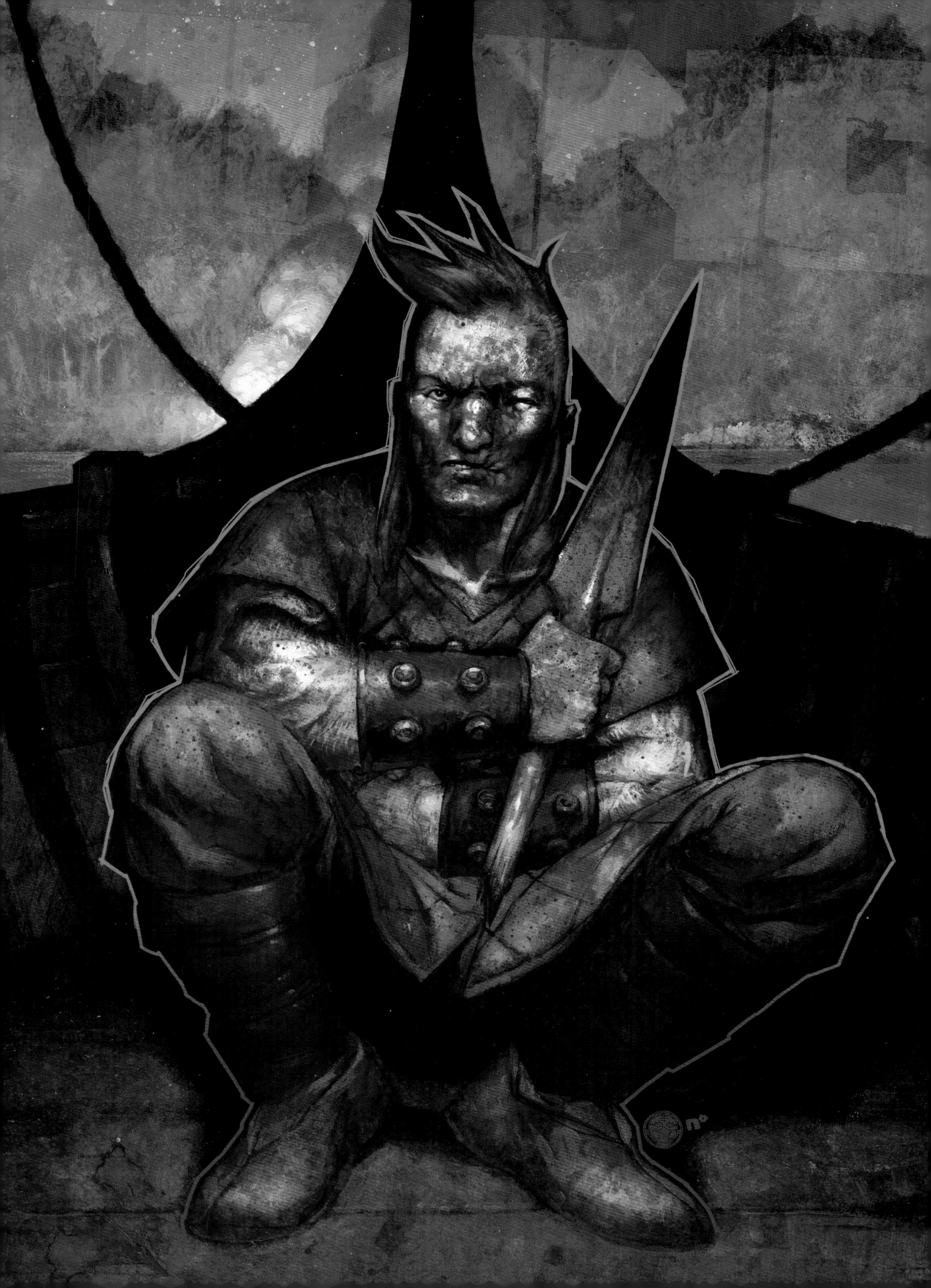

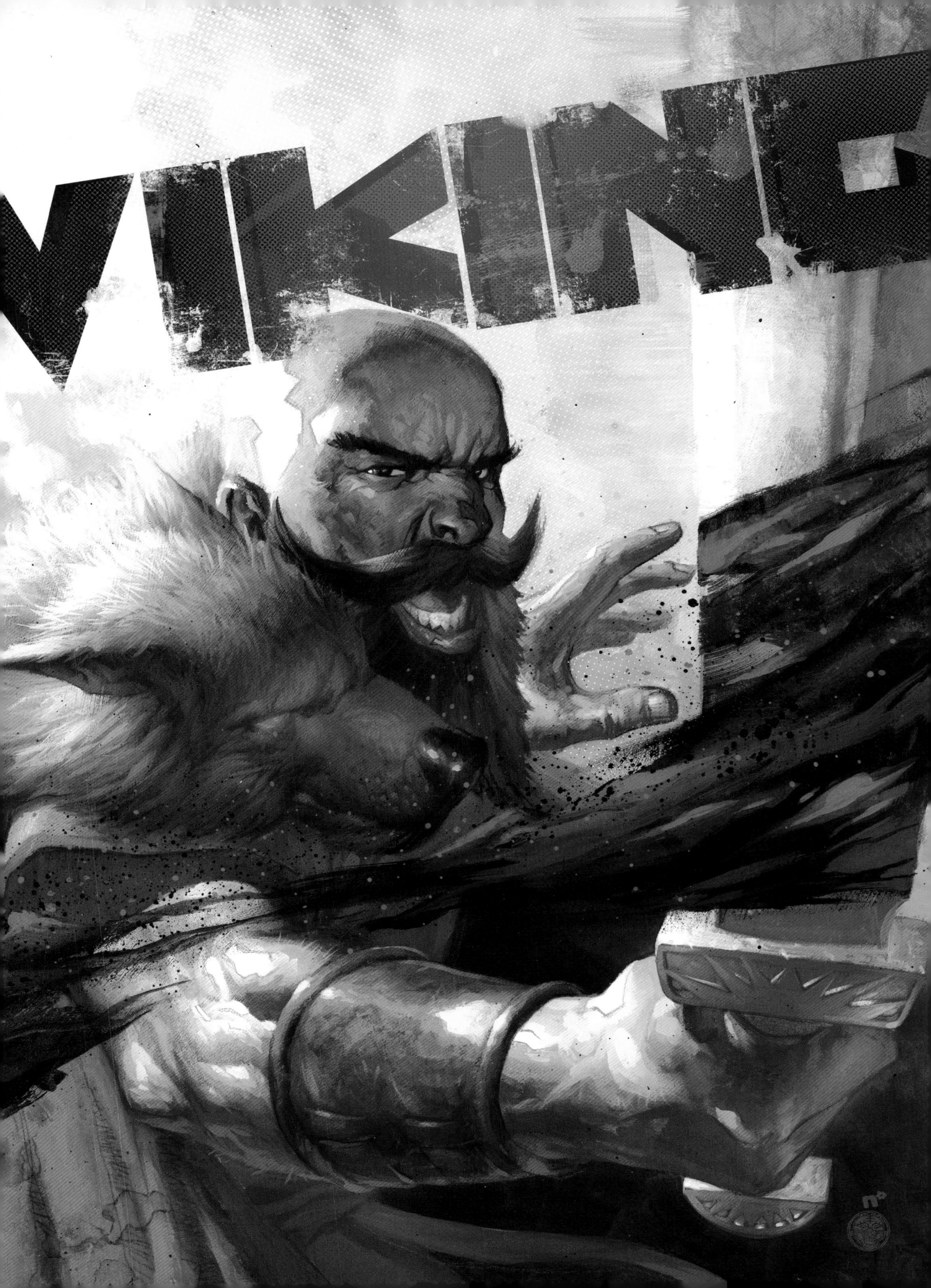
VIKING

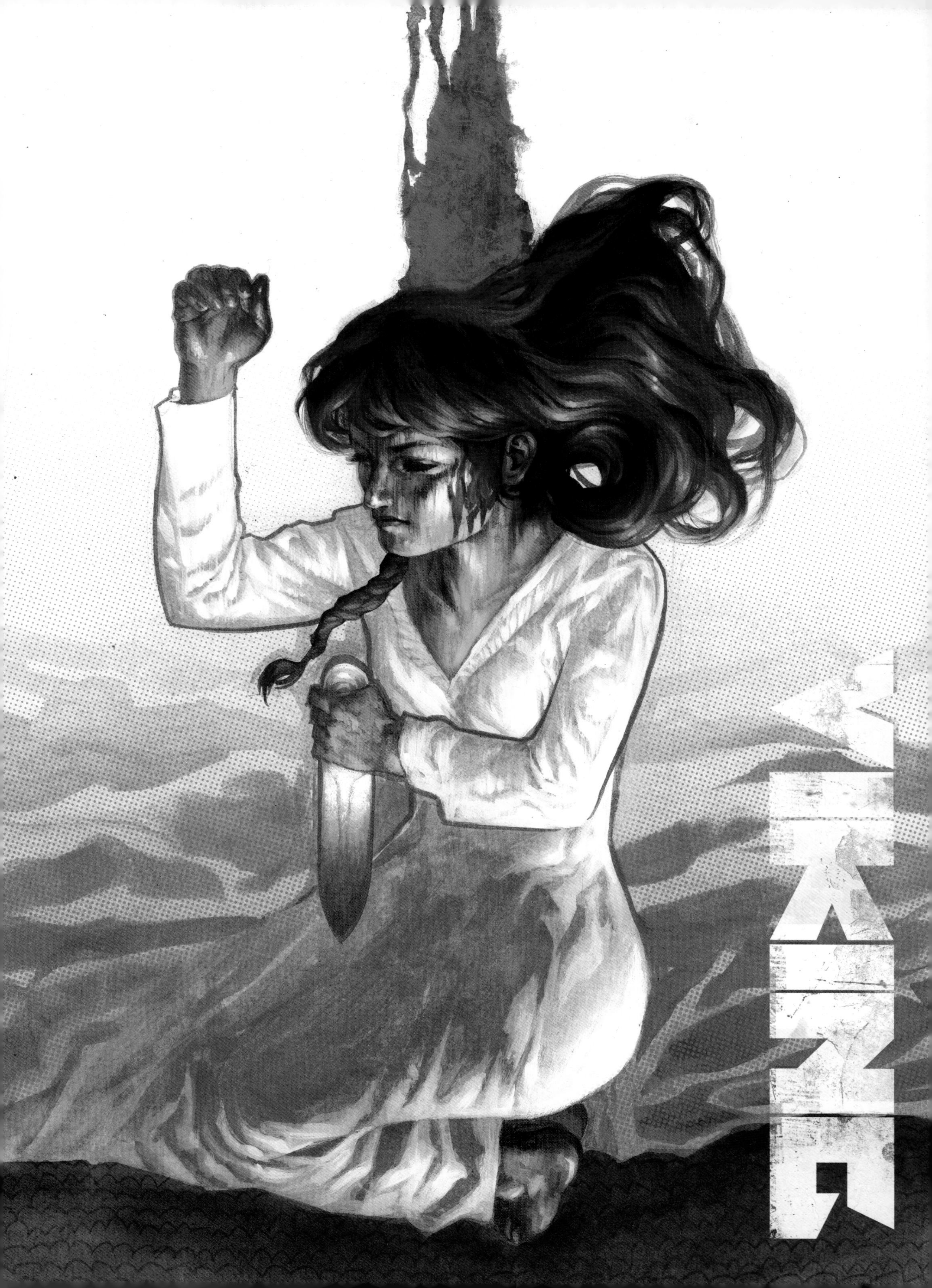
VIKING

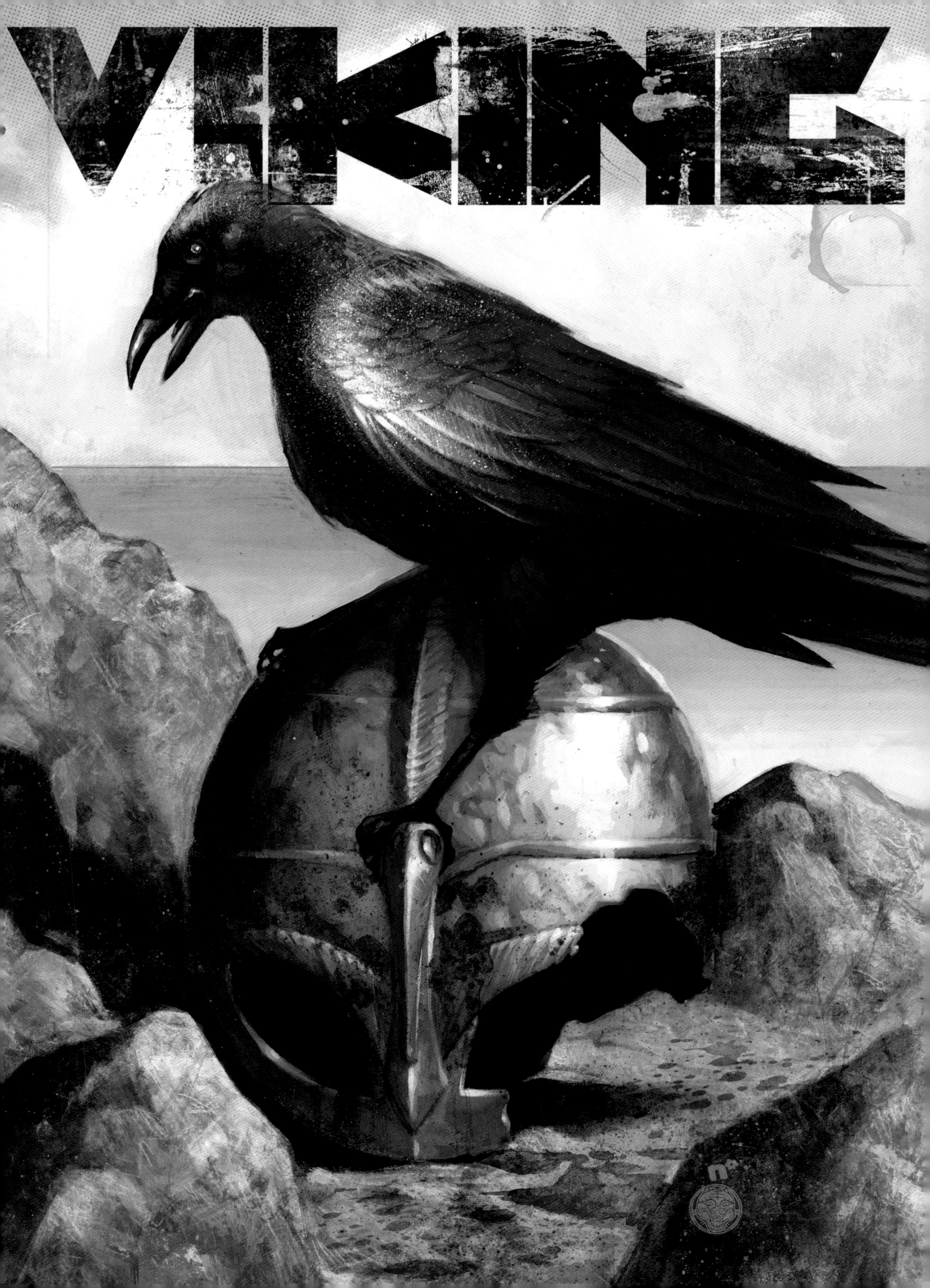
VIKING

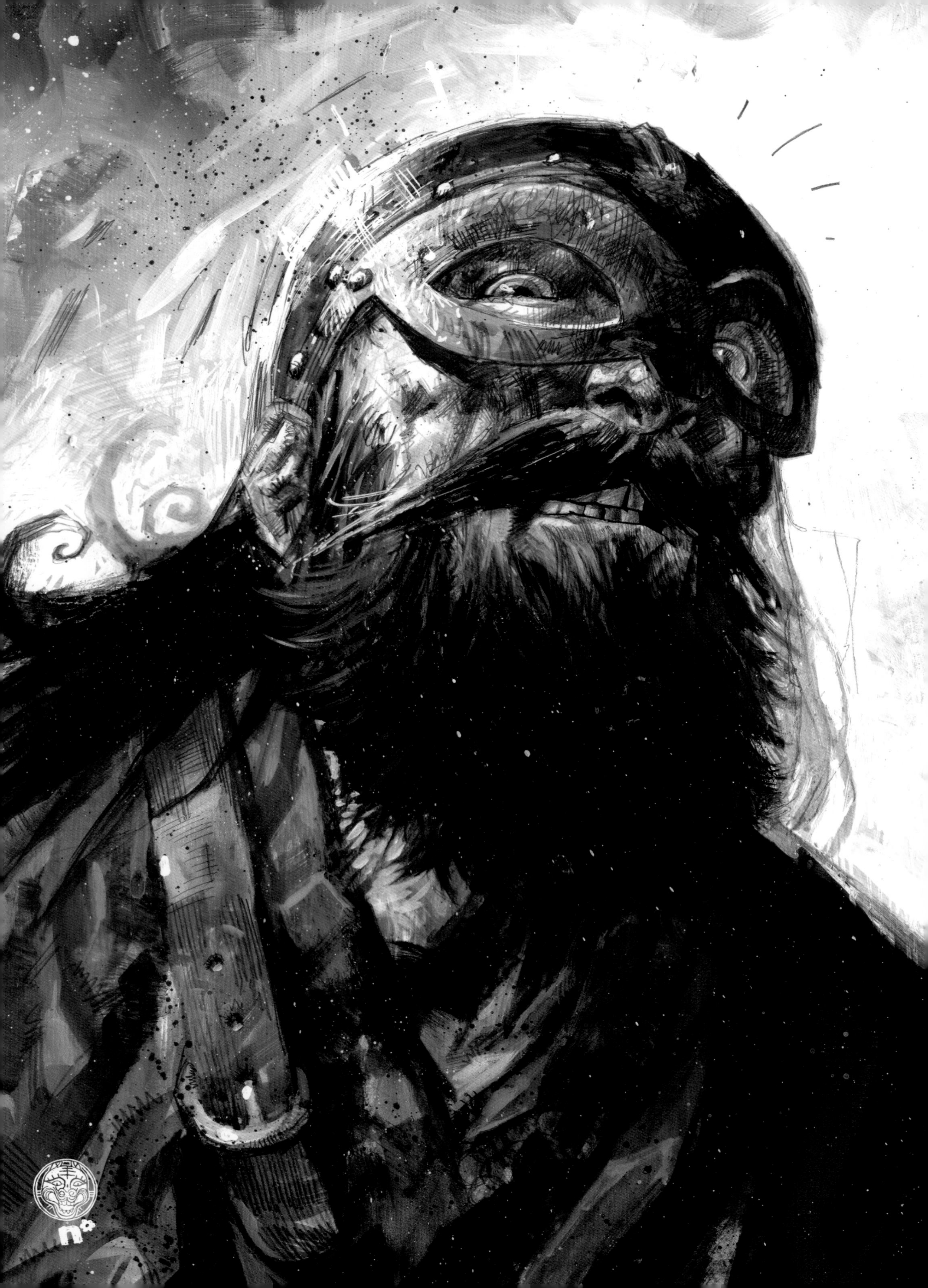

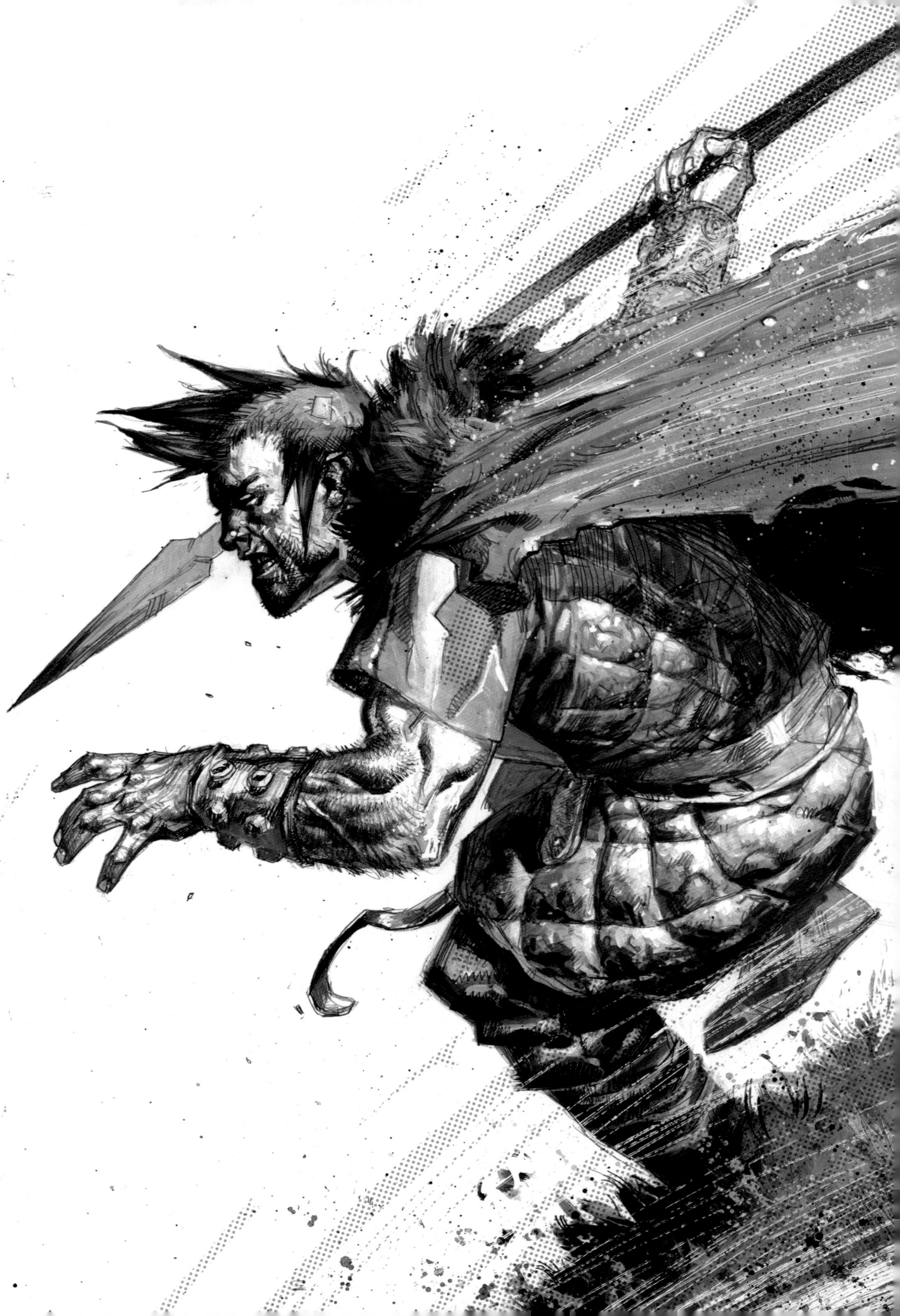

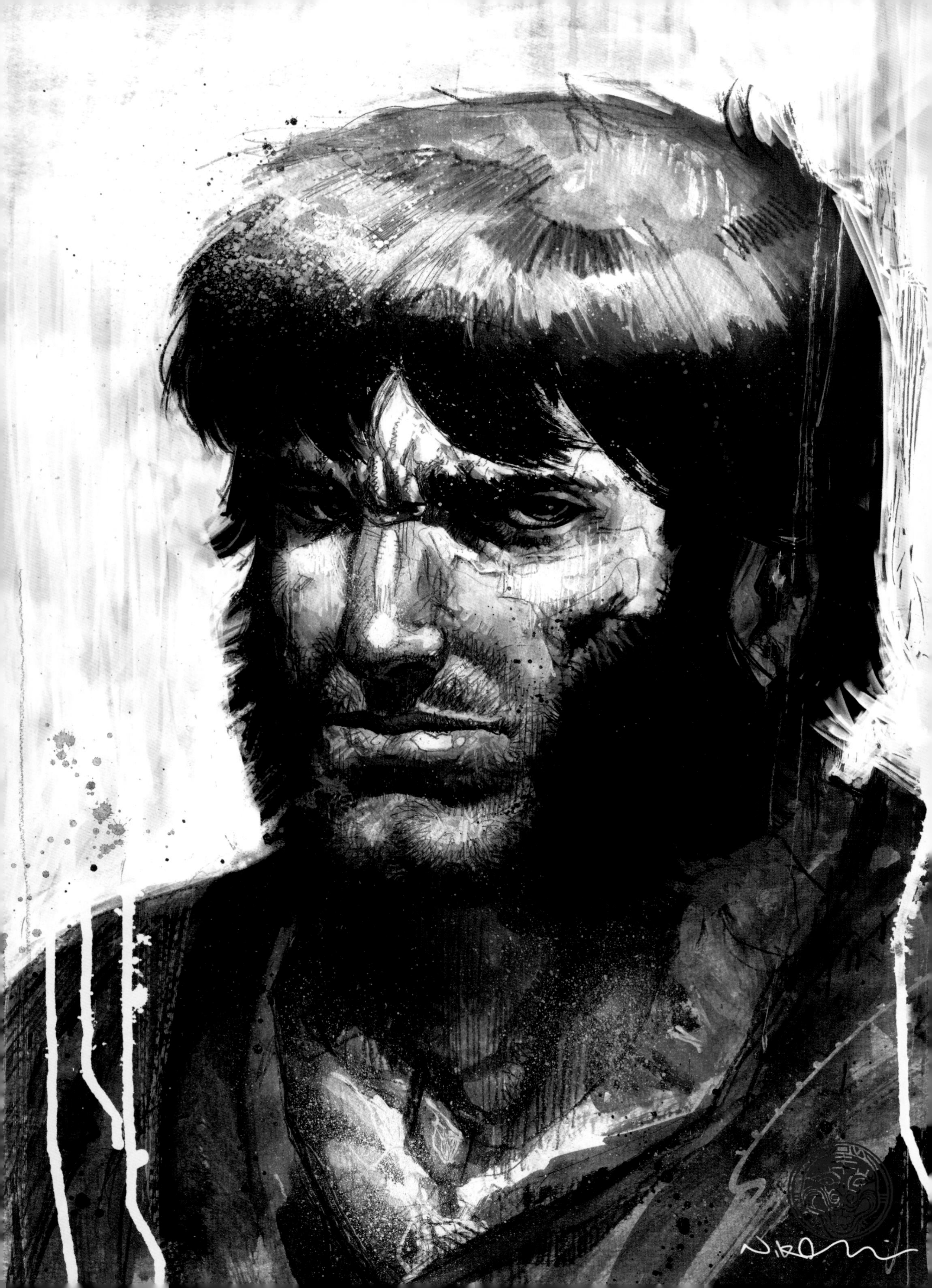

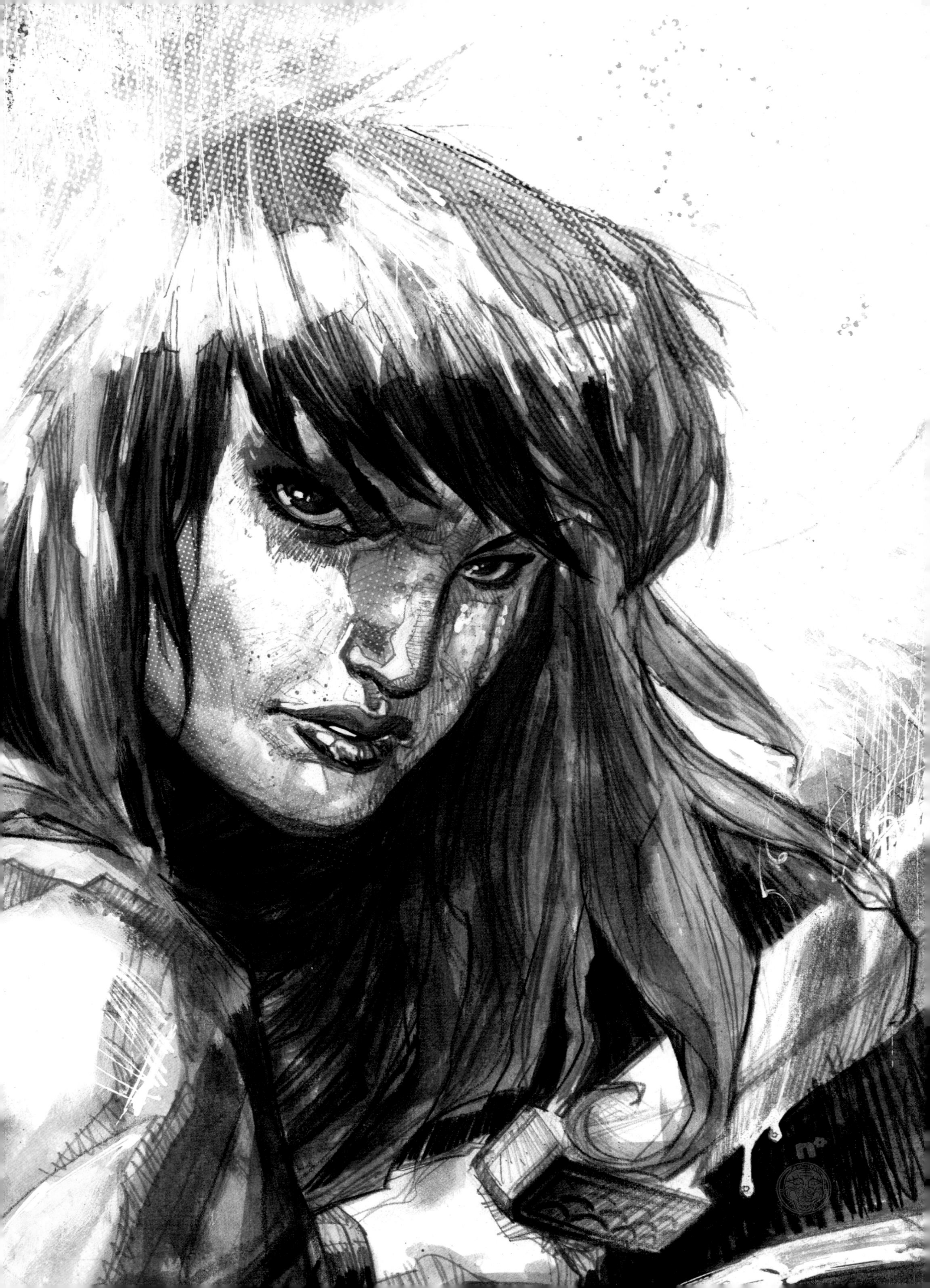

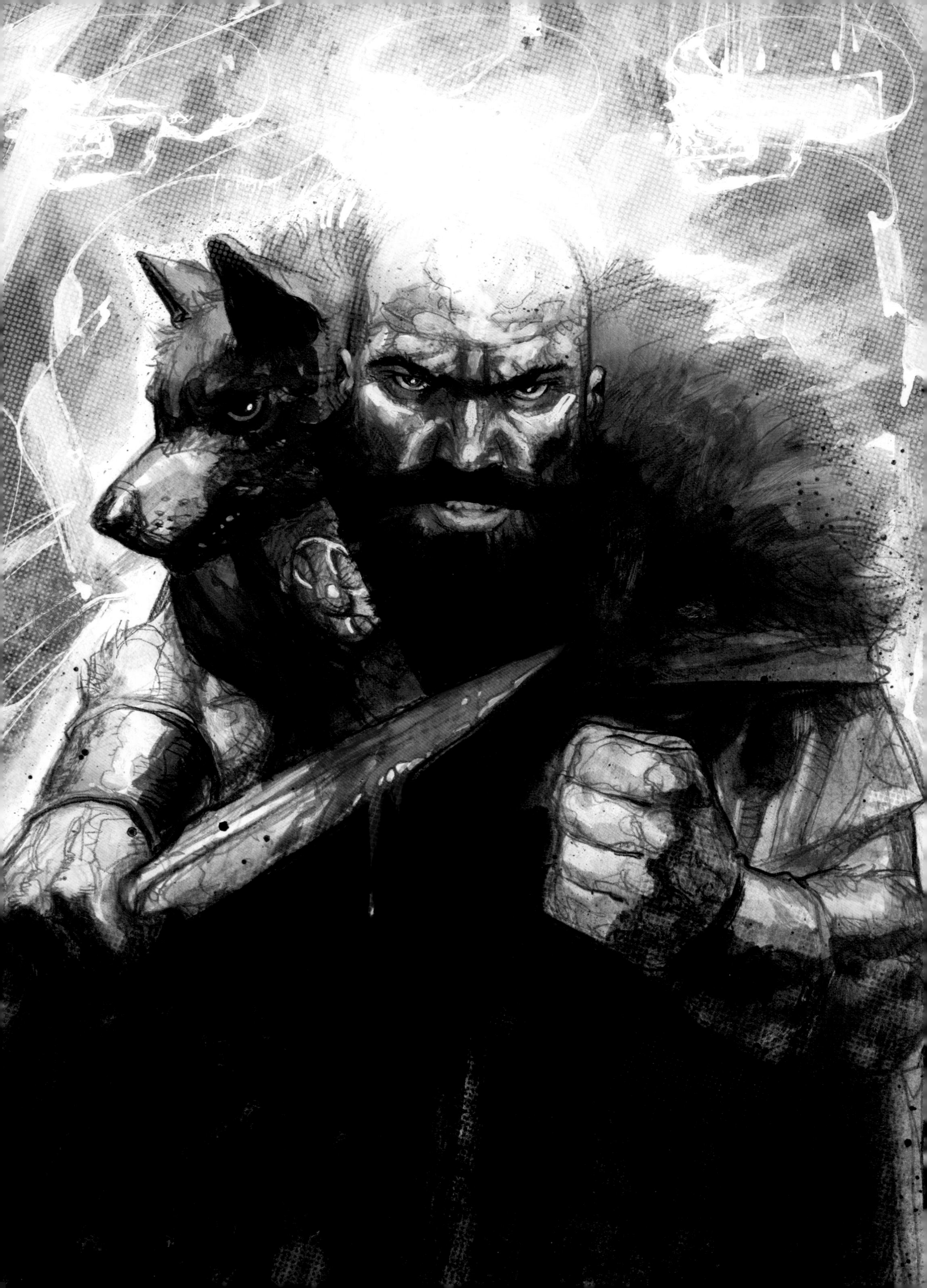

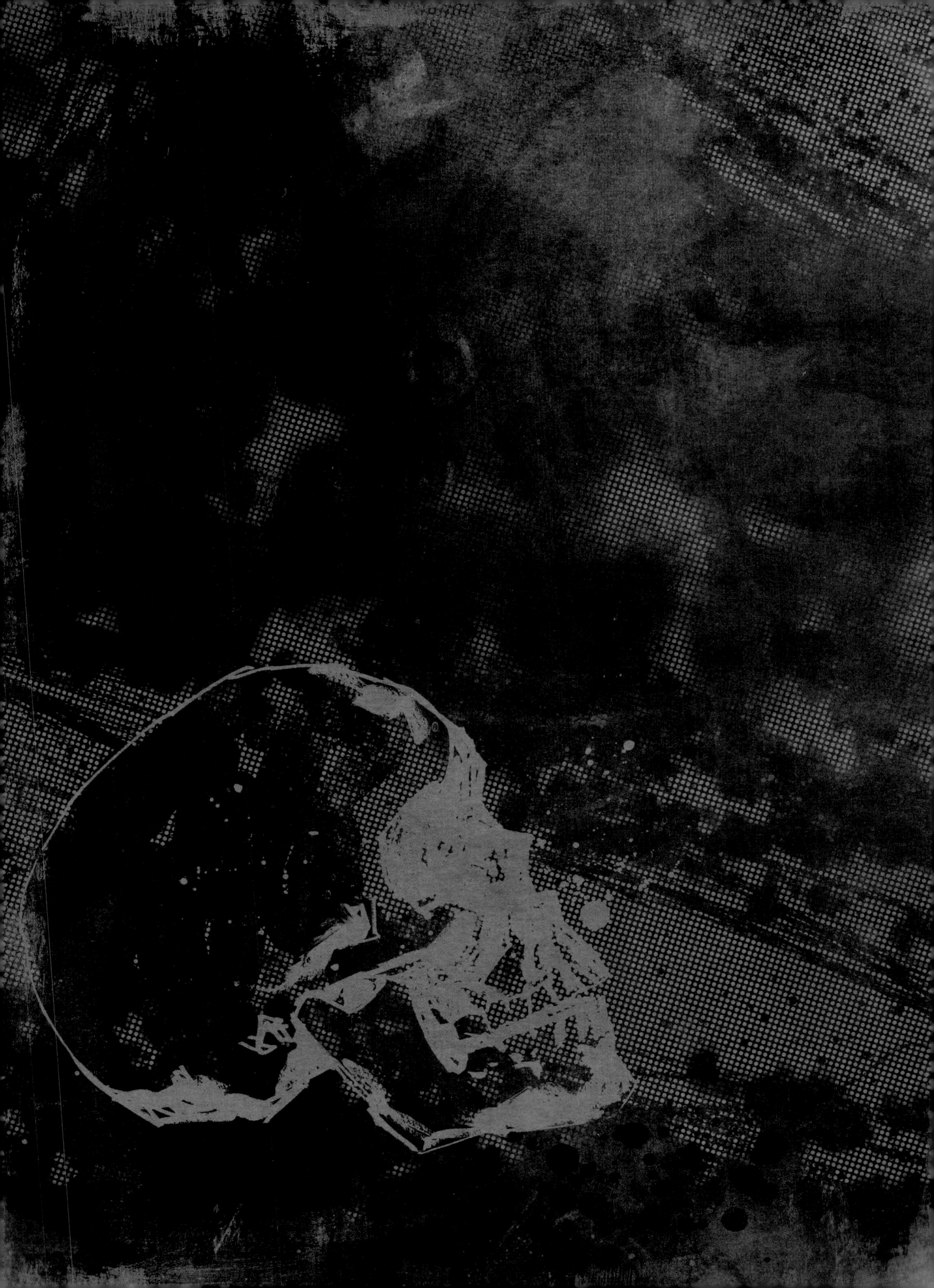

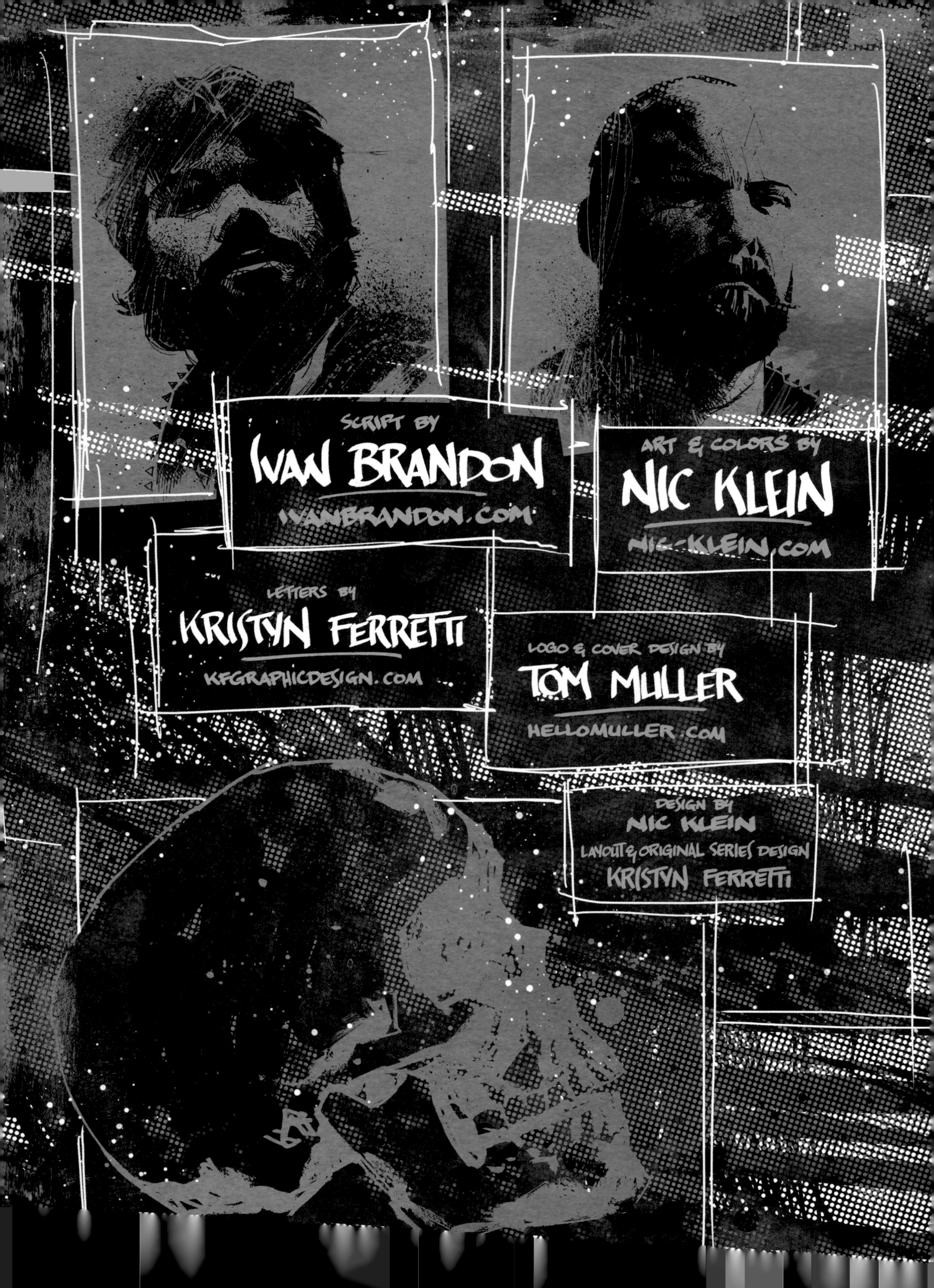

SCRIPT BY
IVAN BRANDON
IVANBRANDON.COM
ART & COLORS BY
NIC KLEIN
NIC-KLEIN.COM
LETTERS BY
KRISTYN FERRETTI
KFGRAPHICDESIGN.COM
LOGO & COVER DESIGN BY
TOM MULLER
HELLOMULLER.COM
DESIGN BY
NIC KLEIN
LAYOUT & ORIGINAL SERIES DESIGN
KRISTYN FERRETTI

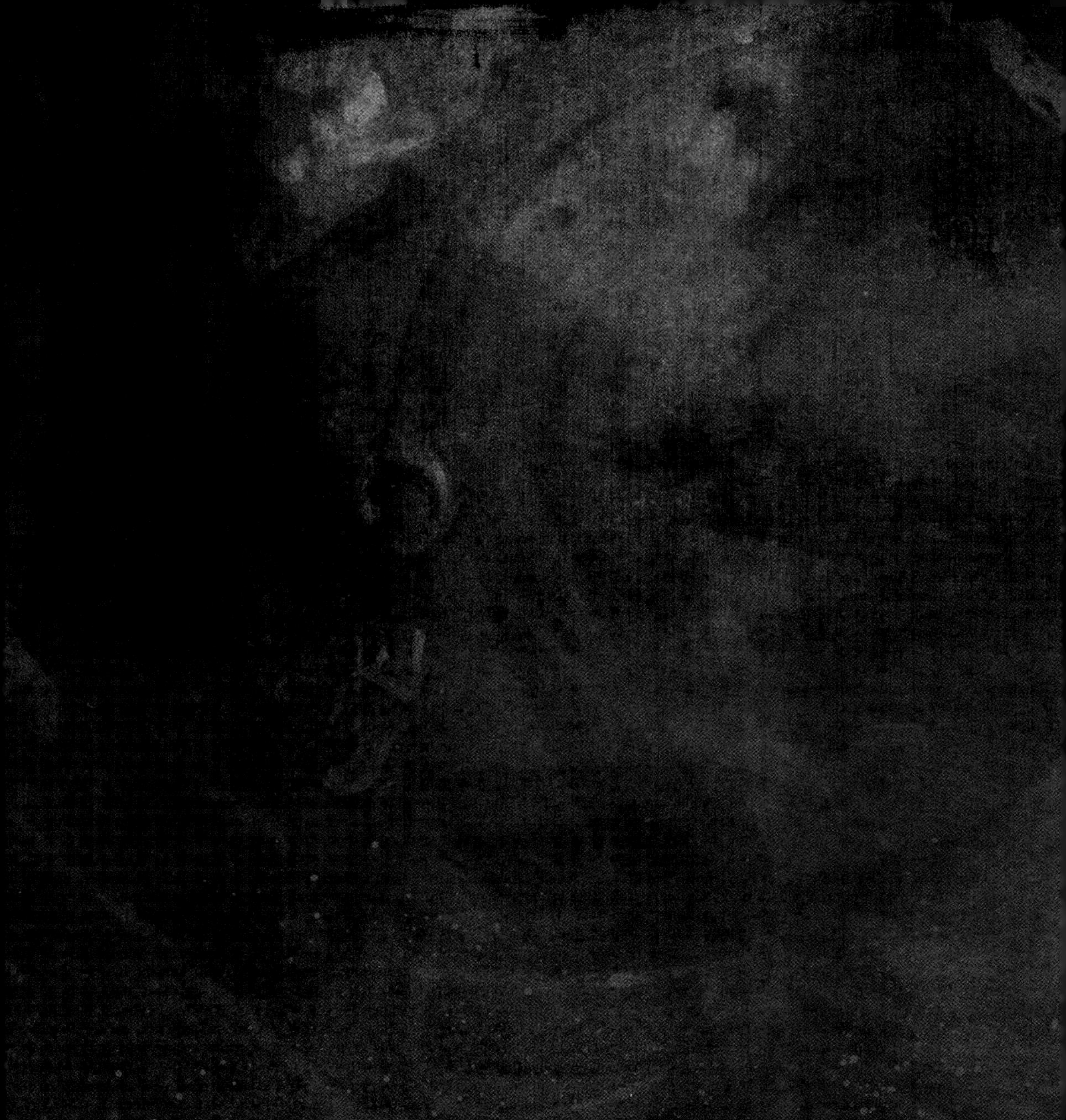

ISBN 978-1-60706-169-4

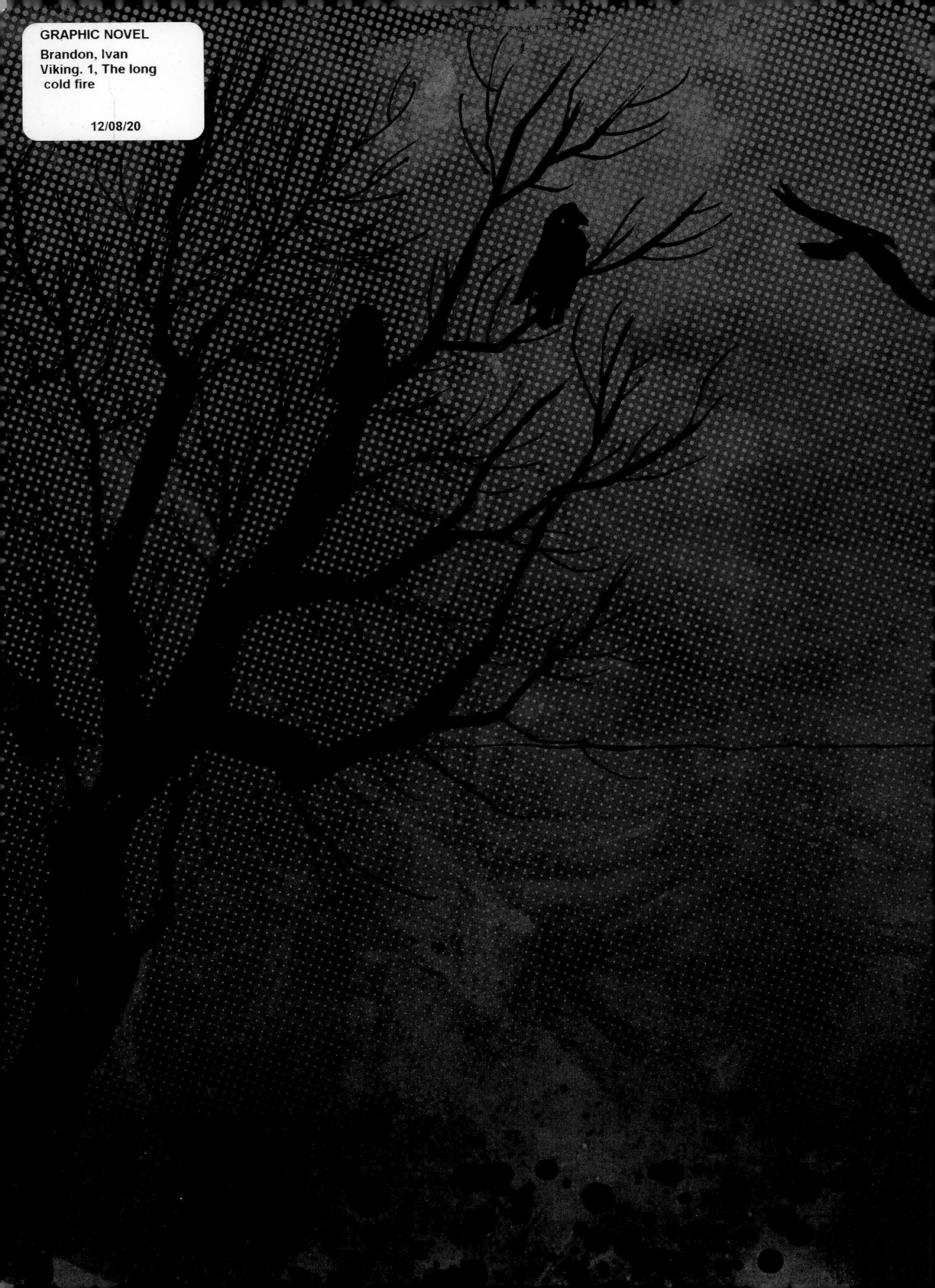